Educational Binds of Poverty

Educational Binds of Poverty tackles the assumptions made by many recent social and educational policy initiatives suggesting that the best way to improve educational prospects of children in poverty is through an increased emphasis upon a culture of control, discipline, regulation and accountability. In this book Ceri Brown presents these assumptions against a review of the research literature and an original ethnographic longitudinal study into the lives of children in poverty in order to highlight the gap between policy discourses and the lived experiences of children themselves.

Through the theoretical concept of a set of 'binds' against educational success, the book explores four key areas that children in poverty have to navigate if they are to be successful in school. These are:

- material deprivation
- the cultural contexts of school, home and the community
- friendship and social capital
- the effects of student mobility through atypical school changes.

In seeking to characterize and explain what life is like for schoolchildren, this book questions why policy makers have a radically different frame of reference in purporting to understand how their policies will change the behaviour of those living in poverty. This leads on to a consideration of what lessons may be learned in order to contribute towards a more appropriate policy agenda that attends to the multiple binds that children in poverty have to negotiate.

Ceri Brown is Lecturer in Education at the University of Bath, UK.

Routledge Research in Education Policy and Politics

The Routledge Research in Education Policy and Politics series aims to enhance our understanding of key challenges and facilitate ongoing academic debate within the influential and growing field of Education Policy and Politics.

Books in the series include:

Teacher Education through Active Engagement
Raising the professional voice
Edited by Lori Beckett

Health Education
Critical perspectives
Edited by Katie Fitzpatrick and Richard Tinning

US Education in a World of Migration
Implications for policy and practice
Edited by Jill Koyama and Mathangi Subramanian

Student Voices on Inequalities In European Higher Education
Challenges for theory, policy and practice
Edited by Fergal Finnegan, Barbara Merrill and Camilla Thunborg

Social Context Reform
A pedagogy of equity and opportunity
Edited by P. L. Thomas, Brad Porfilio, Julie Gorlewski, and Paul R. Carr

Narrowing the Achievement Gap for Native American Students
Paying the educational debt
Edited by Peggy McCardle and Virginia Berninger

Demythologizing Educational Reforms
Responses to the political and corporate takeover of education
Edited by Arthur T. Costigan and Leslee Grey

The Politics of Compulsive Education
Racism and learner-citizenship
Karl Kitching

Educational Binds of Poverty
The lives of school children
Ceri Brown

Educational Binds of Poverty

The lives of school children

Ceri Brown

Routledge
Taylor & Francis Group

LONDON AND NEW YORK

First published 2015
by Routledge
2 Park Square, Milton Park, Abingdon, Oxfordshire OX14 4RN

and by Routledge
711 Third Avenue, New York, NY 10017

First issued in paperback 2016

Routledge is an imprint of the Taylor & Francis Group, an informa business

© 2015 Ceri Brown

The right of Ceri Brown to be identified as author of this work has been asserted by her in accordance with sections 77 and 78 of the Copyright, Designs and Patents Act 1988.

All rights reserved. No part of this book may be reprinted or reproduced or utilised in any form or by any electronic, mechanical, or other means, now known or hereafter invented, including photocopying and recording, or in any information storage or retrieval system, without permission in writing from the publishers.

Trademark notice: Product or corporate names may be trademarks or registered trademarks, and are used only for identification and explanation without intent to infringe.

British Library Cataloguing-in-Publication Data
A catalogue record for this book is available from the British Library

Library of Congress Cataloging-in-Publication Data
Educational binds of poverty : the lives of school children / Ceri Brown.
   pages cm
   Includes bibliographical references and index.
   1. Poor children—Education. 2. Poverty. 3. Home and school.
4. Community and school. 5. Educational sociology. I. Title.
   LC4065.B78 2015
   371.826'94—dc23
   2014027863

ISBN 13: 978-1-138-29111-9 (pbk)
ISBN 13: 978-0-415-71939-1 (hbk)

Typeset in Galliard
by Apex CoVantage, LLC

Contents

	Acknowledgements	vii
1	Underachievement of children in poverty: Scoping the policy context	1
2	The educational binds of poverty	21
3	Clive: School life following relocation, in a single-parent family	42
4	Liza: School life following family break-up and relocation with father	61
5	Megan: School life as a highly mobile Irish Traveller	81
6	Codie: School life after community relocation due to unaffordable housing	101
7	Helen: School life following school change due to bullying	120
8	Robin: School life with a hearing impediment and relocation due to paternal redundancy	140
9	Unpicking the binds: Learning (in) lessons from those that don't	160
	Index	181

Acknowledgements

First and foremost I would like to express my deepest gratitude to my friend and mentor Hugh Lauder for accompanying me along this journey. If it weren't for your support, ideas and encouragement, I'm not sure this book would have got off the starter block and even less certain that it would have made it to the finish line. I would also like to thank my family who continued to tell me it was possible, even when I didn't think it was. Thank you Mum (Lindsay Brown) for your hours of careful proofreading. Thank you Dad (Tom Brown) for reminding me of its importance. Ross Brown your dedication to children and young people in poverty is both inspirational and has driven my curiosity. Andy Merryfield your life's work in addressing social inequalities and injustice has shaped both my political views and understanding of the issues children face. Sam Carr I am indebted to your listening skills, patience and critical insights, which have helped to develop and clarify my claims. I am grateful to Geoff Whitty for his guidance and Pamela Sammons and Silvana Tiani Brunelli for sharing their ideas. I am also very appreciative of all of the staff and pupils at Ivy, Hollybush and the Maple schools, and particularly to Clive, Liza, Megan, Codie, Helen and Robin for letting me in and sharing their lives with me. I hope I have done your stories justice. Lastly, I'd like to thank Santiago Periel Castells for sticking by me and sharing the highs and lows along the way.

Chapter 1

Underachievement of children in poverty
Scoping the policy context

Introduction

This book is about the 'culture wars' between policy makers and children in poverty. It critically examines the cultural assumptions made by policy makers about the behaviour of students in poverty, and contrasts it with their everyday lives: their cultures of friendship and orientations to schooling. In showing how radically different these two accounts are, the book raises fundamental questions about the effectiveness of education policy making. In turn this highlights the issue of the limits and possibilities of policy making. Are there ways in which the insights afforded by studies of youth in poverty can be addressed by policy makers?

The assumptions made by policy makers about those in poverty, and in particular those made in relation to working-class schooling, have changed significantly with the advent of the Coalition government. One way of understanding this change is through the policy framework developed by Ruth Levitas (2005) concerning approaches to poverty. She delineates three perspectives, which she discusses in relation to New Labour. This is a good point from which to start because it enables a discussion of the continuities and discontinuities between New Labour and the Coalition government.

Levitas's first approach is that of RED which stands for redistribution, in which poverty and social exclusion were seen as part of a wider pattern of inequality. In the 1990s, she argued that the idea of policies based on redistribution was joined by two further approaches: a social integrationist discourse (SID) and a moral underclass discourse (MUD). SID understood the key to social integration through labour market participation and it was this approach that dominated under New Labour – so much so that Sure Start for preschoolers was seen as a means of intervention that would eventuate in favourable (paid) labour market outcomes. MUD, in contrast, viewed the socially excluded as morally distinct. This provides a cultural analysis of poverty in terms of moral failings, which sees the way forward in terms of making the poor morally and motivationally 'fit' for the labour market. This approach also penetrated New Labour social policy.

What we see in the discourse of the Coalition government is a greater emphasis on MUD but with elements of New Labour's SID approach; this is especially so in relation to education and its links to the labour market. The Coalition has retained many of the mechanisms of control, which were intended to raise educational achievement under New Labour. The emphasis on testing and the raising of standards of performance through Ofsted inspections have been incorporated into Coalition policy, while there has been some emphasis on school and professional autonomy with respect to Academies and Free Schools. Nevertheless, these apparently more 'teacher friendly' policies have to be set against the MUD policies designed to regulate and control working-class behaviour within school, the family and community. However, as with New Labour, the aim of schooling is to prepare young people for the labour market. The former Secretary of State for Education, Michael Gove, has said that Andreas Schleicher, the Head of Indicators and Analysis for the OECD, which oversees and publishes the results of PISA tests, is 'the most important man in English education'.[1] This is because Gove sees a more or less direct connection between results in these tests and England's economic competitiveness.

What follows is an account of how policy discourses concerning working-class children and their families have shifted in the change from New Labour to the current Coalition government. This shift reflects an increasing blame culture targeted towards those in poverty and the associated need to control, discipline and punish those who don't comply with government policies. The implications of this approach for policy making are then outlined in relation to the current government's social and educational policy. The strategy underpinning this rhetoric and practice is then discussed.

Policy discourses on underperformance

In his speech to the North of England Education Conference (NEEC, 6 January 2012), the then Schools Minister, Nick Gibb, identified the first of three overarching goals guiding current government policy in educational reform: 'to close the attainment gap between those from poorer and wealthier backgrounds'.[2] This is not a new policy interest. Indeed the issue of pupil performance dates back to the 1970s and '80s where growing concern led a number of key educationalists towards advocating major changes to educational policy. By the mid-1990s the situation had escalated whereby large-scale change aimed at improving standards of achievement was on the agenda, taking the form of what was termed 'performance based reform' (Hopkins 2009). As expressed by David Hopkins, Chief Adviser on School Standards at what was then the Department for Education and Skills (2002–2005), it aimed 'to set targets for performance for schools and then hold schools responsible for meeting them' (202). This strategy of increased testing and school accountability has been termed by Lauder, Brown, Dillabough and Halsey (2006) as the 'state theory of learning', or more precisely:

A highly regulated system in which performance can be measured quantitatively by test results. The attendant theory of motivation is that teachers and pupils will be driven to improve against the state determined performance targets.

(Lauder 2009: 200)

Hopkins' claim is that under the New Labour government agenda, this performative based strategy reaped some early gains, in the form of a leap in key stage two performance[3] nationally, between 1998 and 2004. He attributed this success in large part to the National Literacy and National Numeracy Strategies, and to a lesser degree to the 'high challenge, high support' policy framework by which 'under-performing' schools came under very close government scrutiny; this often led to devolved leadership under the auspices of local education authorities, invariably led by 'specialist' core curriculum advisors. However, the claim to success is debatable, as this book will show. Torrance (2009) poses the general question of whether increased performance in national standardized tests is a genuine reflection of a more comprehensive student learning experience, or conversely, a more selective and targeted form of teaching because, as he notes: 'Put desired objectives into testing programmes and teachers will teach those desired objectives' (Torrance 2009: 218).

While Hopkins and Torrance may debate the success of an initial increase in test performance, it is clear that Hopkins (2009) now has doubts about the continued viability of this strategy. Rather he sees that it is time to move beyond centrally prescribed educational reform to a strategy that permeates the hearts and minds of those most closely involved with the daily teaching and learning of students. And to do this the balance must move from one wholly weighted towards prescription and accountability to one weighted towards school-level autonomy and control. The key here, and one that Hopkins pays little attention to, is the question of capturing the hearts and minds of learners, in particular those who come from backgrounds of poverty. As we shall see, to capture their hearts is not easy.

In having moved from a context of a New Labour government to that of a Conservative–Liberal Democrat coalition, the question here is: to what extent, if at all, has the 'state theory of learning' ethos moved on in adapting to in the contemporary social and cultural context of the second decade in the twenty-first century? How is the achievement gap between children from the wealthiest and poorest social backgrounds in England to be closed? In the same 2012 NEEC speech, Gibb cites recent international evidence in order to signal the high profile of this issue:

A PISA study found that England has one of the largest gaps in the world between high and low performing pupils, and a strong relationship between social background and performance . . . A recent report from the OECD also showed that deprived pupils in this country perform significantly less well than deprived pupils in most OECD countries – putting us 39th out of 65 countries.[4]

These are striking figures, yet given the history of attempts to improve education for those in poverty without addressing the fundamental issue of child poverty, the question remains whether educational change can compensate for economic and social inequality. The broad brush of policy is clear: that there will be changes in the structure of education, with increasing numbers of schools leaving local authority control and becoming academies, with a small group of 'free' schools being established by parent and community initiatives concerned with loosening the control over schools, from local authority influence. Furthermore, in the case of 'free' schools, parents can exert greater autonomy through a more direct role in curriculum and pedagogy. These initiatives are nominally about providing greater professional and parental freedom, and the principles of teacher professional autonomy are articulated in the education White Paper, *The Importance of Teaching* (DfE 2010).

Educational reform: In whose interests?

Now formalized in the Education Act 2011, the legislative proposals in the School's White Paper, *The Importance of Teaching* (DfE 2010), represented the Coalition government's position on whole-system educational reform. The paper is organized around three core principles that drive government policy. The first is to raise the competitiveness of the British education and economic system; the second is to increase the quality of teachers and teachers' autonomy, and finally, to raise the achievement of all children, including those who experience poverty. What is so significant about the White Paper (2010) is that after a section on teaching and leadership the next section is devoted to behaviour. It is quite clear from its positioning that the Coalition government sees poor behaviour in school as holding back national educational improvement. Much of this section concerns strengthening the hand of schools in imposing discipline on students.

That this government should identify disruptive behaviour as a key issue in education is part of its wider narrative of what the Prime Minister describes as 'broken Britain'. The response to this perceived national decline is authoritarian, identifying those in poverty as potentially the most disruptive influence. To see why this is, we need to provide a background as to the thinking behind such a view.

MUD and the blame culture

In discussing the notion of 'the poor' as part of an underclass which can be distinguished from the working class, Bauman (1998) has argued that the 'underclass' is not a class at all, given its reference to a social strata positioned outside of the labour market (and therefore the means of production), crucially lacking the possibility of readmission, and above all being 'beyond redemption' (Bauman 1998: 66). While underclass discourses have been traced back to the late nineteenth century (Welshman 2006), the twenty-first century revision of the term has been critiqued for its reduction in the causes of poverty to 'the aggregate product of wrong choices' (Bauman 1998: 71) and, 'as a matter of voluntarily adopted lifestyles . . . unconditioned by economic structure' (Westergaard 1995: 117). In order to contextualize the current Coalition government's blame culture towards those in poverty, it is helpful to consider the evolution of the MUD under New Labour. Both governments can be seen to share a common approach to the social regulation of students from backgrounds of poverty, seeing their underperformance as part of the wider social and economic behaviour of their families and communities.

New Labour's approach to the blame game

A comprehensive account of the state's approach to young people in poverty is given by White and Cunneen (2006). Their argument concerns the role played by the state apparatus in conceptualizing vulnerable groups of young people as 'problematic' populations (17). This rests on the distinction reinforced by state welfare and law enforcement policies, between what they call the 'virtuous poor' and the 'vicious poor'. The former were seen as aspiring towards self-improvement within the parameters of the law, and therefore comprised the deserving recipients of state welfare provision, what in today's political rhetoric are called 'working families'; while the latter were seen as lacking the work ethic. The response is to impose 'varying forms of mutual obligation on the poor – below poverty line benefits and inadequate services in return for work search obligations and imposition of training and employment programme' (White and Cunneen 2006: 22). The implication being that those who uphold their state welfare obligations should be capable of securing employment, whereas those who do not achieve employment are ultimately failing in their contract with the state. Underpinning such a distinction is the assumption that marginalized youth groups represent a form of 'moral category', therefore their status as 'vicious poor' is on account of deviant and harmful lifestyle choices. Such discourses are aligned with theories on youth culture emphasizing individual agency, which simply overlook the effects of economic structures and neighbourhood context, on shaping youth activity. Here, White and Cunneen point to evidence showing that when living in neighbourhoods marked by poverty and high crime, young people are far more likely to remain unemployed (Hunter 1998; Wilson 1996), suffer mental ill health (Burney 2000) and be the victims of crime themselves (Weatherburn and Lind 2001). But consideration of these structural constraints upon the lived experiences of those in poverty, didn't penetrate MUD policy discourses on antisocial behaviour. The bottom line in such blame politics is that: 'Unemployment is reduced to "bad attitudes" and "bad families"' (White and Cunneen 2006: 22).

The solution according to New Labour lay in a communitarian approach, which stressed collective public cooperation, reciprocation and shared responsibilities for each other. In Tony Blair's words:

> In place of an atomised, individualised, selfish society, people yearn for a society that heals itself, a politics that reduces division, intolerance, and inequality . . . individuals realise their potential best through a strong community based on rights and responsibilities.[5]

Here it can be seen how the New Labour rhetoric conforms with the SID, whereby social ills became rendered as a problem of social exclusion: Families are isolated and likely to become problematic if they are excluded from the community. However, the community here is almost synonymous with entry into the paid labour market. Ultimately, it is the labour market that enables integration, even if it does only pay poverty wages. Under this mantra it was, therefore, the responsibility of the community to reintegrate these families into the fold. This informed Blair's policy repertoire for the Social Exclusion Plan launched in 2006, in which he spoke about the need for early intervention with target groups such as looked-after children, teenage mothers, mental health patients and families with complex problems: 'The fact we have yet to succeed with these groups is not for want of spending . . . It is that we need a radical revision of our methods.'[6] One such intervention was the Nursing Partnership Scheme, adopted from a United States initiative to assign a personal health visitor to low-income first-time mothers in order to encourage expectant mothers to give up smoking, bond with their baby, and adopt good parenting practices. While this incited some criticism at the stigmatizing effect of targeting support only towards low-income mothers,[7] such initiatives at least reflected a policy commitment to support socially and economically disadvantaged families, as a way of improving children's outcomes. In the following discussion we will consider how there has been a shift from the SID rhetoric that saw the problem of poverty as being constituted by problem families, which were isolated from the community, to the current MUD rhetoric where problematic families are seen as morally questionable. New Labour perceived that there was a connection between poverty and its material underpinning, although they also saw the issue in terms of individual families. It is this latter element of SID that is the focus of MUD. As such, these families are rendered less fit for community redemption, and more appropriately dealt with under the close surveillance and behavioural management of the state.

The Coalition's approach to the blame game

Even under the Thatcher era, critics observed that the 'New Right' was distinctive as a new wave of conservatism that linked the dual strands of neo-liberal free market economics and the application of these principles into other areas of social life, and neo-conservative emphasis on authority, tradition, and the security and identity of nation (Gamble 1983; Whitty 1990). It could be argued that in the wake of the 2007–08 global economic crisis, and the increasingly bleak prospects of children and young people in poverty, the Coalition government has raised its rhetoric about the problem of the poor, as a rationale for increasing monitoring and disciplining across social and educational policy. We will start by looking at the current government's perspective on the culture of those living in poverty and how that has shifted from New Labour.

The Child Poverty Act was introduced by New Labour to provide a definition and a means of measuring poverty in the UK. However, these have been criticized for focusing solely on income and material deprivation, by the Centre for Social Justice (CSJ), a right-wing think tank, in their report *Rethinking Child Poverty* (CSJ 2012). Their claim was that such a conception overlooks the non-financial antecedents of poverty rooted in family lifestyle choices such as family breakdown, welfare dependency, addiction and personal debt (1). The CSJ vision fits squarely with the Coalition's first strategy concerning poverty, Tackling the Causes of Disadvantage and Transforming Families' Lives, which the CSJ report endorses for its attendance to family circumstances and family structure (8). The report has since been criticized for its omission of in-work poverty, a concession that Managing Director of the CSJ, Christian Guy, himself acknowledges.[8]

Nowhere are the politics of a blame game towards families in poverty as stark as in the government's response to the London riots in August 2011. In his address to the House of Commons concerning the civic unrest, Prime Minister David Cameron made the following statement about the government's position on the antecedents of the 'culture', responsible for the national riots:

> There is a major problem in our society with children growing up not knowing the difference between right and wrong. This is not about poverty, it is about culture. A culture that glorifies violence, shows disrespect to authority, and it says everything about rights, nothing about responsibilities. In too many cases the parents of these children, if they are still around, don't care where their children are, or who they are with, let alone what they are doing. The potential consequences of neglect and immorality on this scale have been clear for too long without enough action being taken.[9]

Despite the Prime Minister's disclaimer, this account speaks all too clearly of the assumed link between poverty and crime. This is signalled in an almost dot-to-dot correspondence between poverty, parental neglect, and antisocial, even violent, behaviour. Cameron goes on to declare that the solution clearly lies in correcting the faults that reside within families, as opposed to addressing the structural conditions leading to poverty:

> There is no one step that can be taken, but we need a benefit system that rewards work and is on the side of families, we need more discipline in our schools, we need action to deal with the most disruptive families, and we

need a criminal justice system that scores a clear and heavy line between right and wrong. In short, all action necessary to help mend our broken society.[10]

This early response to the riots took on an even bolder impetus following the findings from the 'riots, communities and victims panel' (RCVP 2012), commissioned by the government in order to investigate the causes of the riots. Of the five identified areas of responsibility, not one was attributed to the underlying structural causes of poverty and inequality in Britain, despite evidence to suggest that between 59 per cent and 64 per cent of rioters came from the most deprived areas of the UK (Lewis et al. 2011: 5). The primary cause attributable to the riots was 'poor parenting', and included references to 'troubled' and 'rioter' families. Significant responsibility was also assigned to young people themselves, due to individual 'character' failings. Key attributes highlighted as wanting in the rioters included: 'discipline, application, the ability to defer gratification, and resilience in recovering from setbacks' (7). Numerous references were made to punishment and young people were also demonized for their materialism and 'opportunistic looting' of brands (9). No mention was made of the grievances motivating rioters' actions such as an increase in tuition fees, the closure of youth services and the scrapping of the education maintenance allowance, all key factors elucidated through Lewis et al.'s (2011) 270 interviews with people involved in the riots (5).

In effect, the London riots were exploited in providing a public platform to propagate the dangerous face of youth in poverty. As a consequence the government's version of the causes of the riots, reinforced by media accounts of the rioting youths,[11] plugged neatly into the Coalition government's MUD mantra, forming the backbone of the 'Troubled families' programme, which set the background against which much of the following political rhetoric emerged.[12] Speaking in December 2011, Prime Minister David Cameron said:

> I want to talk about troubled families. Let me be clear what I mean by this phrase. Officialdom might call them 'families with multiple disadvantages'. Some in the press might call them 'neighbours from hell'. Whatever you call them, I think we have all known for years that a relatively small number of families are the source of a large proportion of the problems in society.[13]

He then went on to define these 'problems in society' attributable to 'troubled' families as being drug abuse, alcohol addiction and crime. It would be fair to assume, therefore, that these measures are now incorporated into the criteria by which a family is defined as 'troubled'. However, this was not the case. In fact, the characteristics used in order to qualify as being 'troubled' were linked exclusively to material hardship, parental education, and parental mental and physical health, for which families had to exhibit five out of seven indicators.[14] Not one of these measures was directly linked to addiction, crime or antisocial behaviour. What this reflects is a conflation of the factors associated with being in need with those that are attributable to social problems. Through the Russian-doll allegories of the 'broken society', 'troubled families' and 'dangerous/ rioting youths', Coalition rhetoric can be seen to build upon a punitive rationale for addressing youth crime (Goldson 2005; White 1996).

A militant approach to raising educational standards

What we see in the development of MUD in education is a dual approach, in which human motivation in relation to the poor is seen either in terms of a dysfunctional culture, or in terms of families and individuals who are not responding to appropriate incentives and sanctions. In the first case, it is assumed that discipline can be imposed by authoritarian means: what may be considered a traditional conservative response; the second reflects a neo-liberal approach because incentives and spurs are seen in monetary terms (Taylor 2012: 6). With respect to the latter, it has been argued by Foucault in his 1979 lectures (Lemke 2001) that the inspiration for neo-liberal governmentality comes from neo-classical economics, and in particular the work of the leading human capital theorist, Gary Becker. In these lectures on German political economy, Foucault compared the German Ordo-liberalism, which is the form of liberalism expressed in modern Germany, with that of neo-liberalism. His characterization brings out the moral and behavioural assumptions of neo-liberalism that we see manifest in Coalition policies with respect to the poor. Key to this process is the economic imperialism of the Chicago school and in particular Becker (1992), which sought to apply their view of economic rationality to the social sphere. By generalizing economic rationality in this way, Foucault argues, two things are accomplished: 'social relations and individual behaviour are deciphered using economic criteria and within economic terms of their intelligibility [and] second, the economic matrix is also programmatic in that it enables a critical evaluation of governmental policies by means of market concepts' (Lemke 2001: 198).

In so achieving an economic rationality, the neo-liberal argument broke with other forms of explanation of human action including the sociological, anthropological and indeed the psychological. Consequently, from this perspective human beings are always seen as rational in the instrumental sense of being able to calculate means to ends. Therefore, neo-liberal policies always focus on the balance of profit and loss, and seek to apply leverage to the cost–benefit ratio. Hence this analysis can be applied to education, as much to teachers and to parents and families (consider payment by results for teachers and financial penalties for parents whose children do not attend school) as to the economic sphere. The key point here is that for neo-liberals it is the individual who is both morally responsible and economically rational, and in this the subject has 'free will' governed by rational calculation, and reinforced by the punishments and incentives that the government constructs through its policy framework. The moral and indeed political dimension to this is that it is assumed that all rational beings will seek to support themselves through paid work: that is their prime responsibility. If they are parents, it is assumed that they ensure their children are educated for the labour market. And in order to constitute worthwhile moral citizens, this obligation must become incumbent upon children.

Authoritarian and neo-liberal policies in education

There are a range of ways in which the authoritarian nature of Coalition education policy is exerted. The ex-cathedra pronouncements and policies of the now former Secretary of State for Education, Michael Gove, are well known, ranging from a view as to how literacy should be taught, to what students should read. However, there are more indirect, if no less powerful, ways in which this authoritarianism is demonstrated. It is, perhaps, no accident that the head of the government's body for inspecting schools, Ofsted, was a former head of a deprived East London school, which became Mossbourne Academy in 2004. Michael Wilshaw, the head teacher, led the failing school into becoming one of England's best performing. This success was largely attributed to the strict disciplinarian ethos imposed on the school, including methods such as: strict attendance to school uniform policy, no 'special handshakes', no large groups, no hugging, politeness to adults, detentions on Saturdays and even restraining orders for unruly parents.[15] Wilshaw's toe-the-line-or-else philosophy has been appropriated for Ofsted, earning him a disciplinarian reputation in the public eye, with some media journalists even referring to him as 'sergeant major'.[16] This has made him deeply unpopular with many head teachers, for proposals such as dropping 'value-added measures' used to take account of indicators that may impinge on performance, especially in schools in poorer neighborhoods, as 'making excuses'.[17] Many have reflected on the similarities between Wilshaw and the former Secretary of State for Education's policy of tightening discipline and pupil control. This is reflected, most recently, in Gove's guidelines for teachers (DfE 2014) emphasizing measures such as 'screening and searching children' and 'the power to use reasonable force and other physical contact' (4) in order to discipline pupils' misbehaviour inside and even outside of school (3).

However, perhaps the clearest example of an authoritarian response in education to the diagnosis of a 'broken Britain' is the 'troops to teachers' programme, which, although a small part of the overall education policy, speaks volumes as to government thinking.

Troops to teachers (teachers to sergeants?)

The 'troops to teachers' programme was introduced in the Schools White Paper (DfE 2010). It included a variety of different forms of support for service leavers wishing to enter the classroom, such as financial subsidies and a new fast-tracked undergraduate route into teaching. This package has been justified by Michael Gove as:

A huge opportunity for those people who have served their country in uniform to serve their country in our schools. They have many of the virtues that parents across the country feel have disappeared from our schools and need to be restored: self-discipline, a sense of purpose and a belief in the importance of working as a team.[18]

This programme now offers initial teacher training routes for both graduate and nongraduate service leavers leading to qualified teacher status.[19] Ostensibly this measure falls under the 'improving the quality of teaching' aspiration according to Gove, however, this has been publicly received as a measure that speaks far louder in its repercussions for pupil discipline and behaviour control.

Writing for the *Guardian* newspaper, Francis Gilbert reflects that 'the subtext of [Gove's] plans is that our classrooms are so out of control that drastic military action is called for.'[20] The bottom line for Gilbert was spelled out in a statement about military training from an ex-army teaching colleague: 'You simply couldn't allow them to think for themselves.'[21] Gilbert argues that the blind obedience requirement for army personal simply cannot be exported for a school context; 'in the military, independent thought can be fatal, whereas in schools, it's absolutely crucial'.[22]

Furthermore, the claim towards 'improving the quality of teaching' falters somewhat in the face of plans revealed for the Phoenix Free School, a school staffed by former servicemen and women in Greater Manchester. For all intents and purposes, the proposed plans promoted the Phoenix Free School principally on its ability to teach children using military-style discipline. Speaking on BBC Radio 4's *Today* programme, Mary Bousted, general secretary of the Association of Teachers and Lecturers, said she was 'amazed' by the proposal and took issue with the decision to employ unqualified teachers by dint of their military training:

> The idea that you can simply take the skills and abilities you've learnt in war, or on the parade ground, or through armed manoeuvres, and those can be translated undigested into teaching, without any further training is ridiculous. These Free schools aren't free. They are paid for by the public's money and there is no guarantee if you send your child to a Free school that they'll be taught by a teacher.[23]

The inference of the 'troops to teachers' scheme is that the Coalition government values higher the ability to discipline and control than it does the ability to inspire and encourage.

Banning best friends?

Once the focus is so strongly on the top-down social control of behaviour, it can rapidly become internalized by some educationalists in the sense described by

Rose (1989). Following Foucault (1991), Rose understands governmentality to include 'a certain way of striving to reach social and political ends by acting in a calculated manner upon the forces, activities and relations of the individuals that constitute a population' (4). The consequence for Rose is that 'it makes persons amenable to having things done to them – and doing things to themselves – in the name of their subjective capacities' (7–8). In short, that people will enact policies without critically reflecting on what they are doing. An example of the pervasiveness of this culture of control and regulation of children can be seen in the actions of schools and teachers who have encroached upon the private social worlds of children. This is evident in schools' intervention in children's friendships for the disruption that they may have upon their schoolwork. As confirmed by Russell Hobby of the National Association of Head Teachers, the 'ban on best friends' is a controversial measure that has been introduced in a number of primary schools in Kingston, South West London and Surrey.[24] As the name suggests, it is a policy effectively banning children from having best friends, in favour of being encouraged to play in large groups. There will be many that find policies based on the micro-management of social control and blame surprising, especially if it seems to be in near total disregard of the evidence about the lives of those in poverty.

Fines for parents whose children are absent from school

When it comes to the influence of neo-liberal policies in education with respect to those in poverty, then the clearest exemplification are those advocated by Charles Taylor.

In 2012 Taylor was appointed by the Department for Education, as an expert advisor on behaviour, to ensure that the government's disciplinary reforms are fully enforced in schools. Speaking of the significance of appointing a behaviour expert, Michael Gove (2012) acknowledged that the move 'shows how seriously we are dealing with the issue [of behaviour]'.[25] As one of his first key outputs in this new role, Taylor's report on 'Improving Attendance at School' (2012) concerned the findings of a review into the problems and recommendations associated with truancy. In this report Taylor takes issue with 'persistent absence' (PA), which refers to when a child is absent for 20 per cent or more of the school term. In articulating his position on the antecedents of PA Taylor points the finger towards parents:

> [Truancy] is only one dimension [of persistent absence] and distracts attention from the cause of these problems, which is non-attendance in the early years, when approved by parents. This soon becomes a pattern and establishes poor attitudes towards school. The youngest children don't play truant from school, they are off because their parents allow them to be.
>
> (Taylor 2012: 4)

The 'expert advisor' acknowledges that children who persistently miss school are 'more likely to come from the poorest backgrounds' (Taylor 2012: 5). However, he is highly critical of these families, claiming they 'do not value education' (4) and is scathing of the reasons for which parents 'allow' children to be absent from school:

> It is the parents who allow their child to have Monday off because the family is tired after a weekend away, who keep their child back from school because they are waiting for a delivery, or for whom a doctor's appointment in the afternoon becomes a reason for taking the whole day off, who need to be challenged early.
>
> (Taylor 2012: 6)

In understanding the cause of PA for children in poverty to be the consequence of parental apathy, Taylor's punitive response towards such parents who 'exploit the system' (11) has led to the implementation of his recommendations concerning parental fines for school absence (6). Following amendments to the Education (Penalty Notices) (England) (Amendment) Regulations 2013, from September 2013 the fine for parents whose child is absent from school during term-time was raised from £50 to £60, to be doubled if failure to pay extends beyond 21 days, in order for local authorities to act faster on prosecutions.[26] Furthermore, fines can now be issued individually to parents, meaning that a child's mother and father could both receive a separate fine.[27] This conceptualization of pupil absence apparently positions parents as the willing obstructers of their children's education, to be punished accordingly, irrespective of the implications of such financial penalties upon children and their families.

However, Taylor's sights are not only on 'dysfunctional' parents but also the schools that are complicit with them. In critiquing schools' authorization of child absences, he argues that the problem has been compounded because schools are not evaluated on these figures (5). This claim is underpinned by the assumption that primary schools, in particular, are apathetic in being 'a bit too nice and fluffy when it comes to challenging parents on attendance'.[28] For this reason, Taylor proposes that schools should be held accountable for the attendance records of children under the age of compulsory schooling. These recommendations have been applauded by the former Secretary of State for Education, who stated: 'It is clear that poor habits form in the early stages of a child's education.'[29] This has led to changes in regulations for schools, removing the discretionary 10 days' leave afforded to special circumstances such as holidays. Parents will now have to submit an application to the school to remove their child from school, but government guidance insists that this should only be granted in 'exceptional circumstances'.[30]

The appointment of a behavioural specialist, along with these reforms, reflect the growing emphasis of the MUD and the associated policy tools to impose greater disciplinary measures upon children and their families, as well as upon the schools that children attend. The question remains as to why such an approach is seen as effective and indeed politically desirable.

Political collapse and control by damage limitation

In describing the shift in political rhetoric from one of motivating social action through inspiration towards a better vision of society, to one of control through fear of society, Stuart Waiton's (2008) work is helpful. Following Lasch (1979), Waiton argues that politics since the turn of the millennium is in the midst of an identity crisis characterized by an inherent lack of direction and authority, with the associated failure of political leaders to lead and rule. Unsurprisingly, this is coupled with a declining public faith in the power of politics in order to improve society. It is within such a political context, Waiton argues, that a culture of social control via law and regulation emerges. The rationale for this is quite simply that when political leaders have lost the ability to capture people's hearts and minds, they resolve just to control their bodies (Waiton 2008: xvi). Given this intention, politicians merely aim to activate the public spirit, not in addressing a social goal of freedom or liberty per se, but of freedom from fear. For this reason discourses such as the 'vicious poor' articulation of working-class youth (White and Cunneen 2006) can be used to channel the public's fear towards crime and antisocial behaviour.[31] Waiton (2008) challenges the assumption that antisocial behaviour is any more prevalent in contemporary society than it was in the postwar period. He argues that rather it is 'fear of anti-social behaviour' that characterizes current public attitudes. At the heart of such policy discourses lies damage limitation as the central organizing principle (9). In turn, Waiton's thesis chimes well with neo-liberal policy assumptions: where questions of heart and mind are formally eschewed in the development of a framework of punishments and sanctions that are designed to govern people's lives. However, when it comes to education, it can be argued that hearts and minds are critical.

Conclusion, and structure for the following chapters

The aim of this chapter has been to outline the current political rhetoric whereby the daily lives of children of poverty can be seen to play no part in policy making. Underpinning both the social and educational spheres of England's governance is a set of top-down regulatory measures, with increased emphasis upon discipline and control. This permeates the institutions of the school and the family, who are deemed not to measure up to government-prescribed standards, as well as of the children in poverty themselves. In such a political climate, autonomy is viewed as a luxury afforded only to the 'virtuous' schools and families who fall into line, and set within an increasingly competitive market ethos, where schools and indeed children are judged solely on performance, with little recognition of social and emotional well-being, nor of the daily struggles involved in navigating life in poverty.

In building a very different picture to that laid out in current MUD blame discourses, chapter two reviews the literature on the circumstances of children and families in poverty. This chapter rests on the construct of a set of 'binds' against educational success. That is, the multiple barriers faced by children in poverty concerning school and community inclusion. These include: material deprivation and school access, cultural inequalities and symbolic violence, friendship as a means of including and excluding, and irregular school transition (outside of normal school admission and exit points).

In redressing the dominant policy assumptions made about the behaviour of children and youth in poverty, this book documents the lives of six children who have been followed over four years, including the transition from primary school to secondary school. Each chapter looks at the investments involved in the daily navigation of school life, exploring children's friendships and the key role they play in processes of inclusion and exclusion in the classroom, the playground and the illegitimate spaces of the corridors, empty classrooms and hidden territories, which children create as their own. Of most interest, however, is the unchanging nature of children's orientations to school, and the tensions raised in the clash between the expectations of friends and the actions and aptitudes necessary to achieve in school. And it is this last point that is of contemporary significance in the politics of education.

The following chapters will present the schooling lives of these six children. Their focus is on acceptance and friendship, and the stories they have to tell are poignant, as they struggle between the desire for friendship and the demands to conform to teachers' expectations. All the children come from low-income families and are highly mobile. Their circumstances vary but in their own ways can be seen as typical of those in poverty today. Chapter three concerns the story of Clive, who leaves behind home and community to live with his mother in a single-parent family. We will consider the tensions apparent between Clive's aspirations as a talented mathematician with his social identity as a class entertainer and rule challenger. These tensions are amplified post-transition from primary to secondary school, whereby Clive's links weaken between home, school and community, causing him to feel increasingly alienated within school. Chapter four charts Liza's story following family break-up, in moving with her father from London to a small town. Liza also experiences a tension between her bids to gain attention from her friends and teachers. The material strain of poverty is amplified when Liza's father gives up work to be a full-time carer for Liza's grandfather. Following transition to secondary school, Liza's community links strengthen through attending a community art group; however, her artistic talent is not fostered in school given her continuing uncertainty that she can trust her friends and teachers. Chapter five tells Megan's story; a Traveller girl living with both parents and eight of her 11 brothers and sisters. Megan's lifestyle is subject to frequent moves between Traveller sites across England and Ireland due to family commitments, paternal employment and Traveller events. We see how school changes and Traveller culture have resulted in protracted periods of school absence that contribute towards a significant educational gap in her learning, and lead to social isolation and bullying in school. The gulf between school and home cultures can be seen to grow in moving from primary to secondary education. In place of friendships, Megan sees herself to be reliant upon the 'kindness' of her peers, which fluctuates, as well as upon the more reliable help of support staff. Chapter six follows Codie's story, whose family were forced to relocate from London due to uninhabitable social housing and a lack of affordable accommodation. This results in strained relations with her extended family, in leaving them behind in London. Codie's fluctuating moods and temperaments earn her a reputation as an attention seeker and creator of elaborate stories designed to evoke sympathy or interest. Following transfer to secondary school, financial hardship causes Codie to break ties with her previous community. Her sense of displacement in school is considered with respect to the long-term effects of school mobility and losing friends. Chapter seven tells Helen's story, the only one to have lived, with both parents, in the community since birth. We consider Helen's anxiety concerning what she saw as her tatty school uniform, as well as the pressure of court action upon Helen's parents for school absence caused by social exclusion and bullying. Helen's is one of the more positive stories due to the buffering effects of strong community and social ties generating more secure social inclusion. This leads to a greater commitment to learning but only within the culture of a lower-set classroom, rendering formal aspects of school life as mostly irrelevant. The final story, in chapter eight, is that of Robin, whose father's redundancy led the family to move over 200 miles away in order for him to take a low-paid job, forcing them into low-cost accommodation, far from local amenities. This contributes to Robin's sense of isolation from the local and school community, which is exacerbated through his hearing impediment. However, Robin's story represents a point of contrast as the only one able to navigate the binds he confronted with some educational success. His family places a high value upon educational achievement, contributing to Robin's own sense of value in key subject areas where he excels. This is reinforced through his strategy of helping his friends with their work in class and their endorsement of his abilities in key lessons. However, such bonds are not sufficient to bridge outside of the classroom, and Robin remains socially excluded in the playground and the community. In considering the lives of children in poverty through the lens of the four binds outlined in chapter two, such accounts seek to characterize and explain the experience of school life for children in modern Britain.

Chapter nine reflects on the two different accounts of the behaviour of children in poverty: the policy makers, who believe children can be cajoled, regulated and monitored into behaving 'rationally'; and the empirical evidence that demonstrates the binds in relation to school success, which remain. The question is asked as to why the former ignore the latter, and three explanations are canvassed. The chapter leads on to a reflection upon the policy implications as to how we may best support children in poverty. This involves drawing upon the lessons learned from the six stories encountered, considering their relevance within the current agenda for welfare reform, and attending to this in relation to each of the binds detailed throughout the book. The conclusions are lastly reflected upon in terms of likely fruitful directions in researching the educational binds of poverty.

Notes

1. Michael Gove, press release following 'Michael Gove article in "The Independent" on educational reforms', 6 January 2011. Available at www.gov.uk/government/speeches/michael-gove-article-in-the-independent-on-education-reforms.
2. Nick Gibb, North of England Education Conference (NEEC), 6 January 2012. Available at www.education.gov.uk/inthenews/speeches/a00201655/nick-gibb-speech-on-school-improvement.
3. Key stage two is the final curriculum level for primary school children in England, culminating in national standardized assessment tests (SATs) for children aged 11.
4. Nick Gibb, NEEC.
5. Tony Blair, 'Third Sector, Third Way', paper presented at NCVO Conference at Chiswell Brewery Conference Centre, 21 January 1999, London.
6. Tony Blair quoted by Yvonne Roberts, 'Asbos for the unborn', *Guardian*, 17 May 2007. Available at www.theguardian.com/commentisfree/2007/may/17/whatawonderfulboostto [Accessed May 2014]
7. Leading the initiative to be named the foetus asbo, e.g. Roberts, 'Asbos for the unborn'.
8. Christian Guy, quoted by Amelia Gentleman, 'We have missed in work poverty', *Guardian*, 19 June 2012. Available at www.theguardian.com/society/2012/jun/19/christian-guy-managing-director-centre-social-justice [Accessed May 2014].
9. David Cameron, House of Commons address, 11 August 2011.
10. Ibid.
11. E.g. Lee Moran and Allan Hall, 'British youths are "the most unpleasant and violent in the world": Damning verdict of writer as globe reacts to verdict', *Daily Mail*, 10 August 2011. Available at www.dailymail.co.uk/news/article-2024486/UK-RIOTS-2011-British-youths-unpleasant-violent-world.html [Accessed May 2014].
12. This programme was set up in 2011, ostensibly to support disadvantaged families through integrated public services, targeted interventions and channelling resources towards those families most in need.
13. David Cameron, 'Troubled Families speech', 15 December 2011. Available at www.number10.gov.uk/news/troubled-families-speech/.
14. The seven indicators for the 120,000 'troubled families' are defined as: 'no parent in the family in work, the family lives in poor quality or overcrowded housing, no parent has a qualification, the mother has mental health problems, at least one parent has a longstanding limiting illness, disability or infirmity, the household income is below the poverty line, or the family cannot afford a number of food and clothing items'. (DfCLG 2013: 31). Available at www.gov.uk/government/uploads/system/uploads/attachment_data/file/79377/20130208_The_Fiscal_Case_for_Working_with_Troubled_Families.pdf [Accessed 13 June 2014].
15. Susanna Rustin, 'The Saturday interview: Mossbourne Academy's Sir Michael Wilshaw', *Guardian*, 17 September 2011. Available at www.theguardian.com/theguardian/2011/sep/17/michael-wilshaw-interview [Accessed 29 June 2014].
16. For example, Jeevan Vasager, 'An inspector calls: the day the head of Ofsted visited one school', *Guardian*, 28 March 2012. Available at www.theguardian.

com/education/2012/mar/27/michael-wilshaw-ofsted-school-inspector [Accessed May 2014].
17 See Fran Abrams, 'Is the new chief inspector of schools just an instrument of government?', *Guardian*, 23 January 2012. Available at www.theguardian.com/education/2012/jan/23/chief-inspector-schools-michael-wilshaw [Accessed May 2014].
18 Michael Gove, press release, 'Ex-military to be inspiring role models for young people', 28 February 2011. Available at www.gov.uk/government/news/ex-military-to-be-inspiring-role-models-for-young-people [Accessed 11 June 2014].
19 This programme was launched in June 2013. See press release, 'New routes for talented ex-armed forces personnel to become teachers'. Available at www.gov.uk/government/news/new-routes-for-talented-ex-armed-forces-personnel-to-become-teachers [Accessed 11 June 2014].
20 Francis Gilbert, 'Should more ex-soldiers become teachers?', *Guardian*, 24 November 2010. Available at www.theguardian.com/commentisfree/2010/nov/24/soldiers-teachers-michael-gove [Accessed 11 June 2014].
21 Ibid.
22 Ibid.
23 Mary Bousted, audio recording, 'Greater Manchester military style school proposed', *BBC*, 2 September 2011. Available at www.bbc.co.uk/news/uk-england-manchester-14754069 [Accessed 4 May 2014].
24 Harry Hawkins, 'Schools ban children making best friends', *Sun*, 19 March 2012.
25 Press release, 'New powers for teachers to improve discipline in schools', 4 April 2011. Available at www.gov.uk/government/news/new-powers-for-teachers-to-improve-discipline-in-schools.
26 This legislative amendment to regulations 3 and 4 is available at www.legislation.gov.uk/uksi/2013/757/regulation/2/made [Accessed 4 June 2014].
27 This legislative amendment to regulation 13 is available at www.legislation.gov.uk/uksi/2007/1867/regulation/13/made [Accessed 4 June 2014].
28 Charles Taylor, quoted by Julie Henry, 'Schools told to get tough on truanting youngsters', *Telegraph*, 18 December 2012. Available at www.telegraph.co.uk/education/primaryeducation/8963129/Schools-told-to-get-tough-on-truant-youngsters.html [Accessed 7 May 2014].
29 Michael Gove, quoted by Richard Garner, 'Government advisor says truancy crackdown means three-year-olds should have school absence recorded', *Independent*, 16 April 2012. Available at www.independent.co.uk/news/education/education-news/government-advisor-says-truancy-crackdown-means-threeyearolds-should-have-school-absence-recorded-7647716.html [Accessed 7 May 2014].
30 This legislative amendment to regulation 7 is available at www.legislation.gov.uk/uksi/2013/756/regulation/2/made [Accessed 11 June 2014].
31 The policy tools by which those in poverty are cast as morally destitute has, elsewhere, been termed 'poverty of the imagination' (Gilroy 2011; Slater 2011; Tyler 2013) with reference to the contexts politicians draw upon in responding to social issues (such as the London riots, as well as the framing of such issues in political rhetorical terms).

References

Bauman, Z. (1998) *Work, Consumerism and the New Poor*, Maidenhead: Open University Press.
Becker, G.S. (1992) 'Habits, addictions and traditions', *Kyklos*, 45 (3): 327–45.

Burney, E. (2000) 'Ruling out trouble: Anti-social behaviour and housing management', *Journal of Forensic Psychiatry*, 11(2): 268–73.

Centre for Social Justice [CSJ] (2012) *Rethinking Child Poverty*. Available at www.centreforsocialjustice.org.uk/publications/rethinking-child-poverty [Accessed 14 February 2014].

Department for Communities and Local Government [DfCLG] (2013) *The Fiscal Case for Working with Troubled Families*. Available at www.gov.uk/government/publications/the-fiscal-case-for-working-with-troubled-families-analysis-and-evidence-on-the-costs-of-troubled-families-to-government [Accessed 13 June 2014].

Department for Education [DfE] (2010) *The Importance of Teaching: the schools white paper*. Available at www.gov.uk/government/uploads/system/uploads/attachment_data/file/175429/CM-7980.pdf [Accessed 4 September 2013].

Department for Education [DfE] (2014) *Behaviour and Discipline in Schools: advice for headteachers and school staff*. Available at www.gov.uk/government/publications/behaviour-and-discipline-in-schools [Accessed 11 February 2014].

Foucault, M. (1991) 'Governmentality', translated by R. Braidotti and revised by C. Gordon, in G. Burchell, C. Gordon and P. Miller (eds) *The Foucault Effect: studies in governmentality*, Chicago: University of Chicago Press, 87–104.

Gamble, A. (1983) 'Thatcherism and conservative politics', in S. Hall and M. Jacques (eds) *The Politics of Thatcherism*, London: Lawrence and Wisehart, 109–31.

Gilroy, P. (2011) 'Paul Gilroy Speaks on the Riots, August 2011, Tottenham, North London'. Available at http://dreamofsafety.blogspot.co.uk/2011/08/paul-gilroy-speaks-on-riots-august-2011.html [Accessed 12 February 2014].

Goldson, B. (2005) 'Taking liberties: policy and the punitive turn', in H. Hendrick (ed.) *Child Welfare and Social Policy*, Bristol: Policy Press.

Hopkins, D. (2009) 'Realising the potential of system reform', in H. Daniels, H. Lauder and J. Porter (eds) *Knowledge, Values and Educational Policy: a critical perspective*, London: Routledge.

Hunter, B. (1998) 'Addressing youth unemployment: re-examining social and locational disadvantage within Australian cities', *Urban Policy and Research*, 16 (1): 47–58.

Lasch, C. (1979) *Culture of Narcissism*, New York: Norton.

Lauder, H. (2009) 'Policy and governance, introduction', in H. Daniels, H. Lauder and J. Porter (eds) *Knowledge, Values and Educational Policy: a critical perspective*, London: Routledge.

Lauder, H., Brown, P., Dillabough, J.A. and Halsey, A.H. (eds) (2006) *Education, Globalization, and Social Change*, Oxford: Oxford University Press.

Lemke, T. (2001) '"The birth of bio-politics": Michel Foucault's lecture at the College de France on neo-liberal governmentality', *Economy and Society*, 30 (2): 190–207.

Levitas, R. (2005) *The Inclusive Society? Social exclusion and new labour*, Basingstoke: Palgrave Macmillan.

Lewis, P., Newburn, T., Taylor, M., Mcgillivray, C., Greenhill, A., Frayman, H. and Proctor, R. (2011) *Reading the Riots: investigating England's summer of disorder*. London: London School of Economics and Political Science and the *Guardian*.

Rose, N. (1989) *Governing the Soul: the shaping of the private self*, London: Routledge.

Slater, T. (2011) 'From "criminality" to marginality: rioting against a broken state', *Human Geography: A New Radical Journal*, 4 (3): 106–15.

Taylor, C. (2012) *Improving Attendance at School*, Department for Education. Available at www.gov.uk/government/publications/improving-attendance-at-school [Accessed 4 September 2013].

Torrance, H. (2009) 'Using assessment in educational reform: policy, practice and future possibilities', in H. Daniels, H. Lauder and J. Porter (eds) *Knowledge, Values and Educational Policy: a critical perspective*, London: Routledge.

Tyler, I. (2013) 'The riots of the underclass? Stigmatisation, mediation and the government of poverty and disadvantage in Neoliberal Britain', *Sociological Research Online*, 18 (4), 6. Available at www.socresonline.org.uk/18/4/6.html [Accessed 12 February 2014].

Waiton, S. (2008) *Amoral Panics: the politics of antisocial behavior*, London: Routledge.

Weatherburn, D. and Lind, B. (2001) *Delinquent-Prone Communities*, Cambridge: Cambridge University Press.

Welshman, J. (2006) *Underclass: a history of the excluded: 1880–2000*, London: Hambledon Continuum.

Westergaard, J. (1995) *Who Gets What? The hardening of class inequality in the late twentieth century*, Cambridge: Polity Press.

White, R. (1996) 'The poverty of the welfare state: managing an underclass', in P. James (ed.) *The State in Question: transformations of the Australian state*, Sydney: Allen and Unwin.

White, R. and Cunneen, C. (2006) 'Social class, youth crime and justice', in B. Goldson and J. Muncie (eds) *Youth Crime and Justice: critical issues*, London: Sage.

Whitty, G. (1990) 'The 1988 Education Reform Act: its origins and implications', in M. Flude and M. Hammer (eds) *The New Right and the National Curriculum*, London: Falmer Press.

Wilson, W. J. (1996) *When Work Disappears*, New York: Knopf.

Chapter 2

The educational binds of poverty

Introduction

Chapter one outlined the policy discourses concerning families and especially young people in poverty, which have characterized government policy and rhetoric over the last two decades. It was argued that such discourses reflect an increasing emphasis towards the moral underclass discourse, or MUD, which seeks to explain poverty and its effects as the result of moral failings on the part of children and their families. This chapter aims to challenge that view using systematic research to present a very different account of life in poverty for children; one that views children as the victims, albeit not passive ones, of their circumstances, and explores the effects of children's attempts to navigate a set of complex challenges, or binds, in their experiences of school life.

The chapter posits the concept of the 'bind'[1] in order to explain the schooling experiences of children in poverty. The 'bind' refers to a barrier that children experiencing poverty have to negotiate in order to achieve educational success. It is an external constraint that places structural limitations on children's actions and motivations in school. The 'bind' metaphor evokes an encumbrance upon the individual, such that there is very little room for leverage. Children may or may not recognize a 'bind' as an obstruction to educational success; however, they are aware of the consequences for social inclusion. The pervasive force of the bind is in thwarting the child's opportunities to feel a valued learner in school, and interrupting the sense of inclusion that leads to educational success. This is not to say that children are unable to exert agency in striving to be included, but rather that their choices are limited by competing demands, such that the trade-offs inevitably impact upon their educational opportunities and life chances. It was argued in chapter one that MUD attributes educational failure to the actions of the individual, as a result of irrational or poor choices. The bind theory emphasizes the rationality of children's actions in school as a process of day-to-day 'getting by', but, as we shall see, getting by is not the same as 'getting ahead'.[2]

There are four binds advanced in this chapter, selected because of their explanatory power in theorizing educational underachievement for children in poverty. This is not to suggest that these four binds are exhaustive, but rather, that they are arguably among the most pervasive for children in contemporary Britain. The first bind concerns the material penalties of living in poverty and the consequences of material deprivation in excluding children from and within school. The second bind addresses the difficulties that children in poverty encounter in school, which can seem alien to them. This is especially so, if we consider the dominant forms of middle-class cultural capital with which schools connect and foster. Many of the schooling ethnographies of working-class students have centred on the challenges emerging from the cultural clash between school and home. The third bind expounds the social capital penalties for children in poverty. Here there are two related points to be made. The first signals the role of friendship in school life. While government policy has focused entirely on success in a range of tests, the schooling lives of children are much broader and richer such that children's day-to-day lives may be motivated more towards acceptance and inclusion. The second point concerns the implication of friendship in the formation of social capital, in whether friendships can be helpful in achieving educationally or, indeed, the opposite. The fourth and final bind considers the effects of student mobility through atypical school changes, which can affect friendship, learning orientations and educational achievement. Student mobility now affects some 40 per cent of primary school children in England (Goldstein, Burgess and McConnell 2007), many of whom experience poverty. While the four binds discussed in this chapter are discrete, there are clear lines of interconnection, centrally premised on the positioning of children as alien or outsiders in school. The four binds presented in this chapter reflect a theoretical framework by which to analyse and understand the lives of children in poverty in the UK.

Bind 1: Material deprivation and its role in exclusion

While many of us may understand the anxieties and limiting effects of financial hardship upon daily life, Millar and Ridge (2001) provide a systematic set of insights into the effects of material deprivation, through their comprehensive review of the literature on lone parents and low-income couple families with children. Their research shows that despite the different approaches that families may take, there is little evidence to suggest that poor families willfully mismanage their money, but rather that the associated consequences of poverty, including debt, reconstituting family and the ongoing nature of the poverty cycle, 'place a heavy burden on families' capacities to manage' (Millar and Ridge 2001: 73). This is supported elsewhere (Berthoud and Kempson 1992: Kempson et al. 1994; Morris and Ritchie 1994).

Research into the material penalties of living in poverty within Britain points to the associated pressures placed upon families in significantly constraining children's life chances. This has highlighted the impact on basic necessities: health and social and emotional well-being. Millar and Ridge's (2001) findings elucidate the key areas of family life affected by poverty: likelihood to experience health problems, unsatisfactory housing, poor diet, unemployment, financial and social exclusion, and debt. Duration of time in poverty has been found to mediate these experiences, in affecting people's capacities to pay bills and adapt to changes of circumstances including redundancy, divorce and illness (Rowlingson and Kempson 1993).

Many of the issues associated with poverty can become concentrated within disadvantaged neighbourhoods, so that living within an impoverished community has a multiplier effect upon the individual experience. For example, Lupton (2003) has cited the poor service provision and stigma due to fear about antisocial behaviour and crime experienced by residents in the most deprived neighbourhoods of England and Wales. Neighbourhood is also an important mediator in children's access to good-quality schooling. Since the introduction of parental choice within the 1988 Educational Reform Act, low-income families have become more vulnerable to the effects of polarized pupil intakes. In their discussion of 'circuits of schooling' Ball et al. (2001) have showed how for low-income families, practical factors such as space, travel and family organization play a key role in parents' decision-making processes over school choice. Middle-class parents' decisions, on the other hand, were informed by what is ideal and advantageous for their children, on account of school history, reputation and performance. The result is that while families within middle-class neighbourhoods have privileged access to circuits of high quality, often selective-entry state schools, children living in impoverished neighbourhoods can only access circuits of schools with homogenous, low socioeconomic pupil compositions and high levels of deprivation. Given the process implications of managing behaviour, attendance and providing for additional needs and welfare roles, schools in disadvantaged neighbourhoods are likely to provide a lower quality education, even where good management systems are in place (Lupton 2007: 670).

If the material necessities conducive to well being and happiness are so compromised, it takes little imagination to consider how poor health, poor housing and fear and anxiety over unemployment, crime and family income may impact upon children's approach to school. To consider these effects in more detail, it is necessary to turn to the experiences and voices of children in schools.

Ridge's (2002) work into the perspectives of children in poverty is important for understanding how children perceive and respond to the conditions outlined earlier. She highlights the distinctive experience of poverty within an affluent nation and its attendant consumer culture in observing that just as in adulthood, certain commodities represent a means of communication between young people and are essential to ensure social participation (Willis et al. 1990). Money was found to be important for children, not only in relation to possessions such as clothes and music, but also for the experiential value of taking part in school outings and visits to the cinema, shopping or leisure centre. In lacking the commodities of their friends, children in low-income families perceived themselves to be excluded from their peers, and where leisure clothes and school uniforms were outdated or worn, this even led to teasing and bullying. For some children, forgoing material possessions was of secondary importance to the out-of-school and sometimes in-school experiences (in the form of school trips) from which they were often excluded, and which formed a large part of in-school conversation. In reflecting on the significance of missing the school-day trip to France two years earlier, Amy's account reveals the enduring effects of material exclusion: 'even now my friends bring it up and I'm like, "Oh I didn't go, I can't talk about it"' (Ridge 2002: 76).

Social exclusion for children in poverty has been found to extend to children's relationships with teachers, leading them to feel less valued in school (Ridge 2002; Sutton et al. 2007). While the affluent children of the study by Sutton and colleagues (2007) were very positive about school, those in poverty found school to be boring and irrelevant to their lives, and felt less respected and liked by teachers due to their extensive disciplining (19) and coercive control (20). They complained of being 'often shouted at for not knowing what they were supposed to do' (21) and of not feeling heard: 'It's unfair for us because we have to just listen to teachers all the time' (G1 in Sutton et al. 2007: 21).

As the children in Ridge's (2002) study received little or no pocket money, many of them undertook paid employment, and found this to contribute towards their independence. While many young people have some form of paid employment, research suggests that those from low-income families tend to work more than their more affluent peers, either through putting in longer hours or for holding down more than one job (Middleton et al. 1994). Furthermore, for some children, the income generated through their own work was found to make a small but significant contribution to the household income (O'Donnell and White 1998).

The issue of paid employment is important in relation to school success when we consider the data on truanting. In her analysis of the 1997 British Household Panel Youth Survey (BHPYS), Ridge (2002) consulted data on consistent truanting, finding that 11 per cent of children in benefit households were more likely to truant compared with 4 per cent in nonbenefit households. One hypothesis for this is that children in poverty may elect to miss school in order to undertake paid employment. This may explain the finding that 'Children and young people working were nearly twice as likely as non-working children and young people to truant' (Ridge 2002: 116). Considering the importance to their families' finances of missing school in order to work, that children in poverty may choose to do so is hardly surprising.

More recent research into persistent truanting revealed that children in poverty may miss school on account of familial responsibilities or peer pressure. A national study of school absence by the Rathbone charity (2012) found that nearly a quarter of children persistently truanted to care for an ill relative. This is supported by earlier research that uncovered other family demands such as helping to look after a younger sibling, helping with housework, and waiting for a service person (e.g. plumber, electrician) in the absence of parents (Hallam and Roaf 1995). Other social concerns were found to play a significant role in children's decisions to truant from school: almost 30 per cent were bullied so severely they were too scared to return to school, and 46 per cent of respondents had been 'badgered' into skipping school by their peers.[3] These figures explain truanting not as an antieducational and rebellious choice, but rather as a rational response to a high-stress situation in which the truant could exert limited autonomy. Significantly, the study also found that 'for 68% of truants, plans to fine or sanction parents when their children missed class were no deterrent at all'.[4] These findings reflect the constraints to inclusion that influence children's decisions to truant, which hardly suggest an apathetic disregard for school or learning on the part of children or their parents. Such research into the impact of material deprivation provides a sharp contrast to policy responses such as the fines for parents whose children truant, in which the 'solution' rests upon further penalizing families (see chapter one).

This discussion has outlined the material penalties associated with poverty, which may compromise children's potential to succeed in school. This includes the pressure of financial stress upon the home, and the associated responsibilities for children, leading to a sense of 'growing up faster' than their peers (Foster et al. 2008). It also extends outside of the home, in living within communities suffering similar pressures and anxiety. We can therefore understand material deprivation to impact in varying ways upon children's access to quality schooling, in relation to the type of school accessible, factors compromising attendance, and once inside school, the opportunities for inclusion. However, as Gale (2011) has argued, social justice in education is not simply an issue of access to quality education. The next section explores the processes within school that may impact upon the differential experiences for children in poverty from their more advantaged peers, understood through the notion of underclass cultures and the ways that schools respond to these.

Bind 2: The alien culture of schooling

To speak of the culture of schooling as alien for children (and their families) in poverty asserts that the aspiration to achieve educational success should not be equated with the opportunity to realize it (McLeod 2009). As discussed in chapter one, the MUD conception attributes blame to the low aspirations of families in poverty in explaining why children are not successful in school. It is worth noting at the outset that this assumption is not borne out by the evidence. Kempson's (1996) meta-analysis of 31 qualitative studies into the effects of poverty found that families in poverty had the same aspirations as others in society: 'they want a job; a decent home, and an income that is enough to pay the bills with a little to spare' (4). However, she also observed that due to the material consequences brought about by social and economic changes, low-income families were highly uncertain about achieving these aspirations and 'felt deeply pessimistic regarding their own children's futures' (5). More recently, research into the Effective Provision of Pre-School, Primary and Secondary Education

Project (EPPSE) 3–14 study in England (2007–2011) found that students from disadvantaged backgrounds shared generally the same high aspirations for higher education as their more affluent peers (Baker et al. 2014). This was despite such aspirations being 'unlikely to be realized, given existing patterns of continuation rates to higher education and their [children's] levels of educational achievement' (20). If the importance of educational success is recognized as much for those in poverty as for middle-class families, how might the culture of schooling be implicated in understanding parents' vastly different perceptions as to whether schooling will lead to educational success for their children?

One way of understanding the cultural bind confronting children in poverty concerns the processes of *educational* and *cultural* differentiation (Brown 1987). Educational differentiation refers to the difficulties that students in poverty confront when engaging with academic disciplines and the knowledge that they can provide. There has been a major debate concerning this issue (Bourdieu 1974; 1977; Young 2007). Cultural differentiation is intimately connected to disciplinary knowledge, because the cultural modalities in which disciplinary knowledge is taught are middle class. Michael Young (2009) has captured the distinction between the educational and the cultural as that of between powerful knowledge and knowledge of the powerful. Whereas knowledge of the powerful refers to 'who defines "what counts as knowledge" and has access to it' (13), powerful knowledge refers to 'what the knowledge can do – for example, whether it provides reliable explanations or new ways of thinking about the world' (14). Young's argument is that powerful or disciplinary knowledge is essential for all students and particularly those that are considered disadvantaged.

However, it is much more difficult, in practice, to divorce powerful knowledge from the knowledge of the powerful because as Bourdieu (1974) has argued, knowledge and its associated pedagogy is intimately bound up with the culture and the lives of school children of the dominant class. He encapsulates this idea in the notion of cultural capital, in which the culture of the homes of middle-class families, including the books they read, their leisure activities, consumption of culture, and their conversations, are consistent with the culture of the school.

Annette Lareau (2000) has looked at how this account ties in with the everyday lives of middle- and working-class students, especially in relation to their leisure activities. The middle-class children in Lareau's study could be seen to engage in adult-organized activities, which honed their interpersonal skills and confidence, and enabled them to leverage an advantage in relation to school:

> [Middle-class children] spent a lot of time greeting a wide range of other adults, learning to look people in the eye and shake their hands. They spent a great deal of time 'performing' in situations similar to school; as for example, at soccer practice, they lined up, followed directions, performed tasks upon the request of adults and demonstrated their skill in a public setting.

(168)

From this account, it is possible to see how for middle-class children, out-of-school activities translate into dispositions that can lead to school success. Their easy relationships with adults can be applied equally to relationships with teachers. By the same token, schoolwork often involves performing in a public setting in the way they are familiar with. The leisure pursuits of working-class children, however, lacked such opportunities: 'Once home they settled into a flow of activities more under their control, such as television watching, eating snacks, riding bikes, or playing with friends outside' (165). This example illustrates some of the ways in which the lived experiences of middle-class children connect with the cultural expectations of school, preparing them for the performative ideals underpinning school success. In contrast, the more solitary and unstructured nature of working-class children's leisure activities have less resonance with the types of activities that children are expected to engage in at school.

Bourdieu's position can be summed up in his account of symbolic violence: The process of naturalizing dominant symbolic systems into popular culture, through the domination of one cultural group over another (1977; Bourdieu and Passeron 1977). Within school this refers to the marginalization of the cultural values of the working classes, and especially those in poverty, with respect to the dominant values of the school. Symbolic violence can be used to explain the school's role in translating cultural capital into a hierarchy of success and failure in terms of individual capability. In this way, children and their parents are held accountable for their own cultural disadvantage:

> The culture of the elite is so near to that of the school that children from the lower middle [and working] class can only acquire with great effort something which is given to the children of the cultivated classes – style, taste, wit – in short those attributes which seem natural in members of the cultivated classes and naturally expected from them precisely because . . . they are the culture of that class . . . Poor achievement for some groups [and success for others] in a society then, is not something inherent in cultural difference per se, but is an artifact of the way schools operate. Those with the appropriate cultural capital are reinforced with 'success' while others are not.
>
> (Harker 1990: 87)

In considering the operation of symbolic violence it is helpful to turn to the work of one of the most influential sociologists of education, Basil Bernstein, whose analyses of pedagogy and social class provide a complementary account of why school may be perceived as alien for children in poverty. Of key importance here is the significance Bernstein (1966) attributes to the highly differentiated linguistic registers of middle- versus working-class children. Children from middle-class backgrounds are likely to be exposed to what Bernstein calls an 'elaborated' code of speech. Through engaging in in-depth linguistic interaction in the home and community (e.g. in the description and explanation afforded to child questioning) they will be more likely to develop an expansive linguistic register. Working-class children, in contrast, are more likely to be exposed to a 'restricted' code of speech, where dialogue in the home and community is less verbose and more perfunctory. Because schools employ a linguistic register more in line with the elaborated codes of middle-class children, the form and nature of language within school is one way in which children in poverty are less favourably disposed to schooling pedagogies.

While the notion of symbolic violence accounts for the way that students are ranked in ways that are ultimately rigged by social class (Brown 2000), New Labour and Coalition governments have both expected teachers to perform the 'miracle' of equalizing the life chances of students in poverty through a combination of the state theory of learning and an inspection regime which many teachers consider to be a form of hectoring and bullying (see chapter one). While this approach and its consequences dominate public debate, educational researchers have engaged in two approaches to identify and address what has been an intractable problem. The first has reflected on how and under what policy conditions progressive pedagogies may engage working-class students. For example, Whitty (2012) has examined various pedagogical approaches that may create engagement. The second has documented the ways that performative pedagogies, consistent with the demands of the state theory of learning, create passive and conforming learners in working-class schools (Hempel-Jorgensen 2009). While these qualities might be considered desirable to control working-class students (as suggested by the employment of ex-service personnel in schools), they are not the learning orientations required to be academically successful.

To consider the culture of schooling as alien merits consideration of the reasons as to why, and in what ways, schooling pedagogies are alienating for children in poverty. In order to consider how students mediate and negotiate between the cultures of their lives in and out of school, and respond to the material challenges poverty may impose, it is helpful to consider the role of the peer group. It may be that friendships offer a way of countering the excluding effects of symbolic violence and material hardship, in creating solidarity and at times resistance, in school. By attending to the role of friendships we may come to better understand the responses of children in poverty, beyond that of a simple resist/conform duality. Underlying the following discussion of friendship is the insight that dominance relations, of the kind described by Bourdieu (1977), often entail the fragmentation of relationships amongst the dominated, and this can be true of the friendships that those in poverty form.

Bind 3: School friendships and their implication in learning

The claim that friendship can pose a bind against educational achievement does not undermine its fundamental role in rendering meaningful the daily school lives of children. Friendship has been shown to enable assimilation into the school community (Schwarz 1972; Ispa 1981), greater well-being and pro-school attitudes (Ladd and Kochenderfer 1996; Wentzel, Barry and Caldwell 2004) as well as academic achievement (Berndt and Keefe 1995; Wentzel and Caldwell 1997). However, the question of how friendships can be understood to lead to such gains has been explained through their implication in the formation of social capital (Brown 2012). The ways in which friendship can be converted into the social capital for academic success include 'support with classwork, keeping in contact over the phone to discuss homework and . . . helping with revision' (Demetriou et al. 2000: 437). Within the peer group, individual children may be seen as a resource because they are knowledgeable in a particular area, or some may act as intermediaries between teachers and their friends. Alternatively, friendship groups may also obstruct learning through peer group pressure to conform to antieducation behaviour (Demetriou et al. 2000; Galton et al. 1999).

In order to consider how some friendships may lead to an educational advantage while others may not, it is necessary to consider the role of friendship cultures. Research into peer cultures has highlighted the forms and functions of friendship as different for boys and girls, both within sociopsychological perspectives (Rubin 1980; Asher and Gottman 1981; Smilansky 1991) and in the feminist literature (Spender and Sarah 1980; Mahony 1985). While boys' friendships operate in the public spheres of the classroom, street and playground (Sherriff 2007), girls' friendships are more often connected to the altogether more private spheres of social life (Johnson and Aries 1983; O'Connor 1992). Although this may make them less visible within the classroom, it does not mean that friendships are less significant for girls. It may, however, explain why girls were for a long while overlooked by researchers. Recognition of such differences calls for a branching off in the mapping of the ethnographic research, between those interested in boys' and girls' friendships.

The public worlds of boys' friendships

Willis's (1977) seminal study raised the cultural importance of working-class boys' disengagement with school. His analyses distinguished between the school resisters (what he termed the 'lads') and those that went along with the demands of the school (the 'earoles'). The lads did not engage with schooling but sought rather to 'have a laugh'. They effectively 'bounced off' the school because it was not relevant to their future plans for manual work. In turn, the lads' identities as future manual workers were bound up with sexism and racism.[5] Willis's work heralded a series of illuminating ethnographic studies into how some working-class boys respond to the issues of symbolic violence through resistance (Walker 1988; Connell 1989; Mac an Ghaill 1994). This literature has shed light upon the importance of the social group in constructing collective identities that shape boys' orientations to work and education. Not all ethnographic studies found working-class youth resisting, others such as Brown (1987) found that (as with the 'earoles' in Willis's study) many 'ordinary kids' went along with the demands of the school, even if they saw no real point in them. In other words, antischool subcultures were only one of a number of subcultures that working-class youth utilized as a resource in responding to symbolic violence (Bourdieu 1977).

Walker's (1988) five-year study into boys' friendship groups within an Australian working-class urban school followed four groups of boys: the 'footballers', 'the Greeks', the 'hand-ballers' and the 'three friends' across the different sites of school, as well as public spaces such as the street, discos and sports grounds. Unlike many other subcultural ethnographies, Walker was interested in the most dominant of the groups (the 'footballers') for whom the shared activity and culture of sport and racist, sexist and homophobic discourses played a key function in the shaping of their identities as 'true' or 'real' 'Aussies'. Walker's study was significant in exposing the ways in which hegemonic forms of class, ethnicity and sexuality operate so as to oppress and subordinate minority friendship forms. This highlighted the performative element of dominant male friendship groups, and how the domination and contestation of space in the classroom and playground through 'having a laugh' is one way in which boys assert power in school.

In starting to unpack the role of social group identities for boys, it is necessary to shift attention towards the role and interplay of different boys' friendship groups in school. The literature on boys' friendships has frequently resulted in typographies of friendship groups. These included the hard-workers: 'earoles' (Willis 1977), 'Cyrils' (Kessler et al. 1985), 'swots' (Connell 1989) and 'academic achievers' (Mac an Ghaill 1994); the sporty and popular: 'bloods' (Kessler et al. 1985), 'footballers' (Walker 1988), 'cool guys' (Connell 1989) and 'macho lads' (Mac an Ghaill 1994); and lastly, the unpopular nonconformers: 'lads' (Willis 1977), 'three friends' (Walker 1988) and 'wimps' (Connell 1989). Such labels are important according to Sherriff (2007), as boys' behaviour must be read as an identity-making performance in order to affirm peer group membership. He suggests that the more secure the individual's identification with the peer group, the stronger his sense of self-worth. A critical aspect of this performance is in reinforcing the value of one's own group through the devaluation of those outside of the friendship group. This might involve private, but especially public, taunting, teasing and denouncement of another group. Here we may understand how the processes of recognition of peer group status are exclusionary. The individual must demonstrate to those internal to as well as external to the peer group, his own right to inclusive status and other peers' status as nondeserving. There is no status in being part of a group that anyone can join freely! This suggests that inclusion within the social group also results in, and even requires, the exclusion of others. Peer group–to–peer group devaluation is a notable feature of other ethnographic research into boys' friendship groups (Willis 1977; Brown 1987; Pollard 1987). It also helps explain why social groups may conform to the expectations of the school if they are successful in these terms, while those less academically successful may publicly reject them in order to reinforce the social group identity as in opposition to the values and expectations of school success.

The private worlds of girls' friendships

As one of the first in-depth studies into girls' friendships in school, the Harvard Project was significant in attending to the confident voices of girls as moral agents within schooling systems that try to control and silence them (Gilligan 1982; Brown and Gilligan 1992). This work uncovered the ways in which some girls' voices are dominated by more powerful others, and in showing how gendered discourses may legitimize this. However, it has since been argued that in implicating other women as the main perpetrators in the oppression of adolescent girls, this work oversimplified the inequalities between girls and the ways in which they wield power over each other (Hey 1997: 10).

Studying the dynamics involved in girls' social groups is a lot harder given the altogether more private world of girls' friendships, which are often performed outside of the public gaze of the classroom, the street and the playground, in favour of the hidden spaces of the corridors, cloakrooms and bedrooms. Due to the private and intimate nature of girls' friendships, it might be argued that processes of inclusion and exclusion are more formative in shaping girls' experiences *within* the friendship group as opposed to between groups (in the case of boys). This may explain why researchers have been more interested in considering the internal dynamics of girls' friendship groups (Nilan 1991; Quick and Winter 1995; George and Browne 2000).

A sensitive exploration into the private lives of girls' friendships in secondary school can be seen in Valerie Hey's (1997) study, which uncovers themes of intimacy, secrecy and the struggle for acceptance. Hey's research underlines the significant work involved in the daily survival of navigating school. In taking account of the classed, gendered, but also ethicized nature of girls' friendship groups, Hey's work highlighted the ways in which girls' friendships are implicated in the production of cultural hegemony. Through illuminating the inflections of these categories upon the values and social identities of friendship groups, Hey considered the variation in friendship groups lacking in power. Attending to such differences enabled her to reflect upon the tensions evident in consolidating the competing perceived expectations of boys, with an embedded sense of social reputations: 'how to be "lovely (and) gorgeous" without being "slaggy", how to be provocative without "doing it" and how to turn boys on "but not get carried away"'(84).

Limitations upon the opportunities for empowering female friendship identities were also explored in Diane Reay's (2001) work, in discussing the variant, albeit limited, versions of femininity found within one primary classroom. Friendship groupings were positioned within a hierarchy of popularity and validation by which girls, boys and their teachers generally concurred. Reay discussed the social and cultural resources by which girls negotiated discourses of femininities and masculinities, in constructing conforming, as well as transgressive, gendered identities: 'But this is not to suggest that these children have myriad choices of which variant of femininity and masculinity to assume. They do not. Class, ethnicity and emergent sexualities all play their part, and constrain as well as create options' (163). Whereas the friendship groups more closely aligned with conventional notions of femininity were prone to denigration within the wider peer group, the more accepted friendship groups aspired to reject or subvert such conventional discourses, and were active in carving spaces to resist gender subordination. Nevertheless, this did little to challenge the prevailing gender order that it was, in sum, 'better being a boy' (164).

More recent work within the literature of girls' friendship groups has explored the implications for girls in having friendships characterized by more intense emotions in comparison with boys. As discussed in chapter one, recognition of this feature of girls' friendships has led attempts in some schools to discourage children from forming close friendships, on account of the distressing nature of fall-outs, and importantly for schools, the impact that this can have upon learning. George's work (2007) concerned the durability of girls' friendship groups and the stability they offer as a secure resource for inclusion within school. She discussed the propensity for girls' friendships to fluctuate and reformulate, particularly upon transition to secondary school, and suggested that the hierarchical formation of their friendship groups are underpinned by dynamics of inclusion and exclusion, which may well have an emotional cost. As a consequence friendship groups frequently shift and inevitably some girls get left on the fringes. Nilan (1991) has argued that such decisions are 'rational', 'considered', and underpinned by a strict moral code: 'The exclusion of a group member was not an arbitrary event, not just a seasonal "weeding-out" of group members, but was a process informed at every stage by moral justifications that all the girls took very seriously' (167). This challenges the dominant view that fluctuations within girls' friendships reflect the fickle, bitchy or malicious nature of girls' friendships bonds (Davies 1979). On the contrary, Nilan's work shows the extent to which girls took their friendships seriously, and serious too were the consequences for those who defied the moral order of the friendship group.

In considering the dynamics of girls' friendship groups in relation to learning and teacher judgments, George and Browne's (2000) study is particularly illuminating. Supporting previous work highlighting the importance of moral ordering within girls' friendships (Nilan 1991; Hey 1997), this study found the status of best friend(s) to be entrenched within processes of inclusion and exclusion. However, in contrast to Nilan (1991) these processes were constructed not on the basis of mutual trust, but of domination, with the leader exerting emotional power over the other members of the group (see also Quicke and Winter 1995). In explaining this, George and Browne distinguished between the 'inner' circle and 'peripheral' groups, whereby the former were far more secure in the validation of the group, and had greater say in who was in, and who was out. The peripheral groups had, in contrast, far less control over inclusion/exclusion dynamics and were more anxious concerning their group status, particularly in relation to the group leader. Moreover a point of significant interest here was that group leaders were among the highest-achieving girls within the group, a status that was reinforced by teachers' endorsement of their superior ability. This suggests that low-achieving girls may be more vulnerable to social exclusion than low-achieving boys within the friendship group.

Currie, Kelly and Pomerantz (2007) have labelled girls' exclusionary in-group behaviours 'meanness' as a regularity function of group membership, and productive of social identities of being 'in' or 'out' of fashion, favour and respect (36). 'Meanness' as a strategy of asserting power in the school setting, where pupils have little, is seen by Currie and her colleagues to be less a reflection upon individual girls and more as a rational response, 'constitutive, rather than maladaptive of dominant culture' (33).

Balancing peer group and teacher expectations

The findings from the friendship literature presented here suggest that for boys and girls, processes of inclusion and exclusion play a central role in the daily business of navigating school life. Such processes are complex, dynamic and gendered, and further complicated in relation to school achievement. Both within and between friendship groups we can see that children are variously positioned in the power and autonomy they are able to exert, and in their capacity to mobilize the network for social capital gains. Here the work of Francis, Skelton and Read (2010) is enlightening in uncovering the strategies by which boys and girls negotiate the competing demands of school and sociability, and the success afforded those able to 'balance' these effectively. The focus of their study was upon pupils who were exceptionally high achieving and popular with peers and teachers (HAP), yet despite the importance attributed to school success, findings indicated that all of HAP girls and around half of HAP boys spoke of friendship as the single most important part of school. Students' gendered and ingenious strategies maintained an emphasis upon the social, in presenting achievement as 'effortless' and incidental. Among the girls, strategies included 'precociousness' and emphasizing relative maturity above peers (328), and among the boys, 'clowning' as a gentle and nonaggressive form of classroom confrontation (329). While those socially and academically successful at school may be able to balance competing school pressures, the consequences for those boys and girls who cannot were evident in a study by Warrington and Younger (2011). They identified the fear, anxiety and above all, loss of self-integrity young people faced in having to sacrifice their ideals or risk exclusion, perhaps most poignantly expressed in the words of one boy: 'being yourself could ruin your life' (163).

This review of research into boys' and girls' social groups has highlighted the altogether different forms and functions of friendship for both genders. Considering the role of friendships in mediating children's aspirations towards, and performances within, school is helpful in further understanding the tensions apparent between competing expectations of the peer group and the school, and how these may sit with respect to broader cultural backgrounds.

Ambiguities in orientations to schooling for boys and girls in poverty

The purpose of this review into the dynamics of friendships for children in school is in starting to unpack some of the ambiguities apparent in the orientations to school for children in poverty. If popularity with peers and teachers empowers children within their friendship groups in establishing a secure social standing and confidence to participate in learning activities, then we might expect the opposite to be the case for the children on the fringes of friendship groups. And children in poverty are more likely to be on the periphery of peer groups on account of material deprivation (bind 1) and cultural inequalities (bind 2). This enables a more nuanced account of educational failure than if we were to consider any one bind alone. Such ambiguities may be probed further in understanding the orientations to school for children in poverty in the context of highly mobile lives. This leads on to the fourth and final bind, which considers the effects of irregular school changes upon children's inclusion in school, and how this is affected by children's relationship orientations, as a function of inclusionary as well as exclusionary practices.

Bind 4: The impact of 'turbulence' (irregular school moves)

The experience of irregular school transitions has been defined in the educational literature as 'turbulence' or more precisely: 'A child joining or leaving school at a point other than the normal age in which children start or finish their education at that school, whether or not this involves a move of home' (Dobson and Henthorne 1999: 5). Following changes to family and labour market structures, welfare reform, the growth in parental preference policies and a rise in formal exclusions, the number of children who move schools at irregular times has been increasing since the late 1990s. Turbulence is now a major educational issue in Britain (Dobson and Pooley 2004; Machin, Telhaj and Wilson 2006), as it is in many other countries including the United States (GAO 1994) and New Zealand (Lauder et al. 1994). The concern for educationalists is that the majority of studies undertaken in the United States and Britain suggest that turbulence is associated with an educational penalty for children (Simmons et al. 1987; Ingersoll, Scamman and Eckering 1989; Haveman, Wolfe and Spaulding 1991; Wood et al. 1993; Coleman 1988; 1990; Hagan et al. 1996; Pribesh and Downey 1999; Goldstein, Burgess and McConnell 2007). While there are a number of groups of children who change schools at irregular times, including Travellers, the military and what Knowles (2003) refers to as lifestyle migrants (families who elect to move for reasons of social mobility), by far the largest turbulent group are children in poverty (e.g. asylum seekers, refugees, those living in temporary social housing, those escaping domestic abuse and those in families who move to avoid debt). Not only are children experiencing turbulence increasingly likely to be from low-income families, but the negative impact upon educational achievement has been found to be cumulative with each subsequent move (RSA 2013: 5). For this reason it is important to consider turbulence as a further bind upon children in poverty.

Those studies that have aimed to theorize the educational penalty for children experiencing turbulence have appropriated social capital theory (Coleman 1988; Pribesh and Downey 1999; Hagan et al. 1996). Using Coleman's (1988) definition, these studies have emphasized the significance and interconnection for the child, of the relationship between the family, the community and school. This is because social connections between child and adult in different contexts 'can provide the child with support and rewards from additional adults that reinforce those received from the first, and can bring about norms and sanctions that could not be instituted by a single adult alone' (Coleman 1990: 593). Coleman (1988) found that following irregular school transition, pupils were more likely to drop out of high school, arguing that it is the disruption caused by turbulence to family and community social capital that explains the educational penalty. Following relocation, relationships between the child and significant role models in the community (including extended family) are broken, while family relationships are put under strain, resulting in a rupture in the transmission of pro-schooling values to the child in different social contexts. As an additional pressure upon family life, relocation itself can alienate both the child and their family in the school and community. This may be compounded by the particular context in which the move takes place, such as redundancy, illness or family break-up. Given the familial stressors, it takes little imagination to consider why the child's application to schoolwork may be dampened.

Coleman's focus, however, was on the parents and the way they constructed community social capital on behalf of the children. Pribesh and Downey (1999) later developed Coleman's theory in situating the child as an independent purveyor of social capital in their own right. By considering the social networks of the child, these authors identified a more profound educational penalty for school and home moves than either one of these taken in isolation.

The most recent work on turbulence has sought to explain the findings of large quantitative studies through exploring qualitatively the ways in which social capital might operate in school through children's friendships, and how 'turbulent' children's friendship orientations may mediate inclusion/exclusion processes (Brown 2012). In comparing children's friendship orientations with those of their peers who had never moved schools and locations, children experiencing turbulence could be seen to lack trust in four key areas, including confidentiality, honouring promises, endurance following arguments, and reciprocity of trust (232). Furthermore, absence of trust was explained through the effects of severed significant relationships such as grief and loss due to weakened access to friends, family, neighbours, teachers, and community role models (230–31).

Unpacking the lives of children in poverty

In reflecting on the four binds presented in this chapter it is pertinent to conclude in considering potential lines of interconnection. While the experiences of children in poverty may well be mediated by the cultural, political, and social contexts in which children live, there may be commonalities in the ways that poverty impacts on children's social relationships, which may shape their orientations towards school and learning. The social and economic worlds have changed over the period since Willis's (1977) seminal study, and here there are two points to be made. First, children continue in their struggle to negotiate the cultural realm of the knowledge of the powerful. Second, it is in the nature of ethnographic studies that they are situated in a specific time and place, and that while the binds that children encounter in negotiating middle-class schooling may or may not be changing, the meanings, concerns and relationships that help them to navigate these binds will also change.

The following chapters consider the stories of six children in poverty, in discussing the unique ways in which they negotiated the material, cultural and social binds upon their schooling experiences. The stories focus upon the ways in which children navigate through friendship networks, in considering the centrality of peer inclusion in terms of school life. These stories problematize and develop an account of children's schooling orientations and aspirations, in highlighting the tensions and ambiguities apparent within their schooling experiences. It should be stressed that it is in the nature of ethnographic work that we cannot locate all the children neatly within all four binds: some will overcome one or more of them, but even then it is important to see how they do it and what penalties they incur.

Notes

1 Gregory Bateson and colleagues (1956) first proposed the 'double-bind' to describe the situation for children caught in a continuing dynamic of mediating conflicting messages from their parent(s) in which it is impossible to provide a satisfactory response for the domineering party, engendering a sense of powerlessness and lack of control. Over 50 years later psychologist Stephen Hinshaw (2009) appropriated the double-bind theory to describe the pressures affecting contemporary Western girls and young women, in what he calls not a double-bind but a triple-bind. He claims that pressures emerge not only from within the family but also within Western society itself, which explains the increasing range of mental illnesses apparent in the West, including depression, low self-esteem and eating disorders. The specific triple-bind Hinshaw identifies concerns conflicting social pressures; those necessary to be liked (empathy, obedience, helpfulness, nurture); the performative ideals necessary to be admired (success in school, sport and work); and lastly, the narrow set of social standards (concerning appearance and attractiveness) by which to be desired (3). Both these theories conceive of the 'bind' as a set of values and expectations embedded through the institutions of the family, school, community and (new) media. I am advancing a conceptual lens which treats the 'bind' not as an expectation or set of values

per se, but rather as a mediator of children's schooling values and expectations. I retain its sense of imposition whereby there is little space for resistance and little chance of success.
2 Wolf, Lennox and Cutler (1986) have argued according to socioanalytic theory that the forms of self-presentation required to 'get along' (acceptance, approval and popularity) are incompatible with those required to get ahead (power, control and status). Whereas the former concerns the approval of others, the latter is orientated more actively towards personal gain (356).
3 This study has been archived but is available at http://archive-org.com/page/634030/2012-11-12/http://www.rathboneuk.org/newsarticle.aspx?ID=691) [Accessed 26 June 2014].
4 Ibid.
5 Women played a role in Willis's ethnography but only as objects of the lads' desires.

References

Asher, S. R. and Gottman, J. M. (1981) *The Development of Children's Friendships*, Cambridge: Cambridge University Press.
Baker, W., Sammons, P., Blatchford, I., Sylva, K., Melhuish, T. and Taggart, B. (forthcoming 2014) 'Aspirations, education and inequality in England: insights from the effective provision of pre-school, primary and secondary education project', *Oxford Review of Education*.
Ball, S. J., Bowe, R. and Gewirtz, S. (2001) 'Circuits of schooling: a sociological exploration of parental choice of school in social-class contexts', in A. H. Halsey, H. Lauder, P. Brown and A. S. Wells (eds) *Education: culture, economy, society*, Oxford: Oxford University Press.
Bateson, G., Jackson, D., Haley, J. and Weakland, J. (1956) 'Toward a theory of schizophrenia', *Behavioral Science*, 1: 251–64.
Berndt, T. J. and Keefe, K. (1995) 'Friends' influence on adolescents' adjustment to school', *Child Development*, 66: 1312–29.
Bernstein, B. (1966) 'Elaborated and restricted codes: an outline', *Sociological Enquiry*, 36 (2): 254–61.
Berthoud, R. and Kempson, E. (1992) *Credit and Debt: the PSI report*, London: Policy Studies Institute.
Bourdieu, P. (1974) 'The school as a conservative force: scholastic and cultural inequalities', in J. Eggleston (ed.) *Contemporary Research in the Sociology of Education*, London: Methuen.
Bourdieu, P. (1977) *Outline of a Theory of Practice*, Cambridge: Cambridge University Press.
Bourdieu, P. and Passeron, J. C. (1977) *Reproduction: in education, society, and culture*, London: Sage.
Brown, C. (2012) 'Exploring how social capital works for children who have experienced school turbulence: What is the role of friendship and trust for children in poverty?', *International Studies in Sociology of Education*, 22 (3), 213–36.
Brown, L. M. and Gilligan, C. (1992) *Meeting at the Crossroads: women's psychology and girls' development*, Cambridge MA: Harvard University Press.
Brown, P. (1987) *Schooling Ordinary Kids: inequality, unemployment, and the new vocationalism*, London: Tavistock.

Brown, P. (2000) 'The globalisation of positional competition', *Sociology*, 34 (4): 633–53.
Coleman, J. S. (1988) 'Social capital in the creation of human capital', *American Journal of Sociology*, 94: 95–120.
Coleman, J. S. (1990) *Equality and Achievement in Education*, Boulder, CO: Westfield Press.
Connell, R. W. (1989) 'Cool guys, swots, and wimps: the interplay of masculinity and education', *Oxford Review of Education*, 15: 291–303.
Currie, D. H., Kelly, D. M. and Pomerantz, S. (2007) '"The power to squash people": understanding girls' relational aggression', *British Journal of Sociology of Education*, 28 (1): 23–37.
Davies, L. (1979) 'Deadlier than the male? Girls' conformity and deviance in schools', in L. Barton and R. Meighan (eds) *Schools, Pupils and Deviance*, Driffield: Nafferton Books.
Demetriou, H., Goalen, P. and Rudduck J. (2000) 'Academic performance, transfer, transition and friendship: listening to the student voice', *International Journal of Educational Research*, 33 (4): 425–41.
Dobson, J. and Henthorne, K. (1999) *Pupil Mobility in Schools: DfEE Research Report, RR168*, London: DfEE.
Dobson, J. and Pooley, E. (2004) *Mobility, Equality and Diversity: a study of pupil mobility in the secondary school system*, London: UCL, Migration Research Unit.
Foster, H., Hagan, J. and Brooks-Gunn, J. (2008) 'Growing up fast: stress exposure and subjective "weathering" in emerging adulthood', *Journal of Health and Social Behavior*, 49: 162–77.
Francis, B., Skelton, C. and Read, B. (2010) 'The simultaneous production of educational achievement and popularity: How do some pupils accomplish it?', *British Educational Research Journal*, 36 (2): 317–40.
Gale, T. (2011) *Principles from/for social justice policy in Australian education: a potted history*. Presentation to the British Educational Research Association conference, London, 6–8 September.
Galton, M., Gray, J. and Rudduck, J. (1999) *The Impact of School Transitions and Transfers on Pupil Progress and Attainment, DfEE Report*, Norwich: Her Majesty's Stationery Office.
General Accounting Office (1994) *Elementary School Children: many change schools frequently, harming their education*, Report to the Honorable Marcy Kaptur, House of Representatives, Washington, DC, February.
George, R. (2007) *Girls in a Goldfish Bowl: moral regulation, ritual and the use of power amongst inner city girls*, Rotterdam: Sense.
George, R. and Browne, N. (2000): ' "Are you in or are you out?" An exploration of girl friendship groups in the primary phase of schooling', *International Journal of Inclusive Education*, 4 (4): 289–300.
Gilligan, C. (1982) *In A Different Voice*, Cambridge, MA: Harvard University Press.
Goldstein, H., Burgess, S. and McConnell, B. (2007) 'Modelling the effect of pupil mobility on school differences in educational achievement', *Journal of the Royal Statistical Society*, 170 (4): 941–54.
Hagan, J., MacMillan, R. and Wheaton, B. (1996) 'New kid in town: social capital and life course effects of family migration on children', *American Sociological Review*, 61 (3): 368–85.

Hallam, S. and Roaf, C. (1995) *Here Today, Here Tomorrow: helping schools to promote attendance*, London: Calouste Gulbenkian Foundation.
Harker, R. (1990) 'Class, dispositions and Bourdieu', in R. Harker, C. Mahar and C. Wilkes (eds) *An Introduction to the Work of Pierre Bourdieu: The Practice of Theory*, London: Palgrave Macmillan.
Haveman, R., Wolfe, B. and Spaulding, J. (1991) 'Childhood events and circumstances influencing high school completion', *Demography*, 28 (1): 133–157.
Hempel-Jorgensen, A. (2009) 'The construction of the "ideal pupil" and pupils' perceptions of "misbehaviour" and discipline: contrasting experiences from a low-socio-economic and a high-socio-economic primary school', *British Journal of Sociology of Education*, 30 (4): 435–48.
Hey, V. (1997) *The Company She Keeps: an ethnography of girls' friendship*, Buckingham: Open University Press.
Hinshaw, S. R. with Kranz, R. (2009) *The Triple Bind: saving our teenage girls from today's pressures*, New York: Ballantine Books.
Ingersoll, G. M., Scamman, J. P. and Eckerling, W. D. (1989) 'Geographic mobility and student achievement in an urban setting', *Educational Evaluation and Policy Analysis*, 11: 143–49.
Ispa, J. (1981) 'Peer support among Soviet day care toddlers', *International Journal of Childhood Development* 4: 251–69.
Johnson, F. and Aries, E. (1983) 'The talk of women friends', *Women's Studies International Forum*, 6 (4): 353–61.
Kempson, E. (1996) *Life on a Low Income*, York: Joseph Rowntree Foundation.
Kempson, E., Bryson, A. and Rowlingson, K. (1994) *Hard Times? How poor families make ends meet*, London: Policy Studies Institute.
Kessler, S., Ashenden, D. J., Connell, R. W. and Dowsett, G. W. (1985) Gender relations in secondary schooling, *Sociology of Education*, 58 (1): 34–38.
Knowles, C. (2003) *Race and Social Analysis*, London: Sage.
Ladd, G. W. and Kochenderfer, B. J. (1996) 'Linkages between friendship and adjustment during early school transitions', in W. M. Bukowski, A. F. Newcomb and W. W. Hartup (eds) *The Company They Keep: Friendship in childhood and adolescence*, New York: Cambridge University Press, 322–46.
Lareau, A. (2000) 'Social class and the daily lives of children: a study from the United States', *Childhood*, 7 (2): 155–71.
Lauder, H., Hughes, D., Waslander, S., Thrupp, M., McGlinn, J., Newton, S. and Dupuis, A. (1994) *The Creation for Market Competition in New Zealand*, Wellington: Ministry of Education.
Lupton, R. (2003) *Poverty Street: the dynamics of neighbourhood decline and renewal*, Bristol: Policy Press.
Lupton, R. (2007) 'Schools in disadvantaged areas: low attainment and a contextualised policy response', in H. Lauder, P. Brown, J. Dillabough and A. H. Halsey (eds) *Education, Globalization and Social Change*, Oxford: Oxford University Press.
Mac an Ghaill, M. (1994) *The Making of Men: masculinities, sexualities, and schooling*, Buckingham: Open University Press.
Machin, S., Telhaj, S. and Wilson, J. (2006) 'The mobility of English school children', *Fiscal Studies*, 27 (3): 253–80.
MacLeod, J. (2009) *Ain't No Makin' It: aspirations and attainment in a low-income neighborhood* (3rd ed.), Boulder, CO: Westview Press.

Mahony, P. (1985) *Schools for the Boys?*, London: Hutchinson.
Middleton, S., Ashworth, K. and Walker, R. (1994) *Family Fortunes: pressures on parents and children in the 1990s*, London: Child Poverty Action Group (CPAG).
Millar, J. and Ridge, T. (2001). *Families, Poverty, Work and Care: a review of the literature on lone parents and low-income couple families with children, DWP Research Report No. 153*, Leeds: Corporate Document Services.
Morris, L. and Ritchie, J. (1994) *Income Maintenance and Living Standards*, London: Social and Community Planning Research.
Nilan, P. (1991) 'Exclusion, inclusion and moral ordering in two girls' friendship groups', *Gender and Education*, 3: 163–82.
Pollard, A. (1987) 'Goodies, jokers and gangs', in A. Pollard (ed.), *Children and Their Primary Schools*, London: Falmer Press, 165–87.
Pribesh, S. & Downey, D. (1999) 'Why are residential and school moves associated with poor school performance?', *Demography*, 36 (4): 521–34.
O'Connor, P. (1992) *Friendships Between Women: a critical review*, Hemel-Hempstead: Harvester/Wheatsheaf.
O'Donnell, C. and White, L. (1998), *Invisible Hands: child employment in North Tyneside*, London: Low Pay Unit.
Quicke, P. and Winter, C. (1995) '"Best friends": a case study of girls' reactions to an intervention designed to foster collaborative group work', *Gender and Education*, 7: 259–81.
Reay, D. (2001) '"Spice girls", "nice girls", "girlies", and "tomboys": gender discourses, girls' cultures and femininities in the primary classroom', *Gender and Education*, 13 (2): 153–66.
Ridge, T. (2002) *Childhood Poverty and Social Exclusion from a Child's Perspective*, Bristol: Policy Press.
Rowlingson, K. and Kempson, E. (1993) *Gas Debt and Disconnections*, London: PSI.
Royal Society of Arts (2013) *Between the Cracks: exploring in-year admissions in schools in England*. Available at http://www.thersa.org/action-research-centre/learning,-cognition-and-creativity/education/reports-and-events/social-justice/between-the-cracks [Accessed 28 February 2013].
Rubin, Z. (1980) *Children's Friendships: the developing child*, London: Open Books.
Schwarz, J. C. (1972) 'Effects of peer familiarity on the behaviour of pre-schoolers in a novel situation', *Journal of Personality and Social Psychology*, 24: 276–84.
Sherriff, N. (2007) Peer group cultures and social identities, *British Educational Research Journal*, 33 (3): 349–70.
Simmons, R., Burgeson, R., Carlton-Ford, S. and Blythe, D. (1987) 'The impact of cumulative change in early adolescence', *Child Development*, 58 (5): 1220–34.
Smilansky, M. (1991) *Friendship in Adolescence and Young People*, Gaithersburg, MD: Psychological and Educational Publications.
Spender, D. and Sarah, E. (1980) *Learning to Lose: sexism and education*, London: Women's Press.
Sutton, L., Smith, N., Dearden, C. and Middleton, S. (2007) *A Child's-Eye View of Social Difference*, York: Joseph Rowntree Foundation.
Walker, J.C. (1988) *Louts and Legends: male youth culture in an inner city school*, Sydney: Allen and Unwin.

Warrington, M. and Younger, M. (2011) '"Life is a tightrope": reflections on peer group inclusion and exclusion amongst adolescent girls and boys', *Gender and Education*, 23 (2): 153–68.

Wentzel, K. R., Barry, C. M. and Caldwell, K. A. (2004) Friendships in middle school: Influences on motivation and school adjustment, *Journal of Educational Psychology*, 96 (2): 195–203.

Wentzel, K. R. and Caldwell, K. (1997) 'Friendships, peer acceptance, and group membership: relations to academic achievement in middle school', *Child Development*, 68: 1198–209.

Whitty, G. (2012) 'Social class and school knowledge: Revisiting the sociology and politics of the curriculum in the 21st century', in H. Lauder, H. Daniels, M. Balarin and J. Lowe (eds) *Educating for the Knowledge economy? Critical perspectives*, London: Routledge.

Willis, P. (1977) *Learning to Labor: how working class kids get working class jobs*, New York: Columbia University Press.

Willis, P., Jones, S., Cannan, J. and Hurd, G. (1990) *Common Culture: symbolic work at play in the everyday cultures of the young*, Milton Keynes: Open University Press.

Wolf, R. N., Lennox, R. D. and Cutler, B. L. (1986) 'Getting along and getting ahead: empirical support for a theory of protective and acquisitive self-presentation', *Journal of Personality and Social Psychology*, 50 (2): 356–61.

Wood, D., Halfon, N., Scarlata, D., Newacheck, P. and Nessim, S. (1993) 'Impact of family relocation on children's growth, development, school function and behavior', *Journal of the American Medical Association*, 270: 1334–38.

Young, M. (2007) *Bringing Knowledge Back In*, London: Routledge.

Young, M. (2009) 'What are schools for?', in H. Lauder, J. Porter and H. Daniels (eds) *Critical Perspectives on Education*, London: Routledge.

Chapter 3

Clive

School life following relocation, in a single-parent family

Life in primary school

I first met Clive when he was in year five at Ivy school (aged nine). He lived at home with his mother and two brothers in Thornton and had moved from Waterbrook, a large village some 30 miles away, just over a year previously. Clive's experience of living in a low-income family was on account of family break-up and in living in a single parent household. For Clive, the educational binds he experienced were connected to the practical and emotional penalties of family break-up. Clive's parents had separated when he was very young, and for a number of years he had continued to live in Waterbrook and attend the same school. He visited his father, who also remained in the village, on alternate weekends. Clive had approved of these arrangements as he felt warmly about his previous school in Waterbrook, 'Wishing-well', claiming: 'The teachers were nice. Miss . . . my teacher, was called Miss Ketley and she was nice.' However, the cost of accommodation in Waterbrook was no longer affordable for Clive's mother once Clive and his brothers were too old to share a room. She therefore decided to relocate to Thornton, closer to her extended family, where accommodation was cheaper. Clive expressed recognition for both the practical and emotional rationales for the move: 'We just had to come here to sell our flat and so we can see our family more.' This supports research indicating that children in low-income families show a keen awareness of the finances and pragmatics of family matters, as reflected both in the psychological (Benson and Furstenberg 2007; Foster, Hagan and Brooks-Gunn 2008) and the sociological (Ridge 2002) literature.

Wishing well was a small school with previous Ofsted reports indicating only 140 children on roll, and 96 per cent of parents agreeing that 'the school works closely with parents' (64 per cent response rate). Clive enjoyed the small 'family' feel of the school. He felt secure in his friendships and liked the one-year entry: 'But you [were] only one class of each year so that was better for me 'cause I used to never worry about splitting up with my friends or not.' Clive had described feeling 'very sad' about the move of home and school. He had never lived in Thornton, and therefore, the move represented a separation from his father and his friends. Clive continued to visit his father every other weekend and through this contact kept loosely in touch with his previous best friends:

> I leave town and go round my Dad's house 'cause my Dad lives in Waterbrook, and they [Clive's friends] live in Waterbrook, so when I go like to the shop I see them. Yeah and at a school fair, – 'cause I'm still allowed to go to my school fair, – I see them there and the next day they ask me if I can sleep round their house and I say okay, and then I just keep talking to them.
>
> (Clive)

However, these friendships had become a lot looser since the move; Clive did not communicate with them by phone and home visits were limited: 'I never have, I never have sleepovers round my Dad's.' As his account suggests, the material binds of school access can be seen to interrelate with issues of social inclusion in terms of Clive's weakening contact with previous school friends. We will return to this issue later.

School absence following relocation

Upon relocating to Thornton, it was a further two weeks before Clive joined his new school, Ivy. The two descriptors Clive used to characterize his feelings about his first day at Ivy school were 'shocked' and 'worried'. His reticence to start school may have been exacerbated by the protracted period of time it had taken to pack up, move and settle into the new area, which had left Clive feeling unprepared: 'I forgot I had to go to school, then my Mum reminded me on my first day, which wasn't nice.' This extended school absence suggested that the move may have been difficult for his mother, therefore delaying her from registering him in a new school. In this respect the material and emotional pressures of being in a single-parent family might have affected Clive's school and home life, whereby Clive's mother felt both an emotional and financial imperative to relocate.

Pedagogy, cultural capital and knowledge of the powerful

Ivy school was a larger primary than Wishing well. It had 232 children on the roll, which included few children of a minority ethnic background. The number of children claiming free school meals (FSM) was about average for the county at 7.8 per cent of the intake, and there were above-average special educational needs (SEN) at 26 per cent, partly on account of the school's excellent reputation for catering for children with additional learning needs. The school had a mixed socioeconomic composition and drew 40 per cent out of catchment area, primarily from council housing associations.

School inclusion strategies for new students

Now a fairly common practice in English primary schools, a 'buddying' scheme was employed by Ivy school, whereby two children were selected to look after Clive on his first day. This pairing had been effective in assuaging Clive's social uncertainties: 'At the start of the school people were looking after me . . . Marcus and Romain.' This created for Clive a positive introduction to the school in generating an impression that it was 'more friendly'. When asked who he was now friends with, Clive voiced some pride in his apparent popularity, in counting a long list on his fingers of children in the year group:

> Marcus, Romain . . . Laura, Jade, Tristan, Joss . . . and Mark and Mark again and Marcus . . . and all of . . . err . . . and Saul and Zach and Jake . . . Emma and Elaura and Molly and Katy.

Many of these friendships were fairly loose, but Clive's closest friends remained Marcus and Romain. More will be said of his friendships later, but firstly we will consider Clive's inclusion and participation in the classroom.

'Rule challenger' / 'recognized mathematician' dualism

While Clive was popular with a particular group of children, it is notable that the culture of the friendship group clashed with the formal learning culture of the classroom, as can be seen in the class observation below, taken from a silent reading session in his registration class:

> The children have silent reading and Miss Knight tells them to get on with it. They all do and there is a near silent noise level. Clive takes a while to settle and wanders around on the pretence of getting a book. While others are reading he appears to be colouring something in, which Marcus and Saul keep glancing over at, whispering. Miss Knight tells him to sit down a couple of times and at one point he comes over to the front desk to sharpen his pencil or something similar. It doesn't seem entirely necessary and I notice he has no shoes on. I wonder if it's a stunt to show off to Marcus and Saul as they are sniggering.
>
> (English lesson)

The reason that peer endorsement was apparently important for Clive in lessons may have been because he felt unable to be involved in learning. Clive professed to find lessons 'hard' and didn't enjoy them. It was clear that attention was important to Clive who liked to be at the centre of it, both in and out of the classroom, and yet he felt that when he sought the teacher's attention for a valid reason, he was overlooked: ' 'cause every time I put my hand up to ask for help, nobody answers me'. This comment reflects Clive's rejection of what he perceived to be the rules of the classroom culture: passive requests for attention, which he understood to be ineffective for his purposes. This may explain why Clive's response was to disengage with learning and challenge the rules of the classroom. There was but one exception to this lack of interest in learning. Maths was the only lesson that Clive claimed to enjoy. When asked what made him like this lesson he responded, '[It's] something what I'm good at.' For this reason maths represented an important subject for Clive as it was really the only lesson in which he felt he had talent (and he did). Clive was originally in the upper-set maths but at the time of observation he had been recently demoted to the lower set. During an informal conversation Clive's class teacher, Miss Knight, explained to me that this was due to his behaviour in class 'dragging down' the rest of the top group. While she recognized that he had the ability to be in the top group, his classroom behaviour was not considered to be conducive to the pace and performance of the top set. This is an example of what Gillborn and Youdell (2000) termed 'educational triage', which refers to schools' systematic attempts to: 'neglect certain pupils while directing additional resources to those deemed most likely to benefit (in terms of the externally judged standards)' (134). This pedagogic decision was of key importance in considering Clive's access to learning, in that he lacked the cultural capital of classroom behaviour in order to be granted entry into the top maths group. He did not possess the knowledge of the powerful (Young 2009) in terms of an orientation to learning that granted access into the higher class. On the contrary, Clive was unsure whether the down-setting was attributable to his test performance or his behaviour: 'Don't know why I got lowered err 'cause . . . I was naughty, or erm . . . got lowered for my test 'cause I got something like two in my test.' This example supports Bourdieu's (1977) claim that knowledge forms have an associated pedagogy which is intimately connected with the culture of children, such that access to knowledge, in this example, was not a result of meritocracy, but of a behavioural culture. In not understanding the culture of the school, in terms of the rules of inclusion and exclusion into hierarchical learning contexts, the response for Clive was confusion, which dented his confidence in his mathematical ability. This manifested in an anxiety about tests which seemed to have thrown him off balance: 'I'm not very good at maths tests . . . Yeah, I get, I get bad at tests but then afterwards when I go through it, I know the answers.' Clive was clearly upset to be put in the lower set: 'Didn't want to move . . . Yeah, 'cause all my friends are in there [top group].' This wasn't necessarily accurate according to the friendships Clive had named in the interview, where at least three of his friends listed were also in the lower maths group. But the comment reveals that Clive had the aspiration to identify with friends in the top group, perhaps because they were seen as talented, an aspiration that was then problematic to uphold. As Clive felt ignored when he put his hand up, he called out answers that he believed to prove himself to others in the class: 'Some people think I'm like . . . dumb and that so I just call it out the answer and then it's right. Then they think I'm not dumb.' This behaviour is illustrated in the following class observation of a maths lesson taught by a regular supply teacher:

> Clive misses the answer to a question and calls out, 'Is it 0.5?' Mrs Rose replies: 'if you are not going to listen Clive then I'll mark it wrong'. This doesn't require a response but Clive does anyway, 'I'll listen then.' Mrs Rose makes no further response to this comment. She moves on to question two and asks a child to answer (one of the ones with their hands up). As the child explains the answer Clive interrupts and Mrs Rose politely asks him not to call out. He is fidgety and punches his chair muttering, 'I got that one right.' He continues to call out during the activity and Mrs Rose ignores his comments. She continues going through the questions and Clive continues to call out answers exclaiming, 'This is easy.' He gets all the answers correct. A couple of other children are also keen to answer but they put their hands up and get chosen to answer.
>
> (lower-set maths lesson)

Clive's challenging behaviour wasn't acceptable to the teachers at Ivy school and contributed to him being held back from promotion to a higher maths group. He was therefore stuck in a circular pattern whereby all efforts to maintain his identity as a good mathematician continued to prevent him from being formally recognized as talented at maths.

Friendship dynamics and social capital penalties

When asked why Romain and Marcus were his best friends, Clive explained 'they're like me', which he qualified with respect to the common interests they shared, 'cause they all like football . . . and fishing'. It was through the shared practice of such activities that Clive understood 'like' individuals to be defined as a group. Football was one of the primary activities that were practiced in the playground and as Clive noted, particular friends were excluded from this activity: 'Emma we don't normally sort of hang around with Emma 'cause she doesn't like football and we do.' An interest in football was a valued social currency in Wishing-well school because it enabled Clive to play with his friends:

> It was better 'cause erm . . . 'cause my friends, every one like, you can go . . . play with a shed and you had to go in there and get a ball out . . . like they had erm black sacks for the balls. So we used to get them out.
>
> (Clive)

Through understanding the rules and in gaining the skills honed by practice in his last school, Clive had developed a strategy towards social inclusion in Ivy. However, we will see whether this form of social inclusion led to inclusion in relation to the formal aspects of school, or whether like Lareau's (2000) working-class children, out-of-school activities bore no connection to the skills needed to achieve in school.

The importance of conforming to a rule challenging friendship culture

Another reference by which Clive considered his friends to be 'like' him was in terms of outlook and disposition: 'Romain's happy, looks happy. Err Jade's happy, Laura's happy, Emma's happy erm . . . Jake's funny . . . Yeah, Romain's really lively. Marcus is lively, we're all, – my friends, – literally lively.' Humour in boys' friendship groups has been found to function so as disassociate effort from success in academic work (Pollard 1987; Mac an Ghaill 1994; Renold 2001). Unlike the middle-class boys in these studies, however, Clive's 'joker' classroom behaviour reflected no effort to disguise working, but rather can be understood as a bid for collective identity making, to reinforce membership as part of the group (Sherriff 1999). In the playground Clive's peer group culture manifested as a very exuberant group of children with an abundance of energy to run about and test the playground rules where possible. On one occasion Clive and his friends were told off by the dinner-lady for playing on the grass when they were not allowed to. Another aspect of playground behaviour involved teasing and winding each other up, not in a cruel way, but in a playful manner. For example, when I handed out a permission letter to Clive regarding his involvement in the study, his friends responded by taunting him for being a 'teacher's pet'. In Clive's presence Romain told me that 'Clive fancies you miss', and Marcus wrote some 'love letters' on Clive's behalf, which were delivered to me by various girls in the group. As Clive was present throughout it was clear that he was not distressed by this teasing, but played along with it good-naturedly and appeared to enjoy the attention of the group.

Overcoming classroom tensions

As can be seen from the discussion above, Clive's classroom behaviour of disrupting, challenging the teacher, playing the fool and demanding attention served the function of affirming his social group identity of being playful and funny, however, it also translated into disruptive behaviour in the classroom context. Clive was well aware of this quandary and it caused him conflicting loyalties, which at times resulted in him feeling torn between a learning orientation as a recognized mathematician (in striving to conform to behaviour suited to the top group) and in maintaining the support of his friends who would rather be entertained by him:

CLIVE: I have to turn round 'cause he . . . erm I want him [Marcus] to be my friend and then . . . and then I don't, if I don't turn round . . . he, he won't like me that much. So then I turn around and like we be silly and then I laugh like and I get told off.

CB: You're saying that you're worried that if you don't turn round, then he won't be your friend?
CLIVE: He would be my friend but he wouldn't hang around with me.
CB: So you are worried about them not hanging round with you?
CLIVE: I don't mind if they don't, like sometimes Emma doesn't like me and I'm alright with that . . . But it like . . . just don't . . . I like people to keep me company.

Clive was clearly anxious that if he didn't conform to behaviour which complied with the mischievous norm (e.g. distracting behaviour in class) he would lose his social group position. This statement fits with Clive's earlier comments on anxiety about splitting up with his friends.

The conflict between behaving and conforming (so to be recognized by his teachers as a mathematician) and misbehaving and messing around (so to be recognized by his friends as rule challenging and entertaining) caused some contradictory behaviour. Whereas in the example given above, Clive felt compelled to misbehave, on another occasion Clive acted responsibly so as to avoid misbehaviour by striving to differentiate himself from his friends within the classroom. It seemed that these efforts, however, were not always recognized by teachers, such as can be seen in Clive's discussion about having been sanctioned with a 'cross' on account of his friend's intention to distract him. This sanction was displayed on the whiteboard in view of pupils and teachers throughout the day. Two crosses led to a lunchtime detention and three resulted in a letter home and assignment of a one week behavioural record:

> He [Marcus] like . . . erm . . . he like in class he just kinda . . . he made me get a cross yesterday . . . 'Cause he came and sat next to me and then I put . . . I knew I were gonna be silly with him so I pushed him out the way and then I got a cross.
>
> (Clive)

Another example of the conflict between Clive's desire to be valued for his formal and his informal orientations in school, concerned his seating position in maths. Clive had self-elected to be sat on his own away from other children at the back of the classroom. He explained this decision to me as:

> I just like working on my own. I like, I like to work in a group, people in groups if we're really like . . . Erm not naughty 'cause sometimes my friends ask me to mess about and I say "okay then" and I get like a cross, or two crosses. Erm . . . like 'cause every time I sit at the front I always turn, turn . . . err look back to see my friends and if I kind of like sit at the back I can't . . . I just have to keep my eye forward 'cause I can't look back, there would be a wall.
>
> (Clive)

However, even this extreme course of action did not always create the desired behaviour that Clive aimed for in lessons, as can be seen in the example below:

> Marcus and Clive exchange a few comments with each other, although from Clive's seating position they are a couple of meters apart. Emma comes over to Clive's corner to get a couple of pencils from the drawers there. Clive starts to talk to her but she ignores him. Clive calls out the answer again to a question and this time Miss Knight accepts it and asks him how he worked it out, he explains and she praises him. Clive and Marcus both start making noises and Mrs Knight addresses Marcus (who is nearer her) 'Marcus if you do that once more you will be sent out.' He responds to her 'that's not fair, he was doing it as well' (gesturing to Clive).
>
> (lower-set maths)

Putnam (2000) provides a way to understand Clive's social group as a form of bonding social identity to 'reinforce exclusive identities and homogenous groups' (22). This is because of the narrow definition of what constituted group membership, in prescribing specific ways of *being* (funny/lively/rule challenging) and *doing* (football/disrupting classroom behaviour). However, the trade-off from this bonding function was an inability to achieve the bridging social capital, 'crucial for "getting ahead"' (23) through generating 'broader identities' (23) able to cross social cleavages, for example in adapting to the behaviour required to access the top maths class. Clive valued his identity as a recognized mathematician but this aspect of his identity did not gel with his 'rule-challenging' orientation as it manifested in the lower-set classroom, nor with his peer group in registration class lessons. Despite his best intentions, the pull of the peer group inevitably took precedence over being recognized as a mathematician, in generating a 'rule-challenging' and 'entertaining' peer group culture.

Navigating the binds at primary school

In primary school, the effects of turbulence can be seen to interact with the other binds associated with poverty. In terms of the material bind we might consider how financial circumstances led Clive's family to relocate, thus preventing him from continuing in the school where he was happy. Furthermore, issues of access were compounded in the period of absence associated with the move, which not only represented a significant gap in his learning, but also had the effect of breaking his school routine, and may well have been associated with additional difficulties in settling in to the new school. Clive's orientations to the formal and informal aspects of school were also mediated by his orientations, which prioritized social inclusion above inclusion within the higher maths group. This orientation may have been compounded by Clive's anxieties about 'splitting up with his friends', a concern that, by his own account, wasn't present prior to his move of home. The question is, to what extent such orientations persisted or altered following an extended 'settling-in' period and following transition into secondary school, and to consider what effect this had upon Clive's educational achievements.

Life in secondary school: Renegotiating the binds?

I next saw Clive two years later following transition to secondary school, when he was in year seven, aged 11 years old. He continued to live with his mother and brother in the flat they had initially moved into in Thornton. Clive joined the Maple school at the normal admission point at the beginning of year seven, alongside his peers. It was a large secondary school for children aged 11–16, with approximately 1,000 children on roll. The attainment of pupils upon entry was broadly in line with other maintained secondary schools, and the latest Ofsted report rated the school as an overall 'satisfactory' for effectiveness and 'good' for pastoral care and provision. The school streamed the year group according to attainment for English, maths and science. There were six classes of descending 'ability', with a further seventh class for special educational needs.

Continued school absence

Although Clive joined the Maple school on the first day of the school term, the issue of school absence had since arisen again, a concern I was alerted to through Clive's registration class teacher, Mr Harlow. While Clive's mother had provided notes detailing illness, Mr Harlow suspected that these periods away from school did not reflect genuine sickness. The following discussion reflects a disconnect, for Clive, between home and school, such that as Clive retreated more into home life, he felt increasingly isolated from school:

CB: Haven't you been a bit poorly quite a lot recently?
CLIVE: Yeah.
CB: How come?
CLIVE: Dunno . . .
CB: Does that make it hard to go back into school?
CLIVE: Yeah really hard.
CB: Do you prefer staying at home then to going in to school?
CLIVE: Yeah, it's boring [at school].
CB: What do you do at home?
CLIVE: Lie in my bed.
CB: That doesn't sound much fun?
CLIVE: I just fiddle with my gadgets and stuff.

This discussion suggests that Clive found school irrelevant and felt displaced. There was no suggestion of illness that kept him at home (he was still able to play with his gadgets) but rather his connection with his bed suggested the safety of his own company. If Clive's absence was self-elected as opposed to due to genuine illness, this would contradict the government view of truancy as a familial apathy towards school (corrective through financial penalties). In contrast, the reasons for Clive's absence may be more complex and less easily remedied through coercion to attend, as inferred through his response to the question, 'where is your favourite place?':

CLIVE: My room.
CB: What is it about it that you like?
CLIVE: Cozy, cool and I like having my own space.
CB: Do you not feel you have a space at school?
CLIVE: No, 'cause there's everyone around.
CB: Is it important because it's your personal space or your space with your family?
CLIVE: Personal space.

Clive would rather choose social isolation from his friends at school, even if that involved staying in his room where he felt comfortable and had some autonomy. Unfortunately, that only served to make him feel more isolated from school life and lessons, as the following discussion will elaborate upon.

Educational performance, cultural capital and knowledge of the powerful

In considering the success with which Clive had been able to negotiate the binds he had encountered in primary school, it is necessary to consider his educational performance at the end of key stage two, which is the point at which children finish their primary education. Clive's achievements in his key stage two SATs results were:

English:	Level 4
Maths:	Level 4
Science:	Level 4

These results are in line with the national target of level 4 for each of these subjects, which is the minimum grade requirement children are expected to achieve.[1] This suggests that with respect to Clive's national test outcomes at the end of primary school, he had not experienced an educational penalty according to national minimum targets. However, what these test scores do not show is the extent to which Clive's educational success reflected his personal potential, nor do they indicate what were the longitudinal effects of the binds Clive experienced. In order to illuminate these questions, it is necessary to consider Clive's educational performances at secondary school.

At the time of his third term in year seven at the Maple, Clive was currently placed in the middle sets for English, maths, and science (3 of 6). Pupils were also assessed every term at the Maple according to their attainment and attitude towards the subject. Clive's most recent assessments are provided in Table 3.1. Numbers ascend in value both in attainment and attitude, while attainment sub-levels increase from C to A. Attainment grades are measured by key stage tests and teacher assessment in English, maths and science, and purely teacher assessment in all other subjects.

By the end of key stage three (KS3) in year nine, pupils are expected to achieve a solid two levels of progress from their key stage two (KS2) assessments (DfE 2011: 37), which according to the KS2 results that Clive achieved (level 4) would be a level 6. At the end of the third term in year seven (when these assessments were taken), to be on line for this target Clive should be attaining around a level 5B or 5C. These results suggest that Clive was attaining on target for maths and science. However, for all other subjects he was below expectation. Clive's attitude results show a majority response of 2 out of 5. This indicates that his attitude was 'less than satisfactory' for five subjects, including English, and in music Clive's attitude was considered to be 'very poor'. His attitude was considered by teachers to be 'satisfactory' for four subjects including maths and science, and in only one subject, history, was Clive's attitude considered to be 'good'. These attitude assessments are a strong indication not only that Clive was failing to maximize his potential through his learning orientations in lessons, but more significantly, that this had incurred a tangible impact on his attainment since primary school. Indeed, at this point of his key stage three curriculum, Clive was attaining at below the minimum national standard in all but two subjects. The following discussion will revisit the binds Clive encountered at primary school and consider his negotiation of these binds at secondary school, in accounting for the educational penalties he experienced. In unpacking these binds we confront a catch-22 for Clive, in which his very strategy of circumvention made escape impossible.

Table 3.1 Clive's educational achievements at the end of year 7, the Maple school

Subject	Attainment	Attitude
English	4B	2*
Maths	5A	3*
Science	5B	3*
Information Technology	4C	2*
Drama	4C	2*
Art	4B	2*
Design Technology	4B	3*
French	3B	2*
Geography	4C	3*
History	4C	4*
Music	3A	1*

Continued tensions in learning orientations

Although Clive claimed to enjoy playing with the computer at home, this interest did not extend into lessons. The following example illustrates Clive's disengagement with the computer-based learning activity in his maths class:

> Clive is joking and laughing with Miles and James at 11:21. There is collective chatting between the four of them including Trevor. James asks the teacher if they are supposed to be working together, she replies 'No you are not supposed to be working together, Clive I'm going to move you if you don't do your own work'. Clive whines, 'I don't know what to do'. The learning support assistant (LSA) comes over to the group and there is a lot of giggling. Clive and James slouch and make faces instead of listening to her instruction. She responds 'Boys please'. Clive continues to pull faces although this goes unchecked. Trevor gets told off for chewing gum and at 11:26 the teacher tells the group to stand up. 'You are standing up because some of you are not listening to me. I know it's the end of term, but I want to finish top trumps. Who hasn't started yet? Clive? Trevor? Everyone else apart from those two lads carry on' Clive and Trevor are called over, after their instruction they are separated and Clive is moved. When seated Clive pulls apart his keypad and starts to brandish it as a gun. He chats and jokes with his new seatmate and is told off again. Trevor tries to gain Clive's attention but he ignores him. Clive is sent to the corner at 11:34 and the teacher comes and goes through the activity again with him. At the end of the lesson the teacher offers to stay in with the boys over lunch if they would like to finish their top trumps but they decline.
>
> (middle-set maths lesson)

When questioned about this lesson Clive's response was ambivalent: 'I would have done good, but I wasn't here a week, so I didn't really know what they were doing. . . . I was ill with a sickness bug.' This comment indicates a cycle of exclusion where school absence led on to exclusion from learning within school. A further factor in Clive's disengagement with learning was the effect of his friendship culture. Clive's teachers in maths, information technology, geography and science told me that Clive's social group were often separated from each other for misbehaviour, which was clearly frustrating at times for teachers and students:

> Clive is working with two boys on his table Miles and James. They are chatting and laughing instead of working on the game they are supposed to be finishing off. James throws something at Clive and he starts making noises. Mr Harlow addresses the group: 'Er hush please boys, are we going to hire someone to shoot Clive in the head for talking whilst I'm talking?' Another

group of boys respond: 'yeah throw him into a pit of lava'. Clive grins around the group and stops talking.

(middle-set science lesson)

After this lesson Mr Harlow described Clive's group as 'mischievous'. He explained why they were working together: 'You wouldn't put them together at the start of the year but as it's the end of term it's fine. They naturally would choose to work together but they would just mess around.' Mr Harlow went on to explain the fluctuations in Clive's engagement with work:

> Clive I would describe as quite immature, he rushes his work, doesn't do it to the best of his ability. He isn't nasty, just mischievous. Hadn't achieved anything [on the group project] at the end of the first week so had to do book work individually, absolutely hated it and obviously worked on the group project over the weekend and brought in something which had the potential to be very good, but again they've lost the track of it . . . He will get distracted by his friends very quickly.
>
> (Mr Harlow, Clive's science and registration class teacher)

When Clive had the autonomy of his 'personal space' at home he chose to work hard on the school project, however, as soon as he returned to school and among peers, he stopped working on it. This is not to say that Clive didn't recognize the importance of school achievement; on the contrary, when asked what was important about school, he responded:

CLIVE: Maths, English, science, I dunno what others.
CB: Why are they the most important?
CLIVE: I just think they are . . . 'cause my Dad said they're the ones you need really to get a job.

Indeed, maths had continued to play an important role in Clive's learning identity. As he did at Ivy, Clive demonstrated pride (albeit anxious) in his abilities in maths. When asked how he was doing in school, Clive's response indicated that despite his misbehaviour, his performance in formal learning outcomes was still important for him. It also revealed that his perceived maths level was one sub-level higher than his end of term test results:

CLIVE: Well uh, I've got a good maths level, I've got 60. 'Cause when I moved up here I was a 4A and now I'm a 6C.
CB: And how did you feel about it?
CLIVE: Really happy 'cause I got the best in the class.
CB: Was anyone else was happy about that?

CLIVE: Yes my teacher was happy . . . 'Cause in lessons have her in I normally mess around like, I'm like really lazy and then she's like really shocked because I was lazy . . .
CB: So how come you did so well if you weren't listening?
CLIVE: 'Cause when I talk to people I never look at them when I'm talking to them, so that they think I don't listen, but I am.
CB: Why don't you look at them then?
CLIVE: I don't know, don't like to.
CB: Why is that?
CLIVE: (. . .) I don't know, nervous I think.

Clive's comments clearly reflect an anxiety around work and communication with others (possibly those in authority). They also suggest a perception that others have low expectations of him, which might be understandable considering Clive was held in the lower maths group in Ivy school. His pride in performing well in maths seemed in contrast to his disruptive behaviour in lessons.

It is evident that Clive's approach to school did not reflect an outright rejection of schooling of the type seen in subcultural studies such as Willis (1977) but rather, his behaviour can be seen in the context of good intentions. Clive was reflexive of the meaning of secondary education: 'When I moved to Ivy I was really little and now I feel really grown-up'. When asked what made him feel grown up, Clive responded: 'Because I have to wear these clothes and this tie and we didn't wear that at Ivy we just wore a polo shirt and a top'. This change in school attire obviously marked a change in self-perception regarding the association between misbehaving and being childish, and behaving and being grown up. When asked, what difference does feeling grown up mean in terms of moving schools?, Clive responded: 'At Ivy I was really naughty and now I'm grown up and getting better, I'm not good yet, but I'm getting better.' In considering why such good intentions were clearly not followed through, however, we have to turn to a consideration of the role of Clive's friendship groups and the competing drives of social and educational inclusion.

Social capital and the role of friendship in shaping schooling orientations

Clive claimed a number of friends within his year group and this was supported by observation, but his core group shared all his lessons and comprised of 'Me, Jim Miles and James and Trevor', not one of whom was his friend from Ivy school. Clive no longer played football claiming it was 'boring'. It was notable that none of Clive's current friends played football, which may indicate that the activity was more important to him as a means of social inclusion than for its own intrinsic value as a sport. Instead, the main break-time activity for Clive and his friends involved gathering at the pond. This was positioned in a secluded area set away from the other children and out of sight from passersby. As an exception to normal school rules, permission to spend time at the pond had been legitimated by staff, under the condition that Clive and his friends would 'clean it out':

CLIVE: I go to the pond.
CB: What do you do there then?
CLIVE: We just hang around there and clean it out.
CB: Oh really, that's very helpful. Any particular reason?
CLIVE: No we just do it 'cause we're bored and . . . because we get chocolate . . . and it's fun.

The significance of the pond for Clive was later revealed when he was asked what made him feel happy at school, to which he replied:

CLIVE: The pond.
CB: Why is that then?
CLIVE: Because it's fun, its fun hanging out there, 'cause no-one is watching me.
CB: So it feels like your space then?
CLIVE: Yeah.

James et al. (1998) have argued that school spaces are governed by adult processes of control and regulation over children's mind and body, 'through regimes of discipline, learning, development, maturation and skill' (38). Yet Clive's group's contestation of school rules is an example of children's ingenuity in challenging the spatial rules defined by adults (Holloway and Valentine 2000). For Clive and his friends, the importance of the pond territory was clearly separate from the activity of cleaning it out, in fact from observation it was questionable how much cleaning actually took place. Rather, it represented a space in which Clive felt an element of ownership and autonomy, outside of the watchful gaze of authority figures and outsiders to the group. The pond was evidently the territory of his social group and as we will see, the friendships associated with Clive's pond territory had a formative effect on Clive's social identity.

Fear of being ostracized from the friendship group

One of the key tensions in understanding Clive's orientations in secondary school was between the aspiration of being 'good' or 'better' than at primary school, and retaining his position as 'leader' of the group:

CB: I thought you were trying to be good?
CLIVE: I did and then I gave up.
CB: You gave up, why did you give up?
CLIVE: I was good for ages but then when I first got in trouble I gave up.

CB: What was it that made you give up?
CLIVE: I dunno, 'cause when I started to mess around my mates started to mess around too so then I started messing around with em.
CB: Do you think that you're like the ringleader then?
CLIVE: I dunno, maybe.
CB: So whatever you do they do?
CLIVE: Not all the time, sometimes.
CB: So if you were really good wouldn't then they be good?
CLIVE: Doubt it. No they'd probably try to make me mess around.
CB: So do you think that happens then, when you try to be good?
CLIVE: Yeah whenever I try to be good everyone shouts at me, Oh you're a goodie goodie.

Here Clive voices the trade-off he made to avoid social exclusion. He 'gave up' on his aspiration to succeed in school by not conforming to the behaviour required for academic success.

The longitudinal effects of school turbulence

In analysing the tension between Clive's learning and friendship orientations, we might consider the mediating impact of school turbulence upon the stability of Clive's schooling friendships. Clive's former best friends at Ivy also attended the Maple, but when asked if he still saw Marcus and Romain, Clive answered, 'yes, but not so much'. Their friendship had become a looser form of social connection, such as passing conversation in the corridor and playground. This echoes Clive's experiences of friendship after Wishing-well school, which fostered in him some anxiety regarding the continuity of friendships. In the move to secondary school, yet again Clive had lost the formative close friendships he had valued. Yet while Clive's friends had changed, his orientation to friends and friendship had remained the same.

Lack of trust in friends

A key insight into Clive's security in his school friendships emerged within the following discussion:

CB: Who are the people with whom you would trust to discuss a personal matter?
CLIVE: I can't trust anyone.
CB: You cant trust anyone?
CLIVE: Well I can trust my Mum and one of my brothers but not the other one . . . I can't trust my friends, my four friends. [Jim, James, Miles and Trevor.]
CB: How come?
CLIVE: I don't know.
CB: What about the teachers?

CLIVE: Ummm No.
CB: Would you like to be able to trust your friends?
CLIVE: I'd like to.
CB: What do you think would happen if you did tell your friends something that was important to you?
CLIVE: They'll go spread it or something.
CB: What about if someone were to tell you something.
CLIVE: No I wouldn't tell, I know a load of secrets of my mates.

This suggests that Clive recognized the importance of trust in friendships, but felt unable to maintain trust in his current school friends. This insecurity in the continuity of friendships may have explained his continued efforts to conform to the behaviour of the social group. In analysing why Clive's social identity was more durable than the individuals who constituted the peer group, we might speculate that Clive felt more 'at home' in the social identity of being a leader within a familiar rule challenging peer group culture than he would pursuing friends with whom he felt he could trust and rely on.

Conclusion: Educational binds of poverty

So how might we understand Clive's school life of with respect to the four binds of poverty? In Clive's case, the multiple factors of changing school and home, school absence, and a cultural class between the pedagogic expectations of the classroom and Clive's performances to incite recognition, compounded to create an insurmountable tension between his learning and friendship orientations. Here Clive was faced with a quandary, he recognized the need to do well, and drew great pleasure from the occasions when he did achieve highly in maths. Furthermore, under the autonomy of his 'personal space' at home Clive worked hard on his school science project, and produced a good piece of work. Yet, Clive also recognized the negative impact of his misbehaviour, which prevented him from consistently applying himself to his work and achieving. This was reflected in his low attitude scores and his attainment scores that were below national targets in nine subjects. When contextualizing his formal learning outcomes at the end of year seven against his key stage two results, it is apparent that Clive was underachieving to his ability, a reflection of his antiformal learning behaviour in school, and time off for illness.

So how does this account stand up to the MUD position (Levitas 2005) that sees underachievement of children in poverty as synonymous with a lack of motivation? Close attention to Clive's experiences in school reflect concerted efforts within both schools to 'be good' and conform with the pedagogical expectations required in order to achieve in maths. But in the end he 'gave up'. This may be because while Clive presented the aspiration to succeed in school, the behaviour required to do so was not sustainable on a daily basis. Clive's school life was mediated by his role within a 'bonded' (Putnam 2000) yet unstable peer group that demanded adherence to a strict code of conduct. His behaviour to cement group membership therefore precluded his participation in formal learning. Perhaps Clive felt that friendships were inevitably transient? And, in order to manage day-to-day life he felt no choice but to entertain his friends to ensure his insider status (for the time being at least). Even these efforts could sometimes be seen to fall short, in that Clive would rather stay at home in his safe and secure space, where his isolation was an autonomous decision as opposed to a result of his circumstance.

Note

1 These national government standards on educational performance are now available on the Department for Education website at www.education.gov.uk/schools/performance/primary_12/p7.html [Accessed 14 April 2014].

References

Benson, J. E. and Furstenberg, Jr., F. F. (2007) 'Entry into adulthood: are adult role transitions meaningful markers of adult identity?', *Advances in Life Course Research*, 11: 199–224.

Bourdieu, P. (1977) *Outline of a Theory of Practice*, Cambridge: Cambridge University Press.

Department for Education [DfE] (2011) *How Do Pupils Progress during Key Stages 2 and 3? Research Report DFE-RR096*. Available at www.gov.uk/government/uploads/system/uploads/attachment_data/file/182413/DFE-RR096.pdf [Accessed 29 June 2014].

Foster, H., Hagan, J. and Brooks-Gunn, J. (2008) 'Growing up fast: stress exposure and subjective "weathering" in emerging adulthood', *Journal of Health and Social Behavior*, 49: 162–77.

Gillborn, D. and Youdell, D. (2000) *Rationing Education: policy, practice, reform and equality*, Buckingham: Open University Press.

Holloway, S. L. and Valentine, G. (2000) 'Spatiality and the new social studies of childhood', *Sociology*, 34 (4): 763–83.

James, A., Jenks, C. and Prout, A. (1998) *Theorizing Childhood*, Oxford: Polity.

Lareau, A. (2000) 'Social class and the daily lives of children: a study from the United States', *Childhood*, 7 (2): 155–71.

Levitas, R. (2005) *The Inclusive Society? social exclusion and New Labour*, Basingstoke: Palgrave Macmillan.

Mac an Ghaill, M. (1994) *The Making of Men: masculinities, sexualities and schooling*, Buckingham: Open University Press.

Pollard, A. (1987) 'Goodies, jokers and gangs', in A. Pollard (ed.) *Children and Their Primary Schools: a new perspective*, London: Falmer Press.

Putnam, R. D. (2000) *Bowling alone: the collapse and revival of American community*, New York: Simon and Schuster.

Renold, E. (2001) 'Learning the "hard" way: boys, hegemonic masculinity and the negotiation of learner identities in the primary school', *British Journal of Sociology of Education*, 22 (3): 369–85.

Ridge, T. (2002) *Childhood Poverty and Social Exclusion from a Child's Perspective*, Bristol: Policy Press.

Sherriff, N. (2007) Peer group cultures and social identities, *British Educational Research Journal*, 33 (3): 349–70.

Willis, P. (1977) *Learning to Labor: how working class kids get working class jobs*, New York: Columbia University Press.

Young, M. (2009) 'What are schools for?', In H. Lauder, J. Porter and H. Daniels (eds) *Critical Perspectives on Education*, London: Routledge.

Chapter 4

Liza

School life following family break-up and relocation with father

Life in primary school

I first met Liza when she was aged nine years old. She lived at home with her father and older brother in Thornton and had moved from North London almost a year previously. For Liza, mobility in terms of home and school relocation created a bind through a sense of disempowerment, associated with the unwelcome and distressing circumstances surrounding it, and her reluctance to leave a school where she felt valued. Liza joined Ivy school in year four (aged eight) following a traumatic family break-up. Her head teacher at Ivy informed me that Liza's mother had left her father for another woman who was a friend of the family. Her father took this very badly as did the whole family. When Liza was asked why she and her father had moved to the area, she replied: 'Because my Dad wanted to move nearer to his parents and our family.' Although this was similar to the response Clive gave, he had described the decision using the term 'we', suggesting that he felt party to the decision, or at least involved in it: 'We just had to come here to sell our flat so we can see our family more.' In contrast, Liza's response makes clear that the decision was her father's and not something that she was a part of, suggesting she may have felt particularly powerless in relation to the decision to move. This was consistent with her father's account, which indicated that he needed to take care of his father who was in poor health. He perceived himself to have little choice but to move to the area, despite his conflicting responsibilities:

> One of the reasons I took the kids was because they had changed schools so many times, I wanted to give them some stability and so we moved here. But she [Liza] doesn't like change. I don't like change either . . . I grew up here and I went to the Maple (secondary school). I like my comfort zone, I like stability and stuff that I know, and this seemed the best place . . . I had to take care of my Dad, well and my Mum, there was nobody else here to do it, but I guess it was hard on all of us.
>
> (Liza's father)

Memories of Clayroof school

The most recent school Liza had attended prior to moving to Ivy was Clayroof, a large inner-city North London primary with 384 children on roll. Reflecting the high levels of social deprivation in the catchment, two-thirds of children received free school meals, and many had above-average learning difficulties and disabilities. Pupil mobility was very high, and more than seven out of 10 children were from a minority ethnic background. The school was housed in a large three-storey classic Victorian building.

Liza had fond memories of her last school having described it as 'really, really fun'. When asked what she liked about it, Liza's response suggested that her feelings about the importance of the school might have had an effect upon the way she viewed herself there:

LIZA: It was quite, a really big building.
CB: Yeah?
LIZA: It was way bigger than this one, 'cause this is like a big bungalow.
CB: Really?
LIZA: It was . . . the school that I was in, it was like three storeys, not all one storey.
CB: Yeah. Why, why do you like big schools?
LIZA: 'Cause I was at the very top . . . of the whole school, 'cause you would look at the window and everyone were . . . and if you um, shouted 'hello', then everyone would look up and go 'hello' back.

The importance that Liza placed on others' regard for her is a dominant theme in Liza's school life, which will be addressed in later discussion. Liza also had positive memories about her teachers:

CB: What about the teachers, did you like them?
LIZA: Yeah (nods).
CB: Yeah? How come?
LIZA: Because if you were really, really early, they used to give you breakfast.
CB: Really? So you used to go early, did you?
LIZA: Yeah, very, very early and then they used to give you breakfast in the morning. Then if you did, had breakfast in the morning, or you came in really, really late for school, when you didn't have any breakfast at all, they used to get you some toast or something you would really like.

In affording her attention it appeared that Liza interpreted the breakfast provision as evidence that her teachers cared for her and took an interest in her well-being. The consistency of the gesture – even if she was late for school – seemed to be important in illustrating to Liza that the kindness (as she understood it) was unconditional.[1]

The particular context of Liza's school move can be seen to have created a bind in terms of the distress she experienced within her immediate family, and in being forced to leave a school where she felt recognized. In leaving her mother, and in moving closer to her father's extended family, it is therefore unsurprising that the home sphere could be seen to assume a significant role in Liza's sense of security and well-being.

The importance of home and its relationship to school

Liza did not take part in any formal extracurricular activities out of school, and her interests were homebound and family orientated. A particularly special activity for Liza was on Wednesday evening when her aunt cooked for her and her brother, father and uncle: 'Um Wednesdays [at school] are definitely my good day because my Auntie cooks dinner . . . I get really excited when it's a Wednesday so I'm very, very good' (Liza). It is evident that a rather everyday activity of cooking a meal had a big impact on Liza. Maybe family activities were rare for Liza, or perhaps since her mother's departure family time took on an added value and significance. Whatever the reason, this family activity directly influenced her behaviour in school. This is a clear example of the importance of home cultures upon schooling cultures. Here we can see how Liza's happiness out of school could spill over into school. However, the home–school connection in Liza's case was not on account of a synchronicity between cultures, but rather a reflection of the positive effect of home pleasures, mitigating, or blocking out the experience of being in school.

Nevertheless, for the majority of the time she spent in school Liza seemed to feel uncomfortable in the formal settings of Ivy. When asked whether she liked schoolwork, she responded with a straight, 'No', and when probed as to the reasons for this replied: 'Because it's boring, the teachers don't stop talking when they're teaching, they're supposed to shut up past a couple of minutes after talking, but sometimes they're really boring.' This contributed to a sense that the instruction was meaningless for her and she didn't feel able to connect it to her life. This may have been because she did not believe herself to be a deserving learner, but rather out of place in the classroom, in claiming, 'I'm sort of a silly people.'

Liza was insecure in her relationships with teachers and referred to a number of teachers and classroom assistants whom she believed didn't like her. This included her class teacher: 'She's really angry with like with silly people' (Liza). 'Silly' was a word Liza used to describe herself on several occasions, and its meaning unfolded and held relevance across her schooling career. While at Ivy school, being 'silly' clearly had negative associations related to not behaving appropriately in class. Liza gave an example that illustrated both insecurity in her teacher's positive regard for her, and her own recognition that it is not appropriate to express such insecurity to a teacher: 'When I go, "you're my friend" in a silly sort of way, they go "yes Liza" [sarcastic voice]. They think I'm being weird.' Despite feeling 'not liked' by her teachers, getting teachers' attention was evidently of importance. When Liza felt she could gain positive attention from the teacher she engaged in the lesson and attempted to answer questions, even if she was unsure of the correct answers. When she felt out of the teacher's gaze, which was the majority of the time, she switched off and attempted to distract her seatmates, as these classroom observations indicate:

> The teacher asks children to put their pens down and share the words they have been writing as alternatives for 'nice'. Liza waves her hand. Approximately half the class have their hand up. The teacher then starts choosing children to answer. Liza gets chosen third and her word is 'excellent'. Children also have to supply a sentence in using that word and Liza's example is, 'it was an excellent day.' After she volunteers her word, Liza loses interest. She starts colouring her hair in black (she has very blonde hair) and confers with Kez. He seems vaguely amused. She is distracted for the rest of the lesson and continues colouring in her hair and shows Poppy and Eva.
>
> (English class)

In another lesson with a different group and teacher, Liza can be seen to be more engaged with the lesson when she felt that teacher attention was possible:

> The teacher asks about the relationship between three and 12. Presently Liza puts her hand up. Liza can't remember the answer. She doesn't seem to be engaged by the teacher delivery and keeps turning round to talk to Clive; she is drawing on her arm and shows it to Clive. The teacher walks over towards Liza's table and continues asking the class questions. Now she is closer, Liza is more keen to answer questions and puts her hand up several times. As teacher moves away Liza loses interest in the activity. She is working with Hope and seems to be conferring a bit, however on her table she is the most behind. At 2:15 Liza distracts the table by initiating a conversation about the documentary she saw last night, the other children on the table eagerly join in.
>
> (lower-set maths class)

It may be that part of this lack of interest was on account of Liza's anxiety over her ability. When asked about which lessons she was good at she responded: 'I'm not sure, I'm good at art but not that good.' Art was the only subject Liza enjoyed. She could not find anything positive to say about any other subjects, nor her abilities in them. This anxiety clearly grew when end of term reports were pending:

LIZA: I'm kind of scared about my report this year.
CB: Why is that?

LIZA: As much as I've calmed down since year four, like I used to get two crosses [sanctions] at least two crosses every day . . . I'm scared what it's 'gonna' say. You never know what you're doing sometimes . . . I don't like reports 'cause you're not allowed to open it and it has to be signed to come back.

Liza's distracted and disruptive classroom behaviour had resulted in a number of sanctions over the year. It was apparent that these sanctions were only really considered relevant to Liza when they implicated her home life through her report.

The only area of the curriculum that Liza did take an interest in was art, possibly because the lesson provided a link into home through her love of animals:

I'm quite good at art. Because I can draw cats . . . and I can draw rats, 'cause I got two and I can draw dogs. I can draw those little Chihuahuas, those ones with curly hair on their, crimped hair on their ears.

(Liza)

Animals had a special place in Liza's life. She would happily chat away about her pets and when she did so her tone would become warm. In particular, Liza's pets appeared to be significant as something that brought the family together, 'my whole family, we share pets' (Liza).

Liza's father was a talented artist, an interest that he practiced in his spare time. This link between her father's interests and the family pets may have explained why Liza's description of art was one of her most positive descriptions of any lesson. It was also unusual in view of the talent or ability that Liza afforded herself. However, Liza displayed little interest in the importance of high attainment in other lessons. She made no mention of her grades or learning outcomes, and the only comment she made on her ability was when asked why she was part of a group removed for separate group work (external to the class) for numeracy lessons, to which she responded, 'we're the thick group'. This opinion, however, did not seem to have had a strong bearing upon Liza's positive or negative experience of school. When asked how she was doing at school, she replied, 'quite good'. In querying why this account contrasted with her perception of negative teacher opinions, I asked Liza: 'So you don't think your idea of doing well at school is the same as the school?', to which she responded, 'yeah, it's definitely not the same.'

It was evident that for Liza the only aspects of school that she considered important were those with which she could connect with home. Here it's possible to speculate that the source of Liza's anxiety was caused by the disjuncture between what she considered important at school and what the teachers considered important. While Liza understood 'doing well' in terms of positive relationships with others (something which for her was highly variable), she understood the school to see it in terms of appropriate classroom behaviour, something which Liza acknowledged that she didn't conform to, in being, 'silly' instead. This lent to a sense of dislocation and lack of meaning in school, at least in terms of the formal aspects of schooling. In order to consider this further it is necessary to turn to Liza's social relations in school and her orientations to friendships.

Preoccupation with social standing and tenuous social relationships

While Liza had little interest in her academic performance, she placed a great emphasis upon how she was regarded by other people, especially peers, and engaged in an almost daily evaluation of who liked her and who didn't: 'I've got some people who like me and some people don't. Like Clive's OK with me, Rick's okay with me, Codie absolutely hates me, Jade's okay, Emma's okay.' The constantly changing nature of this evaluation resulted in conflicting accounts whereby individual children were at one moment described as friends and in later conversation claimed to dislike her. This suggested that Liza perceived herself within a tenuous and unstable wider friendship group that resulted in insecurity towards her looser friendships: 'We argue about different things like who likes who, we had an argument just a couple of weeks ago about, no that was me and Eva. But me and Codie had an argument a couple of weeks ago.' This argument clearly had a lasting impact upon Liza who had put some thought into analysing why arguments between friends took place: 'Sometimes she, she [Codie] she's mean to me so I'm mean back to her then we get in big arguments.'

One friendship validated through home life

While her wider friendships may have been prone to flux, there was but one friendship within which Liza placed great trust: 'Bonnie is my very, very best friend.' This relationship represented a turning point in that when asked when she began to settle into Ivy school, she replied, 'When I heard that Bonnie was my old cousin.' In fact Bonnie was not a literal cousin, but an 'honorary' one as the daughter of a friend of the family. However, it wasn't so much meeting Bonnie that was important for Liza, but rather getting the affirmation from her family that Bonnie was a person who could be trusted:

CB: Were you friends with Bonnie from the beginning then?
LIZA: No, a couple of days er . . . I sat next to her for a couple of days and then I went home and um, my Dad was on the phone to my uncle John and my auntie was in the living room and they said, there's this really go . . . nice girl called . . . there's this really nice girl called Bonnie still there.

Reflecting a default assumption that the school environment is not one to be trusted, Liza's suspicion towards people in school was only tempered by her family's validation of a potential friend. Through her links with family outside of school, Bonnie represented Liza's only bridge into school, and was her one constant within a precarious social environment: 'Some of them [pupils] I play with, but at the moment I only play with Bonnie.' It is significant the evidence with which Liza felt she could trust Bonnie's friendship: 'Bonnie is really kind to me . . . and [she] lends us things, I lend Bonnie some money sometimes and then she lends me some money sometimes.' Considering Ridge's (2002) findings about the centrality of money in negotiating social inclusion for children in poverty, Liza's account underlines its value in substantiating trust and reciprocity with which she cemented her friendship. Clearly the borrowing and lending of money, for Liza, had far greater currency than the purely financial.

Navigating the binds at primary school

In considering Liza's binds against educational success at primary school, it is evident that their effects were interconnected. Bind two and bind three can both be seen to have caused Liza's schooling experiences to fluctuate considerably. Sometimes this was related to her relationships with others in the school; at other times it related to her emotions out of school spilling into her feelings within Ivy. This instability and dislocation were compounded by her uncertainty in reading her alignment with school culture through teachers' expectations and direct engagement with her. Instead she was reliant on her father to give feedback on her performance in school, who would relay her teachers' evaluations of her upon reading her school report, and whose opinion it would seem mattered far more than any authority figures within school.

It is also possible to consider the interconnections between bind three and bind four in terms of the impact of school mobility in affecting Liza's sense of feeling valued by teachers and peers. Upon joining Ivy, Liza admitted to feeling 'scared', particularly in relation to whether the teachers and pupils would like her. This uncertainty was in contrast to what Liza perceived to be the unconditional validation represented in school provision of breakfast in her previous school, regardless of her time of attendance. With respect to her insecurity in friendships, Liza's response when asked 'how do you feel now about moving schools?' was quite telling: 'I feel sad, because I had most of my friends there.' But, when asked if she kept in touch with her best friend Tasmeena, Liza replied: 'No, I've got her number but I never phone her because I think she's forgotten my name.' Despite having spent a year in Ivy, Liza still considered 'most of' her friends to be from her old school, and yet she didn't feel valued enough to keep in touch with even her closest friend at Clayroof. Leaving the school meant that she effectively ceased to exist for her previous friends; she considered herself to have made so little an impact that her memory would have been erased, right down to her name. This lack of self-worth is illuminating in considering what Liza saw to be the conditionality of her friendships. We will see how this loss developed following transition to secondary school.

Life in secondary school: Renegotiating the binds?

The next time I met Liza she was at the Maple school (year seven, aged 11). She continued to live with her father and brother in the house they had first moved to in Thornton. Liza joined Maple at the normal admission point, alongside the significant majority of other students at Ivy school.

Liza's educational achievements

In considering the success with which Liza had been able to negotiate the binds she had encountered in primary school, it is necessary to consider Liza's achievement in her key stage two (KS2) SATs results:

English: Level 4
Maths: Level 4
Science: Level 4

These performances were in line with the national minimum target grade requirement that children are expected to achieve,[2] which suggests that at the primary level she had not experienced an educational penalty according to national minimum targets. However, what these test scores do not show is the extent to which Liza's educational success reflected her personal potential, nor do they indicate the longitudinal effects of the binds Liza experienced. Here, it is necessary to consider Liza's educational performances at secondary school.

For her year seven 'ability' grouped classes, Liza was placed in the second from lowest group for maths (5 of 6) and lower-middle groups for English and science (4 of 6). In every other lesson students were taught in their mixed-ability registration class groups. Pupils were regularly evaluated in each curriculum subject at the Maple, using a combination of testing and teacher assessment to grade student attainment and attitude. Liza's assessments at the end of her third term in year seven at the Maple are provided in Table 4.1. Both in attainment and attitude, numbers ascend in value, while attainment sub-levels increase from C (the lowest) to A (the highest). In interpreting these figures, the 'attainment' grades are mapped against national curriculum criteria, while 'attitude' ratings reflect teachers' assessments of students' effort. As Liza's registration class teacher explained to me: 'Only if I believe a student is putting in the effort relative to their potential will I rate attitude as good (4), or excellent (5) if I think they are maximizing their abilities.'

Table 4.1 Liza's educational achievements at the end of year 7, the Maple school

Subject	Attainment	Attitude
English	5C	3*
Maths	4C	3*
Science	4B	3*
Information Technology	4C	3*
Drama	4B	4*
Art	5C	3*
Design Technology	5C	4*
French	4C	3*
Geography	4B	3*
History	5C	3*
Music	4C	3*

To be on line for national targets according to her KS2 achievements, at the end of year seven Liza should have been attaining around a level 5B or 5C.[3] Liza's results suggest that she was attaining according to national targets in four subjects, and teachers rated her attitude as 'good' for two of these subjects: art and design technology. This suggests that there was a correlation between Liza's application to work in lessons and her achievement. However, Liza's attainment was below target in seven curriculum subjects. In interpreting the teacher's assessment of her potential, these figures also indicate that Liza may have been underachieving to her ability in nine subjects, for which Liza's attitude was graded as 'satisfactory'. Not one of her teachers felt that Liza was fully 'maximizing' her potential. Using these assessments it is possible to speculate that Liza had experienced an educational penalty by the end of her first year at secondary school, suggesting that the binds she experienced may well have been cumulative. The following account of Liza's school life at the Maple sets about explaining her educational underachievement, through exploring Liza's negotiation of a new bind, and renegotiation of the binds within secondary school.

Skipping lunch and making choices

Since Liza had started at the Maple, her father had given up his job in order to work as a full-time carer for his father, as a result of which financial resources had become scarce.[4] While the effects of financial hardship had been evident in primary school, through the value Liza attributed to money lending, this had not led to social exclusion. However, the value of money had taken on an additional emphasis in secondary school evident through the tactical choices Liza employed in relation to her financial capital. Since leaving primary school she had ceased claiming free school meals, as she had negotiated with her father that he would provide her with money for school lunch, a decision that alleviated some degree of guilt that he felt over having little money to spare:

> She hates the canteen food apparently, and lives off junk food at school by the sounds of it. I don't think it's the healthiest way for a teenage girl to eat, chocolates and crisps and that, but we always eat properly at home, so if she didn't eat all that rubbish she would probably starve! Besides, I do feel guilty that I can't treat her in big ways, the least I can do is provide a bit, so she can eat what she likes, probably whatever her friends are buying.
>
> (Liza's father)

However, it was apparent that Liza was not always using her lunch money to buy food, but choosing to save some or all of it to use for other purposes:

CB: What do you do at break-times and lunchtimes, where do you go?
LIZA: Well at break-times I sometimes go and get a snack from the snack shack and then that's my lunch there, and then at lunchtime me and Kia just link arms and wander round the school, go to the tutor, and then go for a walk.
CB: So what do you do when you wander round? do you eat your lunch?
LIZA: No, I probably ate it at break, or saved the money . . . Just see different people, hug different people, walk round with lots of different people.
CB: Why would you save it?
LIZA: For buying other stuff, or doing things.

Liza felt compelled to make choices between taking part in social activities including buying things for herself, and buying lunch, especially in view of her father's confession that he couldn't afford to treat her to bigger luxuries. This is an example of what Ridge (2002) referred to as the 'negotiating strategies, and alternative sources of income', through which children in poverty try to keep up with peers (42). Research by Hutson and Cheung (1992) found that 16- to 18-year-old adolescents from families who weren't in poverty, even those in part-time employment, continued to receive a regular allowance from parents. This underlines the importance of alternate sources of finance for children from low-income families in 'keeping up' with the buying habits and social activities of their peers. The result for Liza was that lunchtimes lacked a sense of place and purpose, whereby she navigated the playground in an itinerant manner wandering from group to group, consolidating friendships.

Positive affirmation versus educational success

At primary school Liza experienced a disjuncture between her home and school life, whereas at home she felt valued and cared for, at school she felt overlooked and undervalued. Learning and attainment were incidental to the importance of being liked by teachers and peers. This orientation towards school and lessons extended into secondary school. Liza had continued to feel anxious about how her teachers regarded her and as a result felt negatively about most subjects:

LIZA: I don't like science, geography, history, IT [information technology], PSE [personal and social education], French, art.
CB: Why don't you like those?
LIZA: 'Cause the teachers are annoying and they don't like you, and all the lessons are boring twenty four seven.
CB: Why don't you think the teachers like you?
LIZA: 'Cause they scowl at you all the time.
CB: Why do you think they are scowling at you?
LIZA: 'Cause I'm just sitting there doing my work and then suddenly you look over to the side and Miss is there scowling at you and frowning at you. I think it's 'cause I never get anything right.

As at Ivy, Liza had continued to feel uncomfortable in the formal classroom environment and disliked by her teachers. She attributed this to a lack of ability in her work, but it did not seem as if lessons were very meaningful for her. Liza also felt that her orientation to lessons was not well regarded by teachers, and her perceived inabilities in lessons and the disregard of her teachers reflected low self-worth. It is notable that her anxieties of teachers were not borne out by teacher assessments. While only two teachers rated Liza's attitude as 'good' (4), in no instance did teachers define her attitude as 'poor' (2) or 'unacceptable' (1); rather, Liza was most often rated as 'satisfactory' (3). Perhaps Liza was perceived neither to stand out on account of good or bad orientations to work and consequential formal assessments. Therefore, she may have interpreted the lack of interest by teachers as a negative testimony of her worth.

In the absence of teacher recognition, a key factor that affected Liza's confidence in lessons was the endorsement of friends. She recounted a particularly negative recent experience during the school sports competition:

LIZA: At sports day I came last.
CB: So you don't like sports?
LIZA: I love sports, but I don't like sports days, 'cause today we had to do for sports day what we usually have to do [in PE] and I had to do javelin for sports day, and I came very last. I got four flat out, four belly flops.
CB: So how did that make you feel?
LIZA: Sad. I love sports but I don't like it when I lose. 'cause everyone takes the micky out of me, you said you were good at this, but you still lost. Like I love javelin and the usual lesson I get the furthest, not today.
CB: So what was different today then?

LIZA: The fact that we had to do it separately and we didn't have our friends to cheer us on.

I was present for this competition and it was notable that while Liza's best friend Kia was also in attendance, she didn't offer any support for Liza. Indeed, it didn't seem as if either of them were very engaged in the activity:

> During the teacher explanation as to how to hold the javelin, Liza fiddles with the top, she gets told off for doing so as they have been asked not to touch. Each pupil takes their turn to throw the javelin, meanwhile most of the other children watch. Liza is chatting to Kia, although Kia seems more interested in talking to two boys and ignores her. Two other girls walk over, they are not in games kit. Liza runs over to one and hugs her. Kia then comes over to the girls and they start to chat about smoking. Kia and Liza have to be interrupted from their conversation to take their turn with the javelin, neither seems to put much effort in and I notice that whilst Liza takes her turn, Kia is not watching but joking and laughing with the boys. Liza looks at the floor, and shifts from foot to foot in a self-conscious manner. She throws without much focus. It's another 'no throw' as it didn't penetrate the ground.

This lesson observation was a typical example of Liza's distracted behaviour during lessons. Even though Liza was interested in sports, the positive affirmation from her peers took much higher priority, even for such an important event as the annual sports day competition.

In reflecting upon her understanding of the secondary school culture, Liza struggled with the shifting importance of school performance relative to self-worth:

LIZA: Well my geography teacher doesn't like me, but I think she likes me more because at the beginning of the year I used to be really really silly didn't I? and like, she didn't like me.
CB: Do you think there's been a change in you? Or is it just her?
LIZA: I think I know more . . . I've been listening.

At Ivy school Liza connected teacher attention with endorsement, however at secondary school she attributed teacher endorsement to attainment. This posed a problem for Liza in that her orientation towards 'silliness' continued to reflect her dominant behaviour in lessons, as we will see.

The importance of being silly

This issue of 'silliness' was present in Ivy school, in that Liza claimed that her teachers got angry with 'silly' people such as herself, for what she interpreted as inappropriate classroom behaviour. I was interested as to whether Liza retained this identity at secondary school and if it affected her classroom experience:

CB: Do you still think that you are a silly person?
LIZA: Yes.
CB: What does that mean then? What's a silly person?
LIZA: When you don't concentrate on your work and you make the friends that are next to you laugh, it usually works.
CB: And is that a good thing to be or bad?
LIZA: Sometimes, only in some lessons, maths.
CB: Why is it a good thing in those lessons?
LIZA: 'Cause if you're silly in those lessons, the teacher doesn't like it but they don't mind, they just like tell you to get on with your work, you can still make your friends laugh, but they like want you to get on with your work at the same time.

Liza felt that her classroom behaviour was not accepted in other lessons, but was abided by her teacher in maths. This was because Liza perceived her teacher to be more lenient in her tolerance of pupil-to-pupil conversation, including Liza's 'silly' orientation. Liza was positioned in the fifth out of six groups for maths. From observation, there was a good atmosphere in the class amongst pupils and between pupils and their teacher, Miss Bright. More vocal children often called out to the teacher and she would frequently indulge a joke and share stories from home. The pupils evidently respected Miss Bright, as when it did get a bit rowdy (a not infrequent occurrence) pupils generally responded quickly to her raised voice and cross tone. As a default mode she was friendly, cheerful and respectful of her class.

When asked which teachers she trusted, Liza replied that Miss Bright was the only teacher with whom she would feel confident to turn to if she had a problem with her work. A conversation with Miss Bright suggested that Liza's trust was well founded; her teacher felt that she had a good understanding of Liza and was supportive:

> She needs a lot of support, a lot of TLC. I don't think she has very high self-confidence. She sometimes plays up but she mostly tries quite hard. She responds well to praise and encouragement, she does like to be noticed.
> (Miss Bright, Liza's maths teacher)

This perspective was endorsed by Liza's father, who believed that her experience of and behaviour in lessons was underpinned by Liza's relationships with teachers:

> There were a few problems, we talked about the problems with her tutor, in terms of getting on with people and getting on with teachers. She tends to, I

mean I was like this myself, if you get on with someone you excel, and if they give you negative feedback, it just really knocks you, and she's had the same sort of thing. Teachers which she gets on with she gets on in the subjects, and she's changed teachers and done better if she likes the teacher or done worse because she doesn't. There's definitely a correlation with it. I mean if someone came to me and said I'd like her to move up because she's done really well and then Liza said she didn't like the teacher, I'd say no because it has that much of an effect.

(Liza's father)

On Liza's request her father had initiated her down-setting in maths to the lower group because she disliked her teacher in the lower-intermediate class. For Liza and her father, Liza's position in the lower maths class with a friend (Kia) and a teacher she liked was more important than being in a higher maths class. However, Liza felt the need to justify this trade-off in recognizing her down-setting to be a product not of her abilities, but rather of her learning orientation: 'I'm smarter than all of them, it's just my concentration, they're down there because they're not very bright and I'm down there because of my concentration' (Liza).

Discontinuity between home and school values in art

In the three years since last meeting Liza, her interest in art had developed and she had clearly found a therapeutic value in using art as a medium for expression. This may have been fostered through her wider family, as art was an activity they enjoyed together. It was also an activity that Liza engaged in with a wider community, in attending an art club with her father and grandparents:

There's this after-school club with my Nan and my Grandad and lots of other older people. It's for older people only and my Dad, but I'm only allowed to go 'cause my Dad goes and my Grandad goes. And I express my feelings through painting. If I'm annoyed I use dark colours, or if I'm really upset I use dark colours. If I'm happy I use colours like pink and purple.

(Liza)

The emphasis Liza placed upon the word 'allowed' suggested a sense of importance in the exception to the rule that her attendance represented. I inferred from the pride in her tone of voice that she felt an element of being 'special' as part of the adult art club. However, this interest and self-value fostered through art in her community group did not translate into enjoying art lessons. This may have been because Liza's perceptions of her teacher's responses to her classroom behaviour tainted her enjoyment of the lesson:

LIZA: In art we can't make the other person laugh, because if the other person laughs you both get in trouble, that's why I don't like the lesson that I'm

meant to be in now, I'm in art and it's scary because if you just like talk one word, or giggle, she shouts.
CB: See that quite surprises me because one of the things you really seemed to like when I last spoke to you was art?
LIZA: I love art, I don't think I'm good at it but I just don't like the teacher. My Dad always says to me, don't think about the teacher, just get on with the work, but it's hard when they're talking, constantly telling you off.

Paradoxically, teacher assessments rated Liza's attitude in art as good – one of only two subjects rated as such – and yet as far as Liza was concerned, her interest and abilities in art were overlooked by her teacher as a consequence of her intolerable 'silly' behaviour.

Art connection to loneliness

As testimony to Liza's artistic inclination, while she could not connect her interests in art with lessons, she could connect with her artistic sensitivities in the privacy of the art pottery room. When asked 'where is your favourite place in school?', Liza replied 'the pottery room,' which she visited alone in order to attend to dark feelings:

LIZA: If I'm annoyed with someone, or feel lonely, I can just go in there and look round at other people's art. If I go in there . . . I can . . . and they've . . . if it's dark paint on a page, I look at that and sort of feel, say to myself, that's dark colours, that makes me feel better because they feel, they've expressed, and they're dark.
CB: So that makes you feel less alone in your feelings?
LIZA: Yes.

These remarks demonstrate Liza's sophisticated understanding of the role art can play in expressing feelings. It is clear that she had found a resource in art and yet, this had not been fostered through her experiences of art lessons in the school. This reflects a disconnect between home, community and school cultures, as Liza was unable to translate the values and the learning she developed at home and in the community art class into an appreciation of art lessons in school. In understanding why Liza felt prone to such feelings of loneliness it is necessary to consider the third bind for children in poverty: Liza's orientations towards friends in school and their connection to her 'silly' behaviour in lessons.

Social anxiety and unreciprocated 'best friends'

Liza's concern for the way people regarded her had accentuated over the last couple of years. She was very aware of social hierarchies and explained in detail the complex and changing social dynamics whereby friends aligned with each other, fell out and then reformed. When asked who her friends were, she replied:

> Kia, Kathy, Liam, Jane, Cleo, Annie. I have lots and lots of friends. But I don't hang around with Annie outside of the classroom because otherwise Kia gets annoyed with me, 'cause Kia does not like Annie, and the other day Codie took the mick out of Kia's little brother. No one likes Codie, not at the moment 'cause everyone's friends with Kia and no one's friends with Codie, 'cause Kia's in the middle and Codie's out here [indicates to a far away point]
>
> (Liza)

However, within the wider friendship group she had one significant friendship in Kia:

LIZA: 'Cause she's really nice, like one of my best friends. I love her, she gives me hugs and she's always nice to me, she hangs round with me and I think she's my only friend.
CB: I thought you said you had lots of friends?
LIZA: I do but she's my only friend in my tutor, right now.

Liza placed greater emphasis in this friendship than in the others she listed above. Not only did Kia make visual demonstrations of affection (at times), but in being in Liza's tutor group, as well as her maths class, they spent almost all lessons together. Tutor group friends were those with whom Liza spent most lessons with. As with Clive, friendships external to the tutor group were not as strong as those within. This speaks to Brooks's (2002) findings that the grouping strategy, to allocate children from each feeder school to the same tutor group in order to 'consolidate existing friendships during "college" time', increased the longevity of friendships (464). This may be because class-time is such an integral part of schooling; friendships outside of the classroom have less significance on pupils' schooling lives.

While it was important to share classes, it was also important for Liza to continue friendships out of school. Liza told me that 'Kia comes round my house.' This reveals that, as with Bonnie, there was a school–home link between Liza's best friends in school. However, Bonnie didn't feature at all in Liza's discussions of her current friendships at secondary school. Liza's father told me that the two had had a big falling-out shortly after Liza moved to the Maple. When I enquired about Bonnie, Liza replied: 'I sometimes see her lunch-time, break-time, after school, we say hello sometimes that's all.' When talking about Bonnie, Liza's head dropped and the conversation turned to the question of trust. When asked if she trusted any of her friends in school, she replied: 'No. only my parents, well mostly Dad.' Indeed, it was questionable as to what faith Liza might have had in her friendship with Kia, as from observation Kia wasn't overly ready to defend Liza in her absence:

> A boy interrupts the lesson and informs the teacher that Liza's registration class tutor wants to see her. The teacher excuses her and Liza leaves the room with a groan. The students continue their work amid a fairly high level of noise. One pupil from a group of four boys calls over, 'Kia, do you like Liza?' Kia turns and replies in a dismissive tone 'sort of'. The boys start laughing and Kia protests, 'well not really'. The teacher terminates the conversation by calling the class to work quietly.
>
> (religious education lesson)

Liza's father spoke of the precariousness of Liza's social ties and the impact they had upon her happiness and well-being, something which was a repeating feature of her close friendships:

> They [Bonnie and Liza] fell out a while ago now, but even before then she's always been falling out with friends that's nothing new. It's all drama, drama, drama. To be honest I tend to lose track of it now, because of all the drama you get emotionally involved with, whatever argument she's having with whoever, and it goes up and down and up and down and I can't do it. I'm too old! So sometimes I lose track with who she's friends with and who she's fallen out with . . . It's all a bit complicated because they [Liza and Kia] all fall out, we had big upsets the other day because we thought someone had stolen Kia away. I had to explain friends are not like boyfriends. It's getting a bit too much like that.
>
> (Liza's father)

This account reveals that Liza's preoccupation with social relationships was not just confined to her school life, but also permeated home, and had an emotional impact upon her father as well. Friendship could be seen to play an integral part in Liza's life, which may explain why her social investment came at the expense of teacher disapproval of her 'silly' attention-seeking behaviour in the classroom.

The longer term effects of turbulence

In Liza's case, bind four persisted due to the impact of mobility upon her orientations to friendships. In over four years since her initial school move, Liza's patterns of friendship continued to repeat: an intense emotional investment which led onto needy and smothering behaviour, ultimately ending in emotional blow-out and rejection. Such a pattern conforms to Pahl's (1998) concept of 'friendships of pleasure', which aim to replicate the protective and emotionally supportive dimensions of the ideal family. However, he argued that these types of friendships are not reciprocal as they rely on an unequal dynamic of 'cared for' and 'carer'. This may have accounted for the eventual breakdown in Liza's core friendships, and feelings of loneliness and isolation in school, from which she found solace in the empty pottery room. In her search for a safe and secure place it is significant that when asked 'where is your favourite place in the world?', Liza responded 'my bed'. This indicates the importance of autonomy for the child within her home space (Solberg, 1990), but it also highlights the relevance of a private and personal space in which Liza had devised a creative strategy for managing painful emotions:

LIZA: I do most of my stuff on my bed, I sit on it, I talk to my teddies on it.
CB: What are the feelings you have then?
LIZA: Well if I'm sad and annoyed then I just talk to my teddies and if I've just fallen out with one of my friends I lay there and cry. I talk to my teddies and they make me feel better. It seems strange but I talk to my teddies for a reason. I talk to them because I'm sad or unhappy. Like yesterday me and Kia were really upset and she was crying her eyes out, and I was really sad and I wanted to cry for her instead of let her cry. So last night I was just laying there talking to my teddy until 1 o'clock in the morning.
CB: Would you rather sometimes talk to your teddy than a person?
LIZA: Yeah.
CB: Why's that then?
LIZA: 'Cause I love my teddies, I have more teddies than I have friends.

These comments indicate Liza's insecurity in her friendships, both of their authenticity and longevity. A happier or less anxious child may well have cited positive associations with their 'favourite place in the world', yet Liza described a place of refuge from the world, where she felt safe to feel sad, and surrounded by her teddies and pet rats, whose love she perceived to be unconditional.

Conclusion: Escaping the binds?

Liza's story demonstrates the unassailable nature of the binds she faced over her educational career, with the result of an educational penalty. As opposed to escaping the binds she experienced in primacy school, we see that she encountered further challenges in secondary school, in view of increasing financial hardship. Bind two, three and four were interrelated: school and home relocation positioned Liza as an outsider in her school and community. The disconnect between home and school interrupted the development of good relationships with her teachers, and her social investment in friendships was antithetical to her educational progress.

The pervasive affect of these binds was in their interconnection, in preventing a secure and lasting sense of social inclusion. The result, for Liza, was a social orientation in school that was in conflict with an effective learning orientation. Liza's priority was her social relationships. As such she felt that she must constantly invest and remake friendships, aware that, as in the case of her friends Codie and Bonnie and before that Tasmeena, they may be withdrawn at any moment. Liza's strategy was to spread her social net wide, while concomitantly acknowledging one stronger bond at a time. However, no one friendship survived across time or space, and as a result Liza felt unable to trust in her friends.

Liza could not commit to her schoolwork, due to uncertainty in how she was regarded by her teachers and anxiety in her abilities. Achievement in lessons, however, came secondary to peer group acceptance and her focus upon 'being silly' in order to maintain her friends' attention. This applied even in the subjects that Liza enjoyed and showed promise, such as sports and art. As a result she found most lessons to be meaningless and 'boring'. The exception was her lower-set maths, which was the only context where Liza's classroom persona as a 'silly' person was acceptable.

Like Clive, Liza was a 'loner' in school, but while Clive disappeared to the pond, Liza sought out the pottery room, outside of the gaze of her teachers and peers. Here she struggled with her 'dark' feelings, which counterpointed the high times when all was well with her friends and Liza was happy (for a while). Yet such positive moments were hard to draw security from, because they were transient and fleeting, a roller coaster of emotions underpinned by anxiety, uneasiness and fear.

Notes

1 Hoyland, Dye and Lawton (2009), in their review of 45 studies into the effects of breakfast consumption upon the cognitive performance of children and adolescents, found that breakfast consumption is more beneficial to academic performance than going without, although the difference is more apparent in children that are lacking in nutrition. In investigating the effectiveness of school breakfast programmes, they concluded that there was a positive effect upon performance, although this may be partially explained by the increased school attendance such interventions encouraged. Little work, however, has investigated the social and emotional impact of school breakfast provision. Liza's reflection suggests a further benefit may be offered in the symbolic value of breakfast, which for her signified she was unconditionally cared for by her teachers. It may be that the value of similar types of provision is not only physical, but can also contribute towards children's self-worth.
2 These national government standards on educational performance are now available on the Department for Education website at www.education.gov.uk/schools/performance/primary_12/p7.html [Accessed 14 April 2014].
3 The expected grades at key stage three were available at 'Secondary Schools 2006 (KS3)', *National Curriculum Online*, Qualifications & Curriculum Authority, www.dcsf.gov.uk/performancetables/ks3_06/k5.shtml [Accessed in 2008]. This has now been archived due to new government systems and is available only upon request.
4 This echoes recent research in the US and UK suggesting that families move in and out of poverty (US Census Bureau 2011; Aldridge et al. 2012).

References

Aldridge, H., Kenway, P., MacInnes, T. and Parekh, A. (2012) *Monitoring Poverty and Social Exclusion*, Joseph Rowntree Foundation. Available at www.jrf.org.uk/publications/monitoring-poverty-2012 [Accessed 7 April 2014].

Brooks, R. (2002) 'Transitional friends? Young people's strategies to manage and maintain their friendships during a period of repositioning', *Journal of Youth Studies*, 5 (4): 449–67.

Hoyland, A., Dye, L. and Lawton, C.L. (2009) 'A systematic review of the effect of breakfast on the cognitive performance of children and adolescents', *Nutrition Research Reviews*, 22 (2): 220–43.

Hutson, S. and Cheung, W.-Y. (1992) 'Saturday jobs: sixth formers in the labour market and the family', in C. Marsh and S. Arber (eds) *Families and Households*, Basingstoke: MacMillan.

Pahl, R. (1998) 'Friendship: the glue of contemporary society?', in J. Franklin (ed.) *The Politics of Risk Society*, Cambridge: Polity Press.

Ridge, T. (2002) *Childhood Poverty and Social Exclusion from a Child's Perspective*, Bristol: Policy Press.

Solberg, A. (1990) 'Negotiating childhood: changing constructions of age for Norwegian children', in A. James and A. Prout (eds) *Constructing and Reconstructing Childhood: contemporary issues in the sociological study of childhood*, London: Falmer Press.

United States Census Bureau (2011) *Census Bureau Survey Shows Poverty is Primarily a Temporary Condition*, 16 March. Available at www.census.gov/newsroom/releases/archives/poverty/cb11-49.html [Accessed 7 April 2014].

Chapter 5

Megan
School life as a highly mobile Irish Traveller

Life at Hollybush primary school

I first met Megan when she was nine years old, having joined Hollybush junior school one year previously in year four. The school had 169 students on roll reflecting a recent fall in students, and had prompted a shift from a single-year entry to mixed teaching classes in order to accommodate for the loss of one teaching class. Upon joining Hollybush, Megan's class teacher told me there had been some disagreement amongst the teachers over her true age as she looked so much younger, and was considerably smaller, than other children her age. Megan was from an Irish Traveller background and lived at a Traveller site on the outskirts of Thornton, along with her mother and father, and eight of her 11 siblings.

Mobility as a cultural norm

Megan had experienced many changes of school across England and Ireland as part of her cultural heritage. Frequent movement can be seen to be a typical feature of the Traveller culture (Bancroft 2005) and as Hollybush served a nearby Traveller site, the school experienced many Traveller children joining and leaving at irregular times. Teachers at Hollybush voiced frustration in the tendency for Traveller children to be withdrawn from school with very little, if any, notification, which would invariably come through the pupil (as opposed to their parent) on the last day or so of school. Mrs Kelly, a supply teacher and Traveller liaison officer for the school, told me this movement was often related to seasonal employment; visiting extended family in different locations; and in the early summer months, to attend regular horse fairs around the country. The latter in particular often involved children being removed from school for up to three months.[1]

Megan couldn't remember how many schools she had attended previously. As far as she could recall they included: 'one in the North, two in Ireland, and er then Dublin, that was . . . I think there was one or two, can't remember . . . Then before I came [to Hollybush] I was in Littletown, down London' (Megan).

Of her most recent previous school in a suburban town on the outskirts of West London, Megan couldn't remember much detail. She had attended the school for only two months and claimed to 'feel a lot better' upon leaving. Of the school 'in the North', Megan expressed no recollection apart from that she 'just really didn't like it.' Her response was similarly curt of the school in Littletown, in simply stating, 'wanted to go'.

The cultural context of Megan's schooling life and the moving as part of her Traveller lifestyle produced a particular set of interconnections between her binds against educational achievement. First, this will be discussed in relation to her educational lag behind her peers.

Educational penalty following school absence

Megan had no records at Hollybush with details of her prior schooling experience. Mrs Simon, Megan's class teacher and the special educational needs coordinator (SENCO), told me this was common for Travellers at the school. Due to the frequency with which Travellers moved it was notoriously difficult to track previous schooling records. The continual school changes and protracted periods of school absence had contributed towards a difficulty, for Megan, in keeping up with her peers; as such she received a tailored education plan, involving frequent small-group work with a learning assistant, inside and out of the classroom. This provision was difficult for the school to finance as while Megan should have had a statement, this had not yet been possible to procure from the local authority, due to the elongated process of assessment that statementing required. Megan's sister Mia had similar problems in accessing the curriculum.

Reflecting other work highlighting the educational underachievement of Gypsy/Traveller children (Swann 1985; Liegeois 1987; Kiddle 1999), Megan was significantly behind her classroom peers in academic attainment. Upon entering year five (age nine) Megan had been held back in her mixed year 3/year 4 classroom until five months after her peers had moved into the mixed year 5/year 6 class. The decision to move Megan had been a joint one between her teachers and in agreement with her mother: 'It was decided Megan would benefit from being with her peers, having felt some loss of esteem in having been kept behind with children that were much younger' (Mrs Simon, SENCO and class teacher). However, from observation Megan did not settle in comfortably with the other peers her age, as we will see.

Isolated in class

Four months following her promotion to the class above, Megan was quiet, guarded and unsure of herself in lessons. She was particularly anxious in relation to individual and group work, and was reluctant to attempt any activity unaided. Megan preferred to seek out the help of the learning support assistants, or in their absence the teacher:

The teacher writes the definition of 'archaeology' on the board. She tells children to write this down and then proceeds to tell a story about a group of metal detectors in a local town. About half the class are listening and the other half are still writing down the definition, including Megan. The teacher then tells children to gather on the floor. Megan is one of the last to sit down and does so reluctantly on the edge of the group. The teacher explains the learning activity and sends children back to their seats. As the teacher comes over Megan's side of the classroom, Megan gets up and goes and asks where the LSA is. The teacher answers 'she's not here but don't worry I'll help you.' Megan then fetches her literacy book.

(history-literacy lesson)

Megan's isolation in class may have been compounded by the frequent grouping rearrangements. Already that year, Megan had experienced four different table groupings. For all classes, except for literacy and numeracy, children were placed in mixed-ability tables. However, the latest shift had been an improvement on the last one:

MEGAN: There's two girls I don't really like on it.
CB: Why don't you get on with them?
MEGAN: Well, they always whisper and then laugh at me.

She was happier with the more recent grouping with Owen, Nick and Leo in claiming: 'It's alright. Wasn't really, really bad or anything.' When asked why, she explained, 'Cause Leo's on it.' While Nick and Owen were both hard-working and applied themselves, Leo was one of the most disruptive children in the class, who continually sought the attention of the teacher and other pupils. Megan generally ignored any misbehaviour in class, but occasionally colluded in Leo's off-task behaviour, providing it was not overtly disruptive:

MEGAN: I just talk to him [Leo] in class. I don't hang out with him.
CB: What do you talk about?
MEGAN: Play 'It' in class.
CB: 'It' in class? What do the teachers think about that?
MEGAN: Not when they're watching, just when Leo was laughing with his hand behind them all.

Despite her lack of engagement in lessons, Megan did not seek to disrupt lessons. On the contrary she was well behaved and quiet, and tried to go unnoticed by peers and teachers. She made very little effort to communicate with other children in the class and was often lost and alone in group or paired work activities:

The teacher reads the poem and asks the class how they might plan an assembly on it. A couple of children volunteer suggestions. The teacher interrupts a few times to check Leo who is making noises on Megan's table. The teacher then tells children to pair up in order to plan the assembly. This causes commotion but most children are able to sort into pairs or small groups. Someone informs the teacher that Megan hasn't got a partner and she asks Megan in front of the class: 'Who do you want to with'. She replies, 'I don't mind'. No-one volunteers for her to join their group and so the teacher puts her with Lorna, Ally and Sophie. Megan takes a seat on the outskirts of the group. She sits up on her chair trying to hear the conversation between Lorna and Ally. Sophie, in front of Megan, has her elbow on the table and her head on her elbow, her body position is excluding Megan. The teacher notices this and then calls over to Lorna asking if everyone is being included in the conversation. Lorna's group look a bit confused. Presently Megan moves seats and goes to sit next to Lorna. Lorna starts talking to her and explains the activity.

(literacy lesson)

One-on-one learning support

When support was available Megan was removed from lessons to learn separately with Miss George, a learning support assistant (LSA). Occasionally Leo joined them; he also had significant learning difficulties:

CB: What do you prefer out of working out here with Leo and working in the class?
MEGAN: Out. We, outside with Miss George [LSA] and Leo.
CB: Why's that?
MEGAN: Because they don't, that's work more likely for me to do . . . Like, work that I probably, I'm on the level on.
CB: So why's that good?
MEGAN: 'Cause I learn, you, you learn bits and bits at a time.
CB: So do you think you do more learning out here than when you're in the class?
MEGAN: Yeah. A lot, lot more. I don't think I learn anything in class.

When asked about the lesson she liked, Megan replied only, 'numeracy' and when probed if there were any other lessons she enjoyed she replied, 'not really no . . . Boring'. When asked why she enjoyed numeracy, Megan referred to Miss George:

MEGAN: She gives you help and makes it a lot easier.
CB: And why is that good?
MEGAN: Well if I ask what this word says, she'd tell me to try and spell it out yourself . . . and if it takes me a long time, she'll tell me.

Having the support of her LSA gave Megan the confidence, on occasion, to try and take part in lessons. Indeed, this was the only lesson I observed in which Megan would ever put up her hand to answer questions:

> The teacher asks a question and about three quarters of the class put their hands up. Megan whispers in the LSA's ear and she nods and Megan then puts her hand up too. [Has Megan's LSA told her this is correct?] Megan gets selected to answer and her response is correct. Megan smiles at the LSA who smiles back.
>
> (numeracy lesson)

However, without the support and help of her LSA to translate teacher questions and endorse her answers, Megan lacked the confidence to participate in class:

CB: What are the lessons you're more likely to put your hand up in?
MEGAN: Numeracy.
CB: Numeracy? And that's it?
MEGAN: Yeah.
CB: What would make you want to answer questions more?
MEGAN: If there, if there was . . . if I learned a lot more like . . . then I'd put my hand up every question.
CB: What stops you putting up your hand and just guessing anyway?
MEGAN: If it's not right, they might laugh at you.
CB: Why would it matter if they laughed at you?
MEGAN: 'Cause you feel ashamed.

Megan felt distrustful of her peers in class concerning any attempt to become more integrated, although, she clearly wanted to learn and valued the support offered in the tailored tuition she received. However, the relationship she established with her LSA must be considered with respect to her limited friendships, exclusion and even bullying by peers in school. This leads on to discussion of bind three.

Limited friendships with, and exclusion from, peers

Megan's friends in school were 'Josie and Lola'. As a settled Traveller who lived at the site permanently, Lola knew Megan prior to joining school. Josie lived in a nearby council estate. Both girls were the same age as Mia (Megan's sister). Prior to moving into the upper class, Megan had been seated next to Mia, Lola and Josie, in lessons, and the four children often completed group work together with the LSA on the lowest ability table. As in her new class, Megan had been quiet and deferent in lessons. She had been more conversant with her friends in the lower class, however, and seemed less withdrawn than she was in the class she had moved up to.

While Megan no longer shared lessons with her sister and two friends, the four girls continued to stay close together during break times and lunchtimes. They wandered around school as a tight-knit group and were generally lively and bubbly, running around, laughing together, and often were amongst the last to come into the dinner hall to eat. On two occasions I joined the group to eat in the lunch hall. This was a fun experience and the girls seemed confident and gregarious, they asked lots of questions and happily answered the questions I asked them. There was a fair amount of good-natured banter between the group, as they traded food items and chivvied each other to finish so they could go out to play. In summary, Megan could be seen to be far happier out of lessons than she was within them.

Bullying in class

Away from the protection of her friends in the younger class, Megan admitted to feeling vulnerable to experiences of verbal bullying. When asked about her new classroom peers, she responded:

MEGAN: All right. They're not really, really bad.
CB: Just a bit bad?
MEGAN: Yeah. But they're better, they're better than the ones last year.
CB: Why are they a bit nicer in this class?
MEGAN: Er, it all got sorted out 'cause I told the teacher and that's why I changed 'cause um . . . I hate that they call me Tom Thumb.
CB: What's that?
MEGAN: Tom Thumb, do you watch Tom thumb? There's a little girl size of your thumb.
CB: And how did they say that?
MEGAN: Horrible way. And then they called me Maggie [the baby] out of Simpsons, Kevin called me.

It is evident from this account that Megan understood the decision for her to move classes as a reaction against the bullying. This is clearly a negative reason as it infers that the punitive action was against Megan, the victim of the bullying, as opposed to the perpetrators, which she later named as three boys from the previous class. Megan's perception of the rationale behind the move would surely have had different implications were her account to cohere with Mrs Simon's, that Megan had outgrown the younger class? Nevertheless, Megan claimed to feel less distressed in her new class of peers her own age, although the description – 'they're not really really bad' – was far from positive, perhaps reflecting low expectations. As this discussion has illustrated, Megan had very different experiences within the classroom and playground, and although away from her bullies, lessons were uncomfortable in the absence of friends, and given her educational lag behind her peers. This leads to the final bind Megan confronted in Hollybush, that of the cultural clash between Megan's home and school life, which may in part have contributed to her alienation in lessons.

The cultural clash between school and home

Compounding Megan's sense of isolation in school was the huge gulf that existed between her school and home life. Outside of school, Megan didn't take part in any school organized extracurricular activities. She spent all her time with her family, mostly at the site.[2] It was very difficult to gain access to the site as a non-Traveller, as the boundaries were clearly staked out by high fencing. There was only one entrance at the end of a long dusty track that was gated. I was lucky enough to negotiate access to the site in accompanying Mrs Kelly (who was known to the community), on a trip to discuss Megan's reading progress. Mrs Kelly told me that as a stranger to the site community, I would be highly unlikely to gain entrance to the site without an invitation. She also gave me instructions to dress casually and recommended that I remove my matching hat and scarf as this might be seen as 'showy'. The driveway to the entrance was informally monitored in the vetting of approaching cars, by several older teenagers who came cycling up to the gate as we drove up the drive. We were required to stop the car, while these young men asked our business at the site (albeit politely). Mrs Kelly stated that we were from the school and known to Megan's mother (whom she addressed by her full name) and our reason for visiting was to return Megan's exercise book. This entry procedure reminded me of customs control at the airport, and indeed the experience of crossing borders felt strangely similar to entering a foreign country. The site comprised of rows of caravans each with its own small garden area outside. These gardens were meticulously maintained and very neat and tidy. Behind the caravans were several fields where a number of teenagers were riding horses and smaller children played on the track on bicycles. When I entered Megan's enclosure I was surprised to find about seven children milling around, all very well behaved, and Megan was holding hands with a small child who transpired to be her younger brother.

Horse-loving identity

Megan offered to show me her horse and as we wandered out to the paddock I asked her more about how she spent her time at the site. Megan told me she would either help her mother, or play with friends at the site, 'running about and that'. She also spent time caring for and riding the family's horse, Taffy. As we approached the paddock, Megan's older brother (aged 16) was galloping around the field jumping over fences. He was an adept horseman and we discussed the horse and him, both of whom it was evident that Megan was very proud. For the Traveller community, horses have symbolic value rooted in the traditions of

Gypsy/Traveller culture (Bancroft 2005).³ Megan could be seen to demonstrate her love of horses in varying ways within school. This included playground games enacting horse fair scenarios and playing 'wild horses' with Mia, Lola, and Josie:

> The group are galloping around in a corner of the playground. As I approach they stop their game and run up to me. I asked what they were playing and Megan replied 'wild horses'! The game involved the children (as horses) roaming the countryside and having adventures. Megan and her three friends have been braiding each other's hair with matching fluffy hair bands. They told me they were doing each other's 'manes' and the hair bands had been procured from a recent horse fair. Josie also sported one of these bands, which had been given to her as a present from Megan's sister Mia.

While Traveller horse culture had found expression in different and creative ways, in affirming group bonds through various fantasy activities in the playground, this did not extend into the classroom, where such values were effectively eschewed from formal recognition:

> A pupil tells the teacher that Elspeth won a show jumping event at the weekend and she replies, 'Oh well done Elspeth that's excellent,' and instructs the class to give Elspeth a round of applause. After they finish clapping she asks Elspeth: 'Why don't you bring in your trophy for show and tell on Friday?' to which Elspeth nods and smiles. Megan pulls her trousers over her feet and stamps her feet, she tells the classroom assistant that these are Taffy's hoofs. The classroom assistant dismisses the comment with, 'don't be silly' and tells Megan to get on with her work.
>
> (literacy lesson)

While Elspeth was praised for her horsemanship achievements, not once did I observe Megan's teachers engaging with her love of horses. This is an example of the symbolic violence (Bourdieu 1977) by which subordinated cultures, such as the Irish Traveller community, are ostracized from dominant cultures, such as those of the school.

Relative abilities in numeracy

Another example of the cultural clash between home and school was the contextual value of educational achievement, apparent through Megan's mother's perceptions of her daughter's identity as a learner. Reflecting the significantly low literacy rates for various Traveller groups in the UK (Liegios 1987; 1997), Megan's mother was illiterate, and according to teachers' accounts, her daughters' education in literacy and numeracy was a priority for her.⁴ On the occasion that I met Megan's mother at the Traveller site, she was certainly pleased with Mrs Kelly's positive feedback on Megan's progress in numeracy. She told me: 'Yes, Mia's good at literacy and Megan's good at numeracy.' At this praise Megan looked down and shifted her feet in an awkward manner, as if bashful. While in her year group at school Megan had the most significant gaps in her numerical understanding, in relation to her sister (and possibly others in the family) Megan was one of the most knowledgeable. This may have contributed to Megan's enthusiasm and enjoyment of numeracy, with the result that she had generated some sense of confidence in this subject, evident in her understanding of her capacity to help others:

CB: Do you ever help anyone in class?
MEGAN: How can I?
CB: What do you mean?
MEGAN: I can't read . . . I can't do anything . . . Oh, I do help people at numeracy.
CB: So you can help people with numeracy?
MEGAN: I like numeracy a lot and that's it.
CB: Who do you help with numeracy?
MEGAN: Mark. I explain to him stuff what we're doing.

On two occasions I observed Mark turn to Megan and ask questions about the learning activity. These involved clarification over the nature of the task, as opposed to how to undertake the activity. Both times Megan answered politely and smiled. These examples suggest that she relished the opportunity to offer any form of help, even if it required a perfunctory response. This was important to Megan, in challenging her view that she was incapable of providing help.

Close exclusive community bonds

It was evident on seeing Megan in the context of her community, that family and Traveller relational ties were very tight. Only occasionally would Megan venture into town, under the guardianship of an older sibling. When asked if she saw school friends outside of school, or took part in activities in the local town, Megan replied: 'Er, Lola's at my site, she's a nice friend and we always go out swimming together and everything, and Josie's very, very kind.' But when asked, 'Does she come down the site?', Megan replied, 'No.' Having experienced the site entry procedure myself, it didn't surprise me that non-Traveller school friends didn't come into the site; I found the experience to be intimidating as an outsider.

Navigating the binds at primary school

As regards Megan's binds against educational success in primary school, it is necessary to consider their interconnection. In relation to bind four and bind two we can appreciate Megan's Traveller cultural values of nomadism as incommensurate with the 'invisible culture of exclusion' in school (Ivatts 2005: 5). This could in part be attributed to the incremental model for learning and achievement underpinning national curriculum frameworks and government standards (Gillborn and Youdell 2000; Cudworth 2008).[5] Despite concerted efforts towards meeting her needs, the pedagogic arrangements in the school affected both Megan's transference to an age-appropriate class, in which she struggled to access the curriculum, and her increasing dependence upon dedicated learning support to compensate for the educational 'lag' behind her class peers. This led to bind three, in that Megan's isolation from her peers was amplified in having shifted classes away from her sister and Traveller peers, her compensation for escaping the bullying that she experienced in the lower class.

Life in the Maple: Renegotiating the binds?

The next time I met Megan she was in her third term of year seven (aged 12). She had continued to live with both parents and six of her siblings, currently resident at the local Traveller site. Megan had joined the Maple school six months later than the peers in her year group. She did not have an easy transition to secondary school. Since the time I had last spent with Megan at Hollybush, she had changed school a further four times. She did not take her key stage two (KS2) SATs examinations as she was away from school at this time, attending an annual summer horse fair. Therefore, in order to assess the longitudinal effects of the binds Megan experienced and whether she had suffered an educational penalty, it is necessary to consider her educational performances at secondary school.

Upon joining the Maple, Megan had been placed into the special educational needs (SEN) support group for English and maths, and bottom-set group for science (6 of 6). She had remained in these groups since. Megan's teacher assessments of her educational achievement at the end of year seven appear in Table 5.1. Numbers ascend in value both in attainment and attitude, while attainment sub-levels increase from C to A:

National targets expect children to achieve at least a level 4 at KS2 in English, maths and science, and continue to make two sub-levels progress per year across the national curriculum subjects, in order to achieve 5 GCSEs, grade C (or above).[6] To be on line for national targets, pupils are expected to attain around a level 5B or 5C by the end of year seven.[7] These results suggest that Megan's attainment was significantly below target for all subjects except for drama. Indeed, Megan's academic performances were below the minimum requirement at the end of primary school, for all subjects except for design technology. This was in contrast with teacher assessments of her effort, as Megan's attitude was rated as 'good' for seven subjects including English, maths and science. She was rated as 'excellent' in drama, whereas in three subjects (geography, art and European studies) her attitude was considered to be 'satisfactory'. Given that her attainment assessments were so far behind the national minimum target expectation, it can be surmised that Megan had experienced a significant educational penalty. It is possible to speculate that this penalty had increased exponentially over Megan's educational career. We will now revisit Megan's engagement with her educational

Table 5.1 Megan's educational achievements at the end of year 7, the Maple school

Subject	Attainment	Attitude
English	3A	4*
Maths	3A	4*
Science	3B	4*
Information Technology	3A	4*
Drama	5C	5*
Art	4C	3*
Design Technology	4A	4*
European Studies	2A	3*
Geography	3B	3*
History	3A	4*
Music	3A	4*

binds, and consider to what extent she had renegotiated them within her secondary education.

Continuing school mobility

Megan's initial school change from Hollybush was concomitant with a move to Somerset to stay with extended family. This had been instigated by 'a family row in the home' (Megan). This had taken several months to resolve, prior to the family's return to their previous site, at which point Megan rejoined Hollybush. However, there were residual effects following the family feud, in that Megan had fallen out with Lola. This had incurred various negative manifestations, which spilled into Megan's school life at Hollybush:

MEGAN: Now I don't talk to Lola, we have rows and we have fights, everything.
CB: You used to get on didn't you?
MEGAN: Yeah but we had rows and . . . Lola kept telling the teacher stuff that was wrong, that weren't true but she kept making up lies to the teacher.

As a result, Megan's mother had lost faith in the school and decided that she should be moved on to another primary, Old Oak, in her final year. Megan's experience at Old Oak was more positive, on account of a kindly teacher whom Megan had warmed to:

> I reckon Old Oak was better than Hollybush and the Maple, there was one teacher there Mrs Bead, when I finished my work and she let me go on the computers. And if there was a school trip she'd let me help out with the infants, it was really good.
>
> (Megan)

Possibly due to Megan's positive experience at Old Oak it seemed that her mother was reluctant for her to leave the school:

> I went to Old Oak, then my Mum wanted me to get held back a year, and we went to meetings and all and I didn't go to school. When the first year started here I wasn't here [at the Maple]. I was at home 'cause my Mum wanted me to stay at home and then meetings and that went on and then they said I don't need to get held back a year, they said you can go to Maple, but my Mum didn't want me to go, but she finally said I can go.
>
> (Megan)

Megan's transition to secondary, as another school move, must be contextualized against a backdrop of movement and uncertainty with regards to her continuation in compulsory education. The effects of the mobility bind can be seen to interconnect with the other binds that Megan had to navigate in school; first, in relation to her widening educational lag, and second, with respect the local educational authority's ineffectiveness to meet her educational needs.

A widening achievement gap

As with Hollybush, Megan didn't enjoy any lessons at the Maple, ' 'cause they [teachers] mostly give you work that's too hard' (Megan). The educational gap between Megan and her peers had widened to such an extent that the curriculum was completely inaccessible to her in mainstream lessons. Megan had remained without a local authority statement, however, and the school had been unable to provide full-time learning support. Megan's only available strategy was to ask her seatmates for help, but this had proved to be a struggle. When asked whom she asked for help, Megan responded: 'Rosie probably. She's not the best but she's like the best in the class at like helping out.' It was also evident that seeking help affected her morale: 'I want the help but then I don't want it because I feel down.' Indeed, it had become increasingly difficult for Megan to ask for help from her peers as they were disinclined to sit next to her:

> Mostly all the subjects with the tutor group I'm always on my own. They've already got partners then don't, they don't really, not want me, or anything, but they've already got partners. Then there was Carly left and then before we broke up I asked her if I could sit next to her but she said, 'No work with someone else', but no-one else would turn up.
>
> (Megan)

Mr Sherman, Megan's science and registration class teacher, was able to shed some light on her seatmates' reluctance to help Megan, in that he believed they felt that it would compromise their own achievement:

> Megan is totally different [from other pupils in the class], she is isolated in class. There is no point in her being here because she can't read or write, because no one else wants to work with her, because she's a burden. There was one child who would work with her, she helped her, Carly. But it's more like shepherding. I don't do anything for her, I don't teach her anything because I can't. She has no statement or funding associated so she has to be in here, but it must be a nightmare for her. She isn't at their level, she's probably at the level of mid-primary school, but these are not her peers.
>
> (Mr Sherman)

This explanation is important to contextualize Megan's academic performance indicators. While in the majority of lessons Megan's attitude was considered to be 'good', this had little effect upon her formal learning outcomes. If Mr Sherman's account was in line with other teachers, this may have been because teachers felt they were unable to tailor the curriculum to make it accessible for Megan, so that despite her inclination or effort, the gap between her learning and her peers was irreconcilable.

Excluded in and out of the classroom

Even more so than in primary school, Megan could be seen to be isolated and feel overlooked in the Maple:

MEGAN: Yeah I wish I was back in junior schools . . . I would like to stay at the Maple, but if I had a chance to go back to junior school I would go back to Old Oak. It was a really small school, just one classroom with all year sixes, and they were all bonded because there were no other pupils from other classes to pick on you.
CB: And did you bond?
MEGAN: Sort of, they were kind all the time. It's not like here 'cause here they've got other friends so they can't be kind to you all the time, because there's too many people.

In Megan's view, her displacement was as a result of the few pupils, among the many, at the Maple, who expressed kindness and were inclusive. She saw this kindness as a finite resource wielded by her peers. This belief might be explained by the tenuous relationships experienced with the other girls in her class, who oscillated in their attitude towards her:

MEGAN: It's just that the girls here will one minute talk to you and then the next day won't. They won't say anything mean to your face but you can easily tell that they don't want you around them.
CB: The girls here at Maple?

MEGAN: The girls in my class, sometimes it's all right but then sometimes the girls blank you out . . . today Rosie is kind, she's happy now, but some days she won't like you at all.

Despite this inconsistent treatment by the girls in her class, it appeared that this occasional inclusion was the closest Megan felt to any sort of friendship in school. When asked who her friends in school were, she responded:

I can't really call them friends, but erm Rosie and erm I was amazed at this girl Rosie, she said this morning in tutor, can I sit next to you? and I was amazed she wanted to sit next to me 'cause she's one of the girls like the other ones, she don't really like me.

(Megan)

Nowhere was Megan's isolation more apparent than during break times at school: 'I hate break because it's just you feel left out, everyone's got a friend and you're just walking round and everyone thinks you're a loner. So then you're in class and no one hardly notice' (Megan). This experience of break times was a far cry from Hollybush where Megan used to be active and lively. On several occasions I went looking for her and she was nowhere to be found. One lunchtime I found Megan waiting on her own outside her maths class, even though it was 20 minutes before the lesson was due to begin. When I asked Megan why she was stood in the hallway, she answered:

MEGAN: If the tutor [room] is closed I just walk around waiting for lessons to be back on.
CB: Walk around school?
MEGAN: Walk around inside, if I have maths I'll walk around the maths corridor.
CB: What if the tutor room is open?
MEGAN: Sometimes with the girls, they all sit in their own little circle and chat
CB: Which girls?
MEGAN: Rosie, Violet, Ally, Frankie, Bryony, Emma.

Megan was sensitive to the context in which she was more likely to be included or excluded by her classroom peers, and had detected that in sitting in the tutor room during break times, she was more likely to be included in conversation with the girls in her class, despite being literally and figuratively outside of the 'little circle':

CB: Where is your favourite place in school?
MEGAN: Nowhere. Probably just tutor. Because it's just all the children are there . . .
CB: Do you prefer it during break times or tutor group times?

MEGAN: No, I like it during break times . . . Yeah because all the girls in the class just talk to each other in the tutor [group time].
CB: Must be confusing?
MEGAN: Yeah.

This discussion underlines the conditional nature of belonging in school. Megan felt some rights of access into her tutor room through her formal status of being part of the registration class, but the girls in her class only endorsed this during break time. Even then inclusion was only partial, as Megan always sat at the periphery of the classroom, on a table by herself, while the group of girls tended to occupy a circle of tables in the centre. In acknowledging her peers' refusal to respond to her difficulties as a learner, Mr Sherman's account of other pupils' attitudes towards Megan clarifies her perceptions of the conditional nature of her inclusion within the classroom; her appeals for help may have disrupted others' learning.

However, it is perhaps unfair to attribute Megan's exclusion entirely to the pressures of academic expectations, as the following discussion considers to what extent the cultural worlds of school and home were synchronized with respect to Megan's educational achievements and sense of belonging in school.

Limited synergy between home and school cultures

While fear of the 'burden' effect of helping Megan in class may in part have explained her exclusion by peers in lessons, it was also evident that their rejection of her cultural background contributed to her sense of being an 'outsider' in school. Megan recounted experiences of verbal bullying that were not dissimilar to those she experienced in Hollybush; however, in these accounts her ethnic heritage was targeted.[8] When asked if there were any person in the class she didn't enjoy sitting next to in class, Megan responded:

MEGAN: Carly, 'cause she asked me why is all Irish Gypsies leprechauns?
CB: What did you say to that?
MEGAN: I said nothing, she said she didn't say it, but there were two boys sitting next to her and I called over to Trevor who was sitting next to her . . . and he said, 'Yes she did'. I wasn't going to tell the teacher but he said she did say it. But the funny thing about Trevor is he's kind to you but then in science he pulled out my thing and we was rowing and he got detention so then he called us names like dirty Gypsy.

The following comments indicate to what extent the varying binds interacted, resulting in Megan's schooling underachievement. We can see how her educational 'lag' and peer exclusion led her to feel even more demotivated and unable to work:

CB: Do you think that who you sit next to in lessons makes a difference as to how much you enjoy the lesson?
MEGAN: Yeah, because if you sit next to someone who is really really not kind to you it gets harder to do anything every day.

In considering Megan's renegotiation of the cultural differences between home and school, it was a credit to Megan that she had continued to attend school at all. While some of her teachers and peers were unsure of Megan's purpose in school, it seemed that similar mixed messages came from home. In removing Megan from Hollybush, and in her reluctance to send her to the Maple, Megan's mother clearly demonstrated uncertainty as to whether Megan did belong in school. Yet on the other hand it would appear that her mother was very supportive of her education generally, and progress with key skills. When asked how she was doing at school, Megan responded:

MEGAN: Mum said my reading's improved a lot, she said she's happy with what books I'm on and stuff like that.
CB: Is that how you know you're doing well?
MEGAN: If she didn't tell me I wouldn't even know, when I see a word it looks complicated I just guess it, I've got a little bit better but still I'm in the lowest English [class] in the school.
CB: How do you feel about that?
MEGAN: Not really good but you have to be there don't you?

While Megan seemed resigned to the legal requirement to attend school, it was her mother who motivated her with the aspiration of improved life chances. When asked what it meant to do well at school, Megan replied: 'Mum says to get a better job when I grow up'. However, it was questionable as to how convincing this line of argument was for Megan, especially in view of her mother's earlier attempts to block entry to secondary school. Nevertheless, Megan's mother had impressed upon Megan a determinism to make the best of being at school:

> Because my mum's a fair person, she knows kids don't mean that harm, they can do but she knows if they do or not, 'cause she knows better my mum, so if they told me something, like this girl said 'your tights look nice', I thought she was jeering me, I go back to my mum and she said, 'she was just saying they look nice'.
>
> (Megan)

In contrast to Charles Taylor's claims that parents of children who are absent from school do not recognize the value of education, or their children's best interests (see chapter one), Megan's mother was clearly supportive of her educational progress, and celebrated her achievements in maths and English.

'Helping' others in maths

Megan's endorsement by her family may have explained why maths was the only lesson she felt able to learn anything: 'I still enjoy maths because really that's the only subject I can do well, but I'm still in the lowest group, but I can't do anything about it.' Megan learned maths in a small group of seven children with significant learning needs. These lessons included three learning support staff, so children had a high ratio of adult support. Being amongst children working at a similar level of numerical skill appeared to give Megan some confidence to interact with other children in offering help. However, it was questionable to what extent this was valued by her peers, as the following example illustrates:

> The teacher asks children if they would like to play a number game. Laura exclaims in a grumpy voice she doesn't have a pen. Megan offers her a 'spare' pencil. Laura takes it without smiling or saying thank you. The teacher continues to give children simple sums, a couple of boys call out the answer instead of writing them down so the LSA starts to ask pupils individually. Laura is asked a sum she doesn't understand, Megan's LSA has just explained the same sum to Megan previously and she tries to get Laura's attention to tell her what to do. Laura ignores her. Megan turns around and tells me the correct answer. She makes no further attempt to get Laura's attention.
>
> (SEN maths class)

When questioned about this interaction, it was clear that Megan felt able to generate some sense of self-endorsement in her ability to 'help' others, despite the negative responses to her offers:

MEGAN: When I help other people I feel better.
CB: Who do you help?
MEGAN: Laura sometimes. She don't like me though, I just sometimes help anyway.

Endorsement from learning support staff

It was notable that Megan's confidence in maths may have been relative to the support and endorsement she received in these lessons. Megan evidently valued the learning support staff, claiming to 'get on perfect' with them. They also seemed fond of her. On the last day of term, one LSA gave Megan a card congratulating her on her progress, and a gift of a notebook with a hologram of a horse on the front. This one-on-one support must have been expensive for the school without statement support, which presumably was why it was restricted to maths and English.

Conclusion: Getting tied up in knots

Megan's story reveals the long-term effects of the binds she faced against educational achievement. Her Traveller lifestyle and the associated school mobility produced a particular set of interactions that formed barriers against achieving in school, from which she was unable to escape. On the contrary, the effects of these binds were accumulative in manifesting a sense of dislocation and isolation that Megan experienced throughout her schooling life. The frequent school moves and periods of school absence resulted in such gaps in her education, that by secondary school she could not access the curriculum of her peers. This hampered Megan from developing relationships with classmates to such extent that she became a 'burden' on her peers, and even struggled to find a seatmate in class. Megan was also isolated her from her teachers, because while they sympathized for her circumstances they felt unable to teach her. As such she was totally displaced in the classroom without the support of her LSA – the only person within school with whom she had built a bond.

If Megan's cultural heritage was not endorsed in primary school through failing to engage with her love of horses, by secondary school it was actively rejected by all but her LSA. There were also more sinister effects of this cultural clash as demonstrated through the discriminatory behaviour of other pupils at the school, reflecting the kind of prejudice Travellers frequently experience in society (Levinson and Sparkes 2006). As a result Megan had no true friends in her secondary school, instead having to make do with the inconsistent acts of 'kindness' from Rosie or Carly, who could just as easily ignore her as talk to her. Without friends to interact with there was no place for Megan. Instead, she felt she must wait outside the classroom until break time was over, and she was allowed through the threshold, even if her inclusion was only perfunctory. Given her experiences, that Megan was able to maintain a self-valuing identity of sorts in relation to maths, reflected her courage and determination, as well as family endorsement and LSA support.

Notes

1 Since the implementation of the Criminal Justice and Public Order Act in 1994, local authorities have had lifted the obligation placed upon them by the 1968 Caravans Act to provide official sites for Gypsy Travellers who maintain a nomadic lifestyle. As a consequence many Traveller families have been forced into temporary residence within illegal roadside encampments, which increases their mobility to avoid eviction (Bhopal 1994).
2 In support of the strength and significance of close family ties Goward et al. (2006) found that the 'family provided the most support' (320) in Irish Travellers' daily lives, through maintaining regular contact with extended family, and

feeling 'unable to turn to other people in their community for help and support' (321).
3 Bancroft (2005) has discussed the symbolic value of horses for Traveller communities. They are seen to symbolize aspects of the Traveller ideology: reservation and sociability, cleanliness, respect for the inside/outside distinction of animals and people, and central to Gypsy identity, they are intimately associated with travelling itself.
4 Research suggests that traditionally, Gypsy and Traveller groups in the UK and Europe have considered literacy to be a weapon of dominant society that threatens Traveller culture (Levison 2007). In recent decades this conception has shifted whereby Traveller communities now consider literacy as a tool for economic necessity, as well as for social and psychological well-being (Liegieos and Gheorghe 1995). Literacy mastery, therefore, has been cited as a central objective for sending their children to school (Kiddle 1999; Bhopal 2004).
5 Cudworth (2008) has argued that a schooling system based on the requirement for continuous attendance and provision is fundamentally at odds with a nomadic lifestyle. The consequence is that schools find it very difficult to adequately include Traveller children, regardless of positive intentions (363–64).
6 The KS2 to GCSE progression chart is available online at www.education.gov.uk/schools/performance/secondary_11/Guide_to_KS2-KS4_progress_measures_2011.pdf [Accessed 16 June 2014].
7 The expected grades at key stage three were available on 'Secondary Schools 2006 (KS3)'. *National Curriculum Online*, Qualifications & Curriculum Authority, www.dcsf.gov.uk/performancetables/ks3_06/k5.shtml [Accessed in 2008]. This has now been archived due to new government systems and is available only upon request.
8 A wealth of research has documented the psychological and physical bullying of Traveller children in school on account of their ethnic heritage (Save the Children 2001; Jordan 2001; Lloyd and Stead, 2001; Power 2003; Bhopal 2004; Derrington and Kendall 2004; 2007; Derrington 2005; Warrington 2006; Ureche and Franks 2007).

References

Bancroft, A. (2005) *Roma and Gypsy-Travellers in Europe: modernity, race, space, and exclusion*, Aldershot: Ashgate.

Bhopal, K. (2004). 'Gypsy travellers and education: changing needs and changing perceptions', *British Journal of Educational Studies*, 52 (1): 47–64.

Bourdieu, P. (1977) *Outline of a Theory of Practice*, Cambridge: Cambridge University Press.

Cudworth, D. (2008) '"There is a little bit more than just delivering the stuff": policy, pedagogy and the education of Gypsy/Traveller children', *Critical Social Policy*, 28 (3): 361–77.

Derrington, C. (2005) 'Perceptions of behaviour and patterns of exclusion: Gypsy Traveller students in English secondary schools', *Journal of Research in Special Educational Needs*, 5 (2): 55–61.

Derrington, C. and Kendall, S. (2004) *Gypsy Traveller Students in Secondary Schools: culture, identity and achievement*, London: Trentham Books.

Derrington, C. and Kendall, S. (2007) 'Challenges and barriers to secondary education: the experiences of young Gypsy Traveller students in English secondary schools', *Social Policy and Society*, 7 (1): 119–28.

Gillborn, D. and Youdell, D. (2000) *Rationing Education: policy, practice, reform and Equality*, Buckingham: Open University Press.

Goward, P., Repper, J., Appleton, L. and Hagan, T. (2006) 'Crossing boundaries. Identifying and meeting the mental health needs of Gypsies and Travellers', *Journal of Mental Health*, 15 (3): 315–27.

Ivatts, A. (2005) 'Inclusive school – exclusive society: the principles of inclusion', in C. Tyler (ed.) *Traveller Education: accounts of good practice*, Stoke-on-Trent: Trentham Books.

Jordan, E. (2001) 'Exclusion of Travellers in state schools', *Educational Research*, 43 (2): 117–32.

Kiddle, C. (1999) *Traveller Children: a voice for themselves*, London: Jessica Kingsley.

Liegeois, J.P. (1987) *School provision for Gypsy and Traveller children: a synthesis report*, Luxembourg: European Communities Commission, Office for Official Publications of the European Communities.

Liegeois, J.P. (1997). *School provision for Gypsy and Traveller children*, Luxembourg: European Communities Commission, Office for Official Publications of the European Communities.

Liegeois, J.P., and Gheorghe, N. (1995) *Roma/Gypsies: a European minority* (Report No. 95/4), London: Minority Rights Group.

Levinson, M.P. (2007) 'Negative assets: literacy in English Gypsy communities: cultural capital manifested as negative assets', *American Educational Research Journal*, 44 (1): 5–39.

Levinson, M.P. and Sparkes A.C. (2006) 'Conflicting value systems: Gypsy females and the home-school interface', *Research Papers in Education*, 21 (1): 79–97.

Lloyd, G. and Stead, J. (2001) '"The boys and girls not calling me names and the teachers to believe me": name calling and the experiences of Travellers in school', *Children and Society*, 15: 361–74.

Power, C. (2003) 'Irish Travellers: ethnicity, racism, and pre-sentence reports', *Probation Journal*, 30: 252–66.

Save the Children (2001) *Denied a Future. The United Kingdom: England, Northern Ireland, Scotland and Wales*, London: Save the Children.

Swann Report. (1985) *Education for All: the report of the Committee of Enquiry into the education of children from ethnic minority groups*, London: Her Majesty's Stationery Office.

Ureche, H. and Franks, M. (2007) *This Is Who We Are. A study of the views and identities of Roma, Gypsy and Traveller young people in England*. The Children's Society. Available at www.childrenssociety.org.uk/what-you-can-do/resources/publications [Accessed 11 September 2013].

Warrington, C. (2006) *Children's Voices: changing futures*, Ipswich: Ormiston Children and Families Trust.

Chapter 6

Codie

School life after community relocation due to unaffordable housing

Life in primary school

I first met Codie when she was in year five at Ivy school (aged nine). She lived with both parents and her brother, having moved two years previously from West London to Thornton. The circumstances of Codie's move and its repercussions presented a particular set of interconnections between the binds Codie faced at primary school.

Material deprivation and the struggle to find affordable accommodation

Codie did not claim free school meals and brought a packed lunch, but school staff observed that the family struggled to contribute to school events and excursions. Codie's family had moved to the area as they were unable to find affordable accommodation in London. They had been forced to move out of their flat in London due to a leak from upstairs flooding their flat and rendering the property uninhabitable. Her family had wanted to stay in the area but were unable to find anything suitable in their price range. In the end they had to choose between a bedsit in London and their current house in Thornton, but Codie was upset with the decision that was made:

> We had to look at loads of houses and we had about six months we were looking, well . . . and there was a house still in London but it's basically a house where you had to go upstairs in the house to get into the flat . . . and I wanted that one because I was still in my school.
>
> (Codie)

Strain on extended family ties

Codie spoke very positively about her relationships with her mother and father, however, it was apparent that there had been some strain between other extended family members, possibly exacerbated by the distance between them. Codie divulged some problems in the relationship between her grandfather, who lived in London, and her mother:

> My Mum used to get hurt by her Dad, my Grandad and the things he said . . . after we left London . . . and he started . . . being mean to my Mum . . . Saying things like she don't care, and she never goes see him . . . It's really expensive though to get up there and we ain't got a car.
>
> (Codie)

The effects of family tension will be discussed later, but it was evident that relocation and the difficulties with maintaining contact on a low income continued to cause an additional strain on Codie's family, even two years following the move. This leads on to a discussion of the effects of changing school in generating a sense of belonging in her new school, and the challenge of achieving this when Codie was so emotionally tied to her old school, friends and community.

Moving schools and leaving your heart behind

Codie's previous school in London was called the Dove; it was a large primary situated on the outskirts of West London with almost 450 children on roll. The school had a diverse composition, drawing approximately two-thirds of pupils of a nondominant ethnic heritage and half of the pupils had an additional home language. Children were reported to come into the school with, in general, very low prior attainment, and the number of children on free school meals was above the national average.

When asked how she felt about leaving the Dove, Codie replied, 'very sad' because 'all my friends were there that I knew. And then in the end [after moving] I started to realize I should have liked the school more better.' Codie's recollections prior to joining Ivy school were of feeling 'really upset'. In particular she missed her 'gang of friends', and she was still in touch with two of the group, Dana and Polly. She saw Dana regularly in that the two girls attended a Saturday dance school in London. In order to attend these dance lessons Codie took the bus to London where she would stay overnight with her aunt and was picked up and taken to the school by Dana's mother. Maintaining her dance lessons was therefore, clearly a significant effort involving travelling a considerable distance alone every weekend:

CB: That's a long way to go to London every week isn't it?
CODIE: Yeah, but I get to see Dana. 'Cause we've both said we wanna become an actress, and dancer and singer. Um, after I've done a few work at college and leave half way, at 18.
CB: After you've done what at college?
CODIE: Learn make-up and beauty centres and other stuff.

Sharing the aspiration to perform professionally may have been an important part in continuing close bonds with her friend, yet Codie's consideration of a second-option career in make-up and beauty suggests that she may have considered her performer aspirations to be unrealistic.[1]

Codie saw Polly less frequently than Dana but they kept in touch primarily through the ongoing friendship between Codie's father and Polly's father: 'Polly, we will go over and see her or she'll come to my birthday party and stuff like that . . . and I'll go round hers and she'll sleep round mine. My Dad and her Dad have known each other for six years' (Codie).

Codie's continued contact with friends in her previous school was in contrast with her social experiences since. Upon joining Ivy school, Codie conceded that 'I was really shy, didn't speak to anyone. I didn't put my hand up at all.' Her shyness was long lasting, in that it wasn't until 'half way through' the year that Codie claimed to have felt sufficiently confident to speak to others in the school. When prompted to think about the reasons for not talking to other pupils, Codie's response was poignant: 'I don't, I don't belong here, I belong in my old school.' Her sense of displacement in school may well have been exacerbated in that she took no part in local community events or activities, and with the exception of her weekly trips to London for her dance class, spent all her out-of-school time at home.

The limited effects of family endorsement on educational achievement

It is significant that Codie continued to feel like she didn't belong in school, even two years after having joined Ivy. Unlike some of the other children in this book, however, Codie's sense of alienation was in no part attributable to a clash between the values of home and school in relation to educational outcomes. Indeed, Codie's parents were very supportive of her learning in school. They had made arrangements for her to take extracurricular maths tuition classes, following concerns that her maths progress had deteriorated since joining Ivy school. This had connected with a positive effect upon Codie's learning orientation in maths, it being the only lesson she claimed to enjoy at Ivy.

Attempts to be an appropriate learner

When asked how she was doing in maths, Codie replied:

CODIE: Hmmm, good.
CB: Good?
CODIE: Well, quite good.
CB: How do you know?
CODIE: 'Cause I have a . . . um I have er Mrs Branson's husband as my tutor and I get extra help so I think I'm coming along.

The terms of the provision of Codie's 'tutoring' were unclear, in that her family had financial difficulties. However, an arrangement had been agreed upon through Mrs Branson, a friend of Codie's mother. This valuable social capital resource is indicative of the beneficial effect of family–community social bonds on children's educational achievements (Coleman 1988; Sun 1999; Israel, Beaulieu and Hartless 2001). Not only did this additional tutoring evidence the priority that Codie's family's afforded to her learning, but it also had the effect of fostering her belief that she was worthy of receiving 'extra help', which boosted her confidence as a learner. As a consequence there were times in which Codie was switched on and keen to participate in maths lessons:

> The teacher, Miss Kelly launches straight into the lesson, bringing up a stopwatch on the screen and telling children they have 5 minutes to complete the times square with the numbers she's given them. All children seem to be working on their own and not collaborating. When it gets to 5 seconds before the 5 minutes mark, several of the class start chanting out '5,4,3,2,1 stop.' The teacher asks the class who wants more time. Most children do including Codie. The children who have finished queue up to show Miss Kelly, Codie is fifth in line and waits patiently. She gets a house point for being correct. When they have been checked and the extended time has elapsed, Codie calls out: 'Can we play round-the-world'. The teacher does not challenge her for having called out but responds to the class: 'You have to earn playing round-the-world today, if you work hard we will play it at the end of the lesson'. She proceeds to ask the class questions and Codie puts her hand up for all of them, she looks excited and jiggles in her seat, at one point she puts her hand over her mouth, but doesn't call out. The teacher praises the class and starts organising the class for the game.
>
> (lower-set maths lesson)

Codie agreed that this lesson constituted one in which she was more 'settled' and was 'really good'. When asked why she felt she behaved well during this numeracy lesson, Codie replied:

> 'Cause when you are weren't um, like, think you're rubbish at something, you actually are. You get, when you pay more attention, into it like. I pay lots of attentions into maths, I don't like getting a question wrong. So I keep thinking of an answer and keep putting my hands up I keep trying. And I er just really like it.
>
> (Codie)

Demotivating effect of being removed from group work

Codie's participation in class, however, was limited by the school's decision to remove children from some lessons to learn in a special educational needs

(SEN) group outside of the classroom. This was an educational triage strategy (Gillborn and Youdell 2000) to enable the class teacher to extend the learning activities of higher attaining pupils. Ostensibly a member of support staff led this group, but at times it was left unattended. On one such occasion I joined the table and asked Codie and Liza why they were learning outside. Codie responded, ' 'Cause we're dumb-dumbs,' which Liza disputed claiming: 'Teachers would be angry if they heard the name.' Codie looked down and nodded. When I questioned why they would be angry, she replied in a defeatist tone: ' 'Cause we're bullying ourselves, basically'. This exchange reflects not only the negative impact of grouping arrangements upon Codie and Liza's learner identities, but also that teachers had ascribed the fault for this back on to the pupils themselves.

In the following section we will see the ways in which Codie responded to 'not belonging' in school, through seeking to attract attention in whatever ways possible.

Attention seeking

At times Codie's enthusiasm for maths bubbled into over excitement, so that the teacher needed to keep her in check with comments such as, 'simmer down' and 'I'll be with you in a minute', while at other times she was restless, disruptive and attention seeking, as the following extract reveals:

> The children have silent reading and there is a near silent noise level. Codie sits very still with her back straight and staring down at her book. She seems like she's trying to look studious, but her posture looks contrived. The teacher glances at Codie and raises her eyebrow. I think she is suspicious too. A couple of minutes later Codie starts flicking her seat-mate and the teacher calls her by name. She stops. Codie starts gazing round the room and out the window. She then starts chatting to Dale. The teacher tells her: 'Codie stop talking to Dale'. After half an hour the teacher tells children to put their books away and go to their maths places, which involves half the class leaving and the other half joining from the parallel class. Before she goes the teacher calls Codie over and tells her: 'You're not having a very settled day are you? Can you please calm down.'
>
> (English class)

When asked about this occasion Codie agreed that it was an 'unsettled day'. I asked her what this meant and she replied: 'Um, when I'm really like bouncy and really like, all wound up and stuff and not really having a settled day'. Codie's account of being 'unsettled' is evocative of Liza's notion of 'being silly' (chapter four), concerning the shared elements of restlessness and distraction. However, Codie expressed a sense of powerlessness over her behaviour that led to frustration over the 'warnings' and 'crosses' she acquired as part of the behaviour code system:

> It's hard with your behaviour 'cause when you're like one who's like both, it's very hard 'cause you have days when you wanna be really good and no warnings or crosses and there's days where you think: 'oh I'm gonna have to have a warning or cross' like that. And then it's hard because especially me and Liza like that, because we like have days where we're good and then we have days when we're like bad.
>
> (Codie)

By her own admission Codie did try to 'be really good' and managed to be sometimes, but at other times felt that she had lost control of these intentions and was powerless to respond in ways other than those that teachers saw to be 'bad'.

Negative relationship with the teacher

Codie's 'unsettled' behaviour clearly impacted upon her enjoyment of lessons and relationship with her class teacher: 'I've had Miss Kelly for two years now, it's my second year and I'm really like fed up when she has a go at me and my friends, and I just don't like the teacher.' When asked why, she responded:

CODIE: I'm always talking . . . Because we all get bored in class, plus the only reason why I'm silly in class is because I get bored and if I'm entertained and not bored then I'll tell people to be quiet 'cause I'm trying to concentrate. And if I'm watching the TV at home I find I like concentrating on the TV and not anyone around me.
CB: So what do you think's different about the TV and lessons when you get bored?
CODIE: Teachers talk all the time . . . They gossip a lot.
CB: What about?
CODIE: Like people's annoying things.

Codie obviously felt that her classroom behaviour constituted one of such 'annoying things'. She thought that her teacher simply did not like her, with little evidence that I could observe. This appeared to have bred a fear of getting put on report. Codie felt more relaxed with teachers that didn't teach her: 'Because they can't put anything on a report' (Codie) for a pupil not in their teaching class.

Precarious friendships

Reflecting the fluctuations in Codie's behaviour within class and her attitude towards her work, Codie's behaviour out of lessons could be seen to be similarly erratic. She frequently presented with dramatic mood changes that shifted from excitable to angry or sulky, overly confident and then anxious. These ups and downs appeared to be mirrored in her relationships with her friends, in which she was constantly arguing, falling out and sometimes (but not always) making up again: 'Well I get on well with them, Liza, Bonnie, Emma, Rina, but then what would happen is, if we had an argument we wouldn't be friends, but then we can make up' (Codie).

Codie exhibited some anger towards peers in her class, particularly towards previous friends. Harbouring such animosity was clearly as integral to her experience with other peers, as any positive experience with them. This was reflected in Codie's response to the question, 'Who do you get on with in school?', to which she replied: 'Can we tell you who we hate at the end?' These significant fall-outs even extended to her closest friends in school: Liza and Bonnie. It appeared that such fall-outs may have been associated with Codie's anger, as indicated in the following conversation between Liza and Codie, where Liza is telling Codie why a group of girls have fallen out with her:

LIZA: They said that you were really mean and I'm not being mean or anything, but that person you really like said that.
CODIE: Who was it?
LIZA: I can't tell you.
CODIE: You can. 'Cause I'm not gonna tell anyone.
LIZA: Bonnie said you were mean because sometimes you shout a bit, don't you, when you get really angry?
CODIE: Yeah, I shout. Everyone shouts when they're angry.
LIZA: You shouted in her face and that's what made her say it, she got really upset.

Elaborate storytelling

Codie's friendships had experienced significant strain following a false claim that Codie had made, which had implicated Liza. Codie's head teacher and class teachers warned me that Codie had the tendency to create dramatic stories in order to generate attention. In supporting this they had referred to the claim involving Liza, which had caused great concern for the staff at Ivy school. The alleged incident was so significant that the police were alerted to investigate. Teachers assured me that the matter had been resolved with Codie, Liza, their families, and the authorities, that the claim was false and that both girls were safe. However, it obviously had ripple effects with regard to Codie's relationships with teachers and friends.

In a separate incident during my time at Ivy school, Liza and Codie fell out irreparably. Liza explained to me that their friendship had been adversely affected following the false claim in which she thought Codie was 'mean' to her to implicate her:

> I really don't think Codie actually . . . cause she and I sort of, I don't like her a little bit, and sort of do, 'cause . . . she lied to the to the whole school . . . and then told the police that I told her something. Well, the reason why I

don't sort of like her is because I didn't tell her. So that made me feel really sad and that's why I'm not too keen on Codie at the moment.

(Liza)

This suggests that while the incident itself may have been laid to rest, the implications with regard to Codie's key friendships were ongoing.

Feeling overlooked

It may have been that Codie felt overlooked within school. She told me she found teachers 'boring'. When asked why, she responded:

CODIE: But it's actually quite fun talking to you 'cause it's only two children [Codie and Liza.]
CB: So if there's more children that the teacher is talking to it's less interesting?
CODIE: You don't really get a chance to speak.

Navigating the binds at primary school

Through the varying binds of financial hardship, enforced relocation, perceived teacher animosity and unstable friendships, it is understandable that Codie may have felt overlooked, alienated and rejected within Ivy school. Codie's response was to try to gain attention from peers and teachers through a variety of ways. In the more positive moments she achieved this through applying herself within maths lessons to gain teacher approval, but more often it involved classroom disruption and confrontation with peers and teachers, and in the extreme, the invention of elaborate and fictitious stories. In what follows we will explore to what extent Codie was able to renegotiate these binds at secondary school, and what impact this had upon her educational performances and inclusion within school.

Life in secondary school: Renegotiating the binds?

I followed up with Codie two years later when she was starting her first year at the Maple (aged 11). She was still living with her mother, father and brother in the same house that they had originally moved in to in Thornton. She had joined the Maple school directly from Ivy, at the normal admission point at the beginning of year seven.

In considering whether Codie had experienced an educational penalty on account of the binds she faced in primary school, it is necessary to consult her key stage SATs results. These were:

English	Level 4
Science	Level 4
Maths	Level 3

These results indicate that Codie's examination results were in line with the national minimum target for English and science, and yet despite her extra maths tuition and enthusiasm for the subject, she had not achieved the minimum requirement in maths.

Turning to Codie's 'ability' groupings during her first year at the Maple, she had been placed in the lower-middle set for English (4 of 6) and upper-bottom set for maths and science (5 of 6). Her positioning within the lower set for science may be considered surprising in view of her key stage two (KS2) examinations, in which she achieved the national target. This suggests that by the end of her first year in the Maple, her attainment in science had slipped since primary school. In considering more closely Codie's educational achievements in secondary school, it is necessary to consult her most recent assessments. The numerical scores for attainment levels and attitude ascend in value (1–5), while the attainment sub-levels ascend from C to A:

These results indicate that at the end of year seven, Codie was on target for only music and history, and for all other subjects her performance was below target. Codie's 'attitude' results show a majority response of three out of five for seven subjects, which indicates that her attitude was 'satisfactory' for the majority of her lessons. In three subjects Codie's attitude considered to be 'good', and for one subject, English, her attitude was rated as 'poor'. However, it is interesting to consider the fluctuations in Codie's reports in the light of her previous term 2 report:

Over the course of one school term Codie had not made progress in six subjects, including English. More significantly, Codie actually scored lower attainment scores than the previous term in three subjects, including science. In relation to her 'attitude' scores, Codie's performance was similarly erratic. She

Table 6.1 Codie's educational achievements in year 7 term 3, the Maple school

Subject	Attainment	Attitude
English	4B	2*
Maths	3A	3*
Science	4C	3*
Information Technology	4A	3*
Drama	4A	3*
Art	4C	3*
Design Technology	4A	4*
European Studies	4C	4*
Geography	4C	3*
History	5C	3*
Music	5C	4*

Table 6.2 Codie's educational achievements in Year 7 term 2, the Maple school

Subject	Attainment	Attitude
English	4B	3*
Maths	3B	2*
Science	4B	4*
Information Technology	4B	2*
Drama	5C	3*
Art	4C	3*
Design Technology	4A	2*
European Studies	3A	2*
Geography	4A	4*
History	4A	4*
Music	5C	3*

had slipped from 'good' to 'satisfactory' in three subjects, whereas in three other subjects, Codie's attitude had improved from 'satisfactory' to 'good'.

These results reveal that Codie's educational performances and application to her lessons fluctuated significantly at secondary school and that despite achieving the national minimum requirement in English and science in her KS2 examinations,[2] she was not attaining in line with the expected two levels of progress from her KS2 assessments (DfE 2011: 37) in these subjects. Furthermore, she met key stage three (KS3) progression targets in only two subjects, history and music. Codie's underachievement and unstable attitude in lessons does indicate a clear educational penalty, and furthermore, one that may have been exacerbated since primary school. In explaining Codie's educational outcomes, we will consider the ways in which she renegotiated the binds within her secondary education.

Financial hardship and the struggle to maintain previous links

In the five years following the family's relocation to Thornton, bind one and bind four continued to interconnect for Codie, in that financial hardship placed a significant strain on her family's abilities to maintain kin and friendship links with her previous community. It appeared to have taken Codie some time to adjust to life in the small town, and it was clear that she didn't feel totally at home: 'I'm still finding my way around with my Mum, like going shopping and stuff, I mean we've been here for five years but we're doing our best' (Codie).

In terms of relations among her extended family, Codie claimed that things were 'better' between her grandfather and mother, and she had more regular contact with her sister who lived in her 'old town' in West London. Where finances allowed, Codie made regular visits to London every other month to stay with her sister, and also visited her previous neighbours. When asked what she liked doing best out of school, Codie responded that her favourite activity was to visit her family in London: 'I remembered all the short routes and seeing my sister too because she lives quite close to my friend. I just get really excited in case I might see her there.' Codie also recognized, albeit fondly, the contrast between the safety of her new town compared with the danger of her old one:

CODIE: [Old town] is the most dodgiest place, like people get stabbed, asked for drugs, it's been dodgy ever since I've moved there.
CB: So do you feel safer here than in London?
CODIE: When I'm here I think that no-one's going to get me, 'cause it's the country and it's boring and stuff. But I thought it was, just can't get used to the fact that I'm not going to be in a place where I've got friends, loads of friends and good friends that stick up for me. It's like living in a place where I'm not gonna be with friends that I'm comfortable with going out.

In line with 'cotton wool culture' critiques which advocate that exposure to sensible risk is a childhood rite of passage (Jenkins 2006; Guldberg 2009; Layard and Dunn 2009), for Codie there was an excitement associated with her freedom within her previous community in London and her social relations there, that translated into warmth and attachment.

Solitary out-of-school activities

The sense of boredom or frustration that Codie felt towards Thornton may in part be explained through her lack of connection with her local area and her solitary out of school activities:

CODIE: [Out of school] Erm I do trampolining, I don't do it in school, out from school, I kind of teach myself a bit, I've got my own trampoline . . . I like to learn new things as well, like computer I'm always on it, out of school.
CB: Do you do that with someone else or on your own?
CODIE: On my own I go on my sims [computer game] and stuff and I go on power point and word, act like a teacher.

A major blow for Codie was in being forced to cease her dance lessons in London a year and a half previously, because they were too expensive for her family's budget. This decision had evidently put some strain on her relationship with her mother:

CODIE: My Mum didn't want to renew it [dance lessons] anymore because it was too much money.
CB: How did that make you feel?

CODIE: It made me feel: 'Why didn't I get told this? and Why didn't I get my say?' I mean I don't want everything dumped on me, I don't want to be told what I have to do, I just want a say in everything. I want to see my best friend and do the thing I love.

Codie's sense of unhappiness in Thornton could be seen to permeate her home life. In referring to her parents' expectations, she claimed that 'I can't be how I want to be.' When asked how she would want to be, Codie replied:

> Well a girl who learns and just learns to be how she, what she wants to be, and not to be nagged at about stuff, really, when I'm at home I get nagged at to do homework, log off computer, get in the bath, dinners ready, empty the dishwater.

It could be speculated that spending so much free time at home might have created an additional strain on familial relationships and prevented Codie from accessing opportunities in which she could develop a fulfilling sense of self. This endorses Coleman's (1988) view of the stress caused by relocation upon interfamily bonds. In this case, the lack in Codie's community forms of social capital may have created additional pressure upon her interfamily social networks. The interconnection between bind one and bind four were ongoing in that material deprivation continued to put a strain upon Codie's resources in maintaining links with her previous community.

The following discussion considers how Codie's previous experiences of changing schools may have impacted upon her experience of normal transition into secondary school.

Comparison with previous move

The move to secondary was a significant step for Codie. Before joining the Maple she was 'nervous' and found the thought of secondary school 'scary', raising negative experiences of her previous turbulence. Codie knew people from Ivy and from out of school that were joining the Maple at the same time, but when asked if she found this helpful, she replied: 'Not really, I just thought that it's gonna be a bit the same as moving from the Dove to Ivy.' It was clear that the trauma and loss associated with her previous move continued to raise strong emotions and reluctance to let go of her old life:

> First day at Ivy was more frightening because I had to leave school and I had to leave all my friends and all the teachers that I grew really fond with, and kind of coming to Maple was getting to know teachers and I still don't remember their names and I still don't remember their faces, unless I see them in the shopping centre. I wasn't used to be in a different school with different uniform and different friends, I was still trying to remember every

last bit that I had of the Dove, and when I went to Ivy I think I cried for the first two weeks 'cause I missed so much of my friends. I still do.

While retaining strong attachments with her previous life may have significantly affected Codie's ability to feel included within her new community, a further element in reinforcing a notion of outsider was in Codie's relationships with teachers and peers in the school. We will now turn to consider the ways in which Codie renegotiated her social interactions in secondary school.

Fluctuating friendships and social exclusion

The precariousness of Codie's friendships in the Maple was in parallel with her experiences at Ivy. Out of the five friends she cited previously, she had fallen out with all but one, Bonnie. Furthermore, they did not have any lessons together and did not appear to socialize in school. Often I saw Codie during lunchtimes and break times arm-in-arm with another girl, Ellen. This friendship was fairly recent as previously Codie was closer to another pupil, Donna. However, since her falling out with Donna, Codie and Ellen appeared from observation, as well as from Codie's own account, to be inseparable, in school at least.

CB: So who's your best friend now?
CODIE: Erm I would say Ellen out of those in school.
CB: And why is she your best friend?
CODIE: Erm I just think we get along better than I did with Donna and I think whatever she does I do.

As with Liza, this account echoes Pahl's (1998) friendship of pleasure, which he saw as an unhealthy dynamic whereby tight emotional bonds lead to codependency and reliance. Codie was clearly anxious in her friendship with Ellen and sought to keep Ellen's company for herself. This emerged through a discussion when Codie was asked: 'Where is your favourite place in school?':

CODIE: I would say when I'm out at break and lunch.
CB: Whereabouts physically?
CODIE: Just walking around really, 'cause that's all I really do with Ellen, we walk around, go to the toilets, that kind of thing, is the main thing we do.
CB: So if you could choose one bit of the school that was your favourite?
CODIE: I would say out by the hall.
CB: Why's that?
CODIE: 'Cause like no-one really goes there. They only go there for the food and then they stay there and then they've gone after a while.
CB: So you like the hall when it's empty?
CODIE: Yeah it feels like there's only a few people left walking past and we can really use it and think we've got the place to ourselves.

Codie's friendship with Ellen also represented an example of Putnam's (2000) bonded social network. The 'exclusive' element of their relationship was clearly evident in that Codie only seemed to feel secure within it in the absence of peers. This may to some degree be explained through the alienation she felt from her other peers at school, particularly those within her registration class.

Alienation within the tutor group

Time with Ellen may have been precious because the two girls were assigned to different tutor groups. This was significant, as apart from maths, English and European studies, Codie shared all lessons with her tutor group:

CB: Is there anyone you sit next to that you particularly don't like?
CODIE: Basically my whole tutor when I'm with 'em,
CB: Really? Your whole tutor?
CODIE: No um, I've been out with like half of them, and none of them like me now, so everyone like hates me.

One year on from this interview it was notable that Ellen did not cite Codie as even one of her loose friends in her sociogram diagram,[3] which suggests that as with Donna and certain classmates, Codie's friendship with Ellen may have been short-lived as well.

Bullied by peers in the year group

While Codie's friendships appeared to lack longevity, it could be seen that grievances were long lasting, for example the feud between Codie and Liza. However, what was a personal rift went on to implicate other peers, leaving Codie with a sense of victimization by other pupils in her year group:

CODIE: You know Liza, well we're like not friends. Apparently I was taking the mick out of her mate's brother for being disabled which I wasn't, but apparently five people have gone up to her and said that I have. Like probably they hate me, but they didn't see it, just wanted to stir it up.
CB: So you think there are people in the year which stir things up then?
CODIE: Load of people, Liza will stir it up, loads of people they wanna get involved and just stir it up, so the person who hasn't done anything will get blamed for doing it. And it's just about trying to focus on who to trust like to tell secrets and see what they say and do.

Codie appeared to be caught in a repeating cycle of distrust. As discussed in chapter four, Liza also felt unable to trust in her friends, particularly in relation to their durability. Research into the dynamics of girls' friendships highlights trust as a key part in processes of inclusion and exclusion within the friendship group (Nilan 1991; Brown 2012). It may be that one way to earn trust within the group is to maintain the exclusion of others. This could in part explain Codie's victimization as the result of trust breaking regarding the story she invented involving Liza, and in part on account of Liza's attempts to stay inside the group. The repercussions for Codie were that she was left with no peers in which to place her trust, and dependent upon the school pastoral provision in order to discuss any personal matter. For such purposes Codie found the 'pupil support' service to be a helpful resource in which to confide, however not overly effective in terms of tackling the bullying:

CB: If [you had] an issue to do with friendships who would you go to?
CODIE: Erm I think pupil support, sometimes my tutor, mainly pupil support because like my tutor has to deal with stuff that happens in the classroom and how I behave, but here [pupil support] I can talk about stuff like a secret people are spreading, like saying I've started my periods and stuff like that I would come here, because I want it sorted. I don't want anyone knowing my private stuff . . . I talk to them about like if I'm getting bullied stuff like that, and I do trust them and they do sort it but it just carries on, the people who are bullies they don't listen, they just want to do it to wind you up and to get you on their level.

This is interesting, as Codie appeared to perceive a clear dualism between the formal and informal parts of school with their associated lines of authority and accountability. Whereas she ascribed to her registration class teacher the responsibility for behaviour in the classroom, she believed his interest was confined only to this sphere. If Codie experienced problems in social aspects of her school life she believed that the pastoral support advisers were the only viable authority available to her.

It is little wonder then that the fluctuations and lack of security within her friendships and classmates may have effected Codie's learning orientations. As the following discussion illustrates, it was in the classroom where Codie felt the least included.

Disillusionment with learning

While Codie had been able to find some form of inclusion during break times through her friendship with Ellen, she clearly felt a sense of displacement within class time. When asked whether she enjoyed lessons, Codie replied:

It depends, like if I go into tutor and someone says something really bad about me, it would be on my mind all day, really annoying. And I'm just worried that they're gonna say it again it's gonna get out of hand. I'm going to lose my temper and shout in their face and all that lot and then get sent out of class. I just worry about that and then I just disbehave in the lesson.

(Codie)

Here it can be seen that a key factor determining Codie's enjoyment of lessons was her social interaction, which directly impacted on her behaviour in class, and if negative, made her guarded and aggressive. This insight provides a lens in considering her oscillating attainment and attitude assessments across the two terms.

Another factor that contributed to Codie's sense of exclusion was her removal from French lessons taught within the tutor group, to learn European studies, a small group taught by learning support assistants in the learning support room. This group consisted of children across the year group with low attainment. Codie explained to me her feelings about being removed from mainstream lessons to take European studies:

I prefer being in the class, um I hate the teachers they treat you like two years olds and the work is so easy . . . I just act like it's so hard that I just ask for help and also its so boring, 'cause like . . . if they want to treat us like two year olds then why not let us act like it.

(Codie)

It is evident that being part of this group had a negative impact upon Codie's sense of self-esteem. It is notable that Codie's attitude of feigned ignorance and helplessness was in contrast with her reactive orientation within other lessons. This account suggests that Codie may have given in to teacher expectation and assumed a more passive learning orientation in this class. It would appear that this learning orientation was interpreted positively by the teaching staff, as Codie's attitude was rated 'good' for this subject, an improvement on her previous term's score of 'poor'.

Relationships with teachers

While Codie's approach to lessons could be seen to fluctuate according to her social interaction, it was clear that relationships with teachers also bore significance:

Depending on the way they are towards me. I ended up having an argument [in science] with the teachers about it and then I just get sent out for it . . . Teachers don't see that the innocent person tells the truth, they don't tell lies 'cause they don't want to get into trouble.

(Codie)

It is clear that as well as feeling victimized by other pupils, Codie also felt persecuted by some of the teachers. This may well have inflamed her sense of injustice and contributed towards her unsettled and disruptive behaviour in class.

It is notable that in science and geography, both with teachers that Codie hated, her attainment had dropped, so that she was currently attaining lower scores than she had achieved the previous term. This demonstrates the dramatic effect that Codie's relationships with teachers had upon her formal learning outcomes. However, Codie's sense of persecution by teachers was not supported in observation. Their treatment of her was consistent with their attitude towards others in the class. It was notable that in some lessons Codie's outspoken behaviour was more tolerated than in others, and by her own concession, was alternatively erratic, playful or aggressive, according to her relationships with peers and teachers at the time.

Good intentions with regards to work

So pervasive was the influence of social relationships on Codie's experience of lessons that they even affected her enjoyment of the lessons that she had previously valued at primary school: 'I do like it [maths], I just think it's the people that are in my class' (Codie). Yet Codie was open about the frustration this caused her, as she plainly recognized the value of education and considered it important to do well in her work:

> If I sit next to someone I like then yeah I get on really better, if it's someone I hate then I just don't do the work 'cause I'm just focusing on what they are doing that I can get into trouble . . . but otherwise than that then I don't care what the lesson is really, I just get along 'cause I want a good education and a good career when I'm older.
>
> (Codie)

The following classroom observation of a maths lesson illustrates Codie's restless and distracted behaviour:

> Codie walks into class loudly and takes a seat on her own at the back of the classroom. The teacher asks the class to quieten and explains the activity. Codie starts whispering to Annie at the desk in front of her. She gets told off by the teacher for talking, which she ignores. Annie is not interested and gives her short answers. Codie loses interest in the conversation and calls out to the teacher to ask about the activities for the last week of school: 'Can we have a party tomorrow, play a bit of bingo and eat popcorn? no?, well can we watch a video then?' The teacher responds in a kindly manner, that they might be able to play number bingo. There is a lot of noise in the classroom, but children appear to be working alongside their chat. Codie gets pulled up for chewing gum and told to spit it out.

Codie plainly liked her maths teacher, Miss Bright, and it is clear that while some behaviour was unacceptable to the teacher (for example the gum chewing), other behaviour (like calling out) was tolerated. Like Liza, Codie felt that she was accepted by Miss Bright, whose classroom culture was more in harmony with her behaviour in lessons.

Conclusion: The multiple binds of poverty

Codie's is a story of a pupil who has struggled to manage the binds of financial hardship, relocation, and unstable social relationships, and who failed to achieve educational success and happiness in school. It is difficult to separate the effects of these binds, in that financial hardship led to an unwelcome move of home, school, and location, and placed a significant strain upon maintaining social relations in her previous community. As with her 'old' friends in London, her more recent friendships remained tenuous, with the result that Codie felt alienated and victimized within school.

Reflecting the precarious nature of social relationships with both peers and teachers, Codie was anxious and frustrated by not feeling accepted in school. This connected with fluctuations in her social and learning orientations, between her desperation to gain approval, and frustration and indignation towards the peers and teachers whom she felt rejected her.

While relations may have been strained in areas of her extended family, it was clear that Codie's parents were supportive of her education, in providing extra tutoring lessons and supporting her learning. However, any benefit to Codie's confidence as a learner may have been undermined by her exclusion from mainstream lessons, both through the maths SEN classes in primary school, and the European studies lessons at secondary school. Codie also felt excluded within mainstream lessons, and responded with attention seeking and off-task behaviour. This may well have further contributed to her sense of exclusion, as unlike the off-task behaviour of Clive or Liza, Codie's behaviour was not acceptable to her peers. Yet there was a difference between Codie's attitude in lessons with teachers that she liked to those that she disliked. While still loud and outspoken in her maths lessons, Codie did not express the aggression and frustration characteristic of her behaviour in the European studies room, or in arguing with her science teacher.

Apart from Megan, Codie was the only child who had no friends within her tutor group and as such represented an extreme case of an isolated pupil. Codie's inability to assimilate into the school culture in Thornton may have reflected and compounded her dislocation from community life. Despite spending almost half her life in Thornton, Codie generated little sense of identification or affiliation with either school or the community, neatly encapsulated in her reflection: 'I don't belong here, I belong in my own school'; in heart and mind, it would appear that she did.

Notes

1 The low educational and career aspirations of working-class secondary school–aged children has been well documented (Willis 1977; MacLeod 1987; Cook et al.

1996), but even aged 10, Codie tempered her dreams to succeed as an actor or dancer with what she saw to be more achievable aspirations.
2 These national government standards on educational performance are now available on the Department for Education website at www.education.gov.uk/schools/performance/primary_12/p7.html [Accessed May 2014].
3 The sociogram is a friendship-mapping exercise whereby the participant places their name in the centre of a piece of paper and indicates significant relationships using a line to connect each friend's name to the centre. The closer the relationship, the closer the line between friend and participant (see Brown 2014: 86).

References

Brown, C. (2012) 'Exploring how social capital works for children who have experienced school turbulence: What is the role of friendship and trust for children in poverty?', *International Studies in Sociology of Education*, 22 (3): 213–36.
Brown, C. (2014) 'Researching children's schooling identities: towards the development of an ethnographic methodology', *Review of Education*, 2 (1): 69–109.
Cook, T. D., Church, M. B., Ajanaku, S., Shadish, Jr., W. R., Kim. J.-R. and Cohen, R. (1996) 'The development of occupational aspirations and expectations among inner-city boys', *Child Development*, 67 (6): 3368–85.
Coleman, J. C. (1988) 'Social capital in the creation of human capital', *American Journal of Sociology* 94: S95–S120.
Department for Education [DfE] (2011) *How Do Pupils Progress During Key Stages 2 and 3?* Research Report DFE-RR096. Available at www.gov.uk/government/uploads/system/uploads/attachment_data/file/182413/DFE-RR096.pdf [Accessed 29 June 2014].
Gillborn, D. and Youdell, D. (2000) *Rationing Education: policy, practice, reform and equality*, Buckingham: Open University Press.
Guldberg, H., (2009) *Reclaiming childhood: freedom and play in an age of fear*, London: Routledge.
Israel, G. D., Beaulieu, L. J. and Hartless, G. (2001) 'The influence of family and community social capital on educational achievement', *Rural Sociology*, 66 (1): 43–68.
Jenkins, N. (2006) ' "You can't wrap them up in cotton wool!" Constructing risk in young people's access to outdoor play', *Health, Risk and Society*, 8 (4): 379–93.
Layard, R. and Dunn, J. (2009) *A Good Childhood*. London: Penguin Books.
MacLeod, J. (1987) *Ain't No Makin' It: leveled aspirations in a low-income neighborhood*, Boulder, CO: Westview Press.
Nilan, P. (1991) 'Exclusion, inclusion and moral ordering in two girls' friendship groups', *Gender and Education*, 3: 163–82.
Pahl, R. (1998) 'Friendship: the glue of contemporary society?', in J. Franklin (ed.) *The Politics of Risk Society*, Cambridge: Policy Press.
Putnam, R. D. (2000) *Bowling alone: the collapse and revival of American community*. New York: Simon and Schuster.
Sun, Y. (1999) 'The contextual effects of community social capital on academic performance', *Social Science Research*, 28 (4): 403–26.
Willis, P. (1977) *Learning to Labor: how working class kids get working class jobs*, New York: Columbia University Press.

Chapter 7

Helen
School life following school change due to bullying

Life at primary school

I met Helen during year six at Ivy school (aged 10). She lived at home with her older sister, mother and father, in the house she had lived in all her life, in Thornton. Helen had moved to Ivy from Hollybush school in the middle of year five. Her story is unique as the only one of the six children who had asserted a choice in leaving and joining schools. As such, for Helen school change represented the chance for a welcome fresh start, and an escape from the bullying she experienced.

Financial hardship and shame

The staff at Ivy suspected Helen to be eligible for free school meals (FSM) but her family did not claim them and Helen brought a packed lunch. Such judgments were informed by Helen's parents' requests for a second-hand uniform, and returned forms to the school office to say she was unable to contribute to school trips. Upon first joining Ivy, Helen had been given a spare uniform, and staff noted that it did not appear to have been replaced since she first joined the school, in spite of the holes and in being too small for her. This had caused Helen some shame as regards to how the pupils and teachers at Ivy would receive her, in view of her tatty uniform:

> Well, I woke up [on her first day] and I, I got changed 'cause I had different clothes and, um . . . Yeah, I like it, but I had like a logo on but I haven't got one now, it's even worse. And, um, 'cause my sleeves were all wrecked and that so I was nervous. . . . of what they thought . . . So I went into my new class and . . . and . . . then I just like got on with my work real quiet.
>
> (Helen)

For Helen, the strategy to offset any negative attention was to aim to go unnoticed. This coheres with other research into the child's perspective of poverty, concerning the shame and stigma associated with visual signs of poverty and demarcation of difference (Lister 2004; Ridge 2009). Ridge (2009) has discussed how visual markers of poverty can lead to social exclusion and even bullying, and sadly this was the case for Helen, to such an extent that she had felt compelled to change schools, as we will see.

Moving schools to escape bullying

Helen moved from Hollybush to Ivy as she felt persecuted by the children, as well as the teachers at the school. In over a year since joining Ivy, it was apparent that Helen still felt very negatively about her past schooling experiences:

> Didn't really like Hollybush, children were horrible and . . . yeah, to me. Um, and, um, the teachers kept shouting at me all the time, for no reason that much . . . I wanted to leave 'cause I didn't really go to school that much 'cause the people.
>
> (Helen)

This illustrates the interconnection between absence from school and the further bind of moving school. As Helen admits, self-elected school absence brought about by her social exclusion resulted in her ultimate desire to change schools. In contrast to the other children encountered in this book, Helen felt 'kinda happy' before joining Ivy, possibly as negative associations from Hollybush prompted her to feel she was leaving for something better. Helen's parents had also grown up in Thornton, and as such Helen had the advantage of prior relationships with children at her new school, Samantha and Kirsten, forged through local community links: 'Samantha I met at a pub [with their parents] and we became friends. And then I met Kirsten . . . Oh yeah, my Mum and her Mum are fr . . . friends and then me and her met, each other.' Her positive aspirations of Ivy were tempered, however, by trepidation about starting her new school, provoking such anxiety that she ended up leaving school early on her first day:

> My Mum came in but I felt I was still at Hollybush, and my Mum came in here to ask if, get some papers and that. Filled 'em in, I think she took 'em back, or, I went there but then I felt sick and so, so I came in the, next day.
>
> (Helen)

When probed as to why she felt so anxious, Helen admitted that she was concerned about, 'well the children really'. At the root of Helen's bullying at Hollybush were her unstable relationships with friends, which resulted in frequent disruption:

HELEN: Some of them kept changing our. . . . Our, um, yeah my best friend, and, she was like, 'I don't like you' and all, kept going on . . . We fell out.

CB: What about?
HELEN: Nothing really . . .
CB: So you were friends as well at times?
HELEN: Yeah, but I never knew when it would be horrible, or OK.

While such ups and downs with friends could be argued to be a common feature of girls' friendships (Nilan 1991; George 2007), the emotional burden must have been extreme for Helen to lead to school absence and even transfer. In contrast to the other children who had felt positively about pre-transition schooling experiences, Helen's school move was made with sole reference to her social relationships. Accordingly, like the other children in this study, social inclusion played a far more relevant concern in relation to Helen's happiness and purpose in school life than educational success, a theme that continued throughout her time in Ivy.

The importance of home–community–school connections

When asked what surprised her most about Ivy, Helen responded: 'I thought the teachers were nice and some children were nice.' The change in her social relations, in particular, was significant and lasting:

CB: Do you prefer being at Ivy or Hollybush?
HELEN: Ivy.
CB: What are the reasons for that?
HELEN: Well the children are here, they play with me and the children there don't really bother.
CB: So the most significant difference was the children?
HELEN: Yeah.

Despite Helen's oldest friends, Kirsten and Samantha, having moved up to secondary school at the start of the academic year, she still saw them out of school, as well as Lorna, who was in the parallel year six class. Lorna was introduced to Helen through her friend Kirsten. Her description of the friendship group indicated that similarly to Hollybush, there were fall-outs and exclusions within the group:

> Well, we've had a fall out. Well, those two have, [Kirsten and Lorna] Um, those two had a fall out and . . . And, um, they've had a fall out and, um, I like both of 'em really. But those two won't get together 'cause Kirsten said, 'no. I don't wanna be her friend anymore'.
>
> (Helen)

Although Helen spoke of a number of friends she had at Ivy school, it was significant that none of Helen's core group of friends were in her lessons. Only Connor, Lorna's boyfriend, was in the same class as Helen, who in spite of being 'a bit annoying' in 'trying to nick' her pencil case, was a valued member of the friendship group:

HELEN: Um, Connor's really funny and I always hang around with him. Lorna, she's my best friend, so is Kirsten 'cause, um, I sleep round Lorna's house.
CB: Do you see Kirsten out of school?
HELEN: Yeah, she lives just up the road from me.

Helen, Lorna, Connor, Kirsten and Samantha were part of a group that socialized out of school together, not through any formal out-of-school clubs, centres or activities, but in informal settings.[1] One particular place where Helen and her friends socialized out of school was 'the Brook'. This was a secluded space set away from any public areas, and constituted a meeting ground for children from the local primary and secondary schools:

HELEN: [Connor] Tries to annoy me all the time but I see him down the Brook sometimes, hangs around with him there.
CB: Where's that?
HELEN: It's near here. Um, it's near [Thornton] swimming pool in, behind, near the pub.
CB: What is it?
HELEN: Just somewhere to hang out.
CB: Like a recreation centre?
HELEN: No, just our place.

The head teacher and Helen's class teacher told me that they had been quite concerned that she was falling in with this older crowd out of school, who were known for displaying 'anti-social' behaviour:

> In terms of her social group she's quite old for her age, she tends to mix with some of the children from the year above from secondary school, which have been known to be a bit unruly, smoking and drinking.
>
> (Head teacher at Ivy)

Helen had a boyfriend, Tony, who was part of this social group. She also knew a number of other children who were part of 'the Brook' crowd, but the fact that she didn't know what school they attended suggested the limited degree to which school featured in conversations between them. There also appeared to be links between the crowd that went to 'the Brook' and a wider intergenerational group, which socialized at the local pub. Helen spoke with pride when she referred to the pub, which suggested there was some kudos associated with liaising in this adult environment:

HELEN: Well, I meet Kirsten round the pub. I don't really meet Tony. I don't know his Dad. But, I see Kirsten.

CB: Who do you go there with?
HELEN: My Mum, my Dad and sometimes my sister.
CB: Is that a weekend or an evening thing?
HELEN: Evening and weekend.
CB: Is that a place where you hang out with other young people as well?
HELEN: Yeah. Yeah.

These social networks through the pub and 'the Brook' were clearly important for Helen, as they connected her to her local area and her family. Having met Kirsten several years previously through their mothers' friendship, it was evident that Helen, like Liza, felt that a potential friendship was validated through family endorsement. It was apparent that the home–school–community link was a key factor in reinforcing friendships, as also indicated in Helen's previous friendships with Mia and Tania, both in her class at Ivy. The importance of connecting friends and home life can be contextualized against Helen's negative experiences with these previous friendships. At the beginning of the school year Helen told me that her best friends were Tania and Mia. However, both friendships deteriorated on account of Mia's upsetting remarks about Helen's home, which must have been all the more poignant considering that Helen was already sensitive about visual signs of poverty:

HELEN: Tania, I was friends with her, just me and her before and I used to, er, go round her house for dinner.
CB: How long were you friends for?
HELEN: Bout a month. Well, about two months or three.
CB: And Mia?
HELEN: Mia? Well, she slept round my house once and then w . . . after, when it was school, she was like being horrible with Tania and that about my house.

These upsetting remarks may have also had an impact upon her friendship with Tania:

CB: Are you still friendly with Tania?
HELEN: No, 'cause sometimes goes and tells on me for something I don't do.
CB: For no reason?
HELEN: Yeah, and it's really annoying. She like comes and bothers me and all that, then she tells the teacher that she, that I bother her.

This experience suggests that while family–friends endorsement may be important to Helen, the reverse was also evident in terms of friends–home endorsement. Spending time together with friends at each other's houses was a central component in consolidating friendships, perhaps through signifying that friends accepted and valued Helen's home life.

Since her best friend had left Ivy school, and in view of the fall-outs with her friends in her class, this may explain that while Ivy was clearly an improvement on Hollybush, school life held little relevance in the absence of friends. This was supported by Helen's class teacher, Mrs Duthie:

> It may be that Helen feels like she's outgrown [Ivy] school in that her main social group is outside school. She can be restless and disengaged in class, and I think she's just looking ahead now to starting secondary school.

The lack of connection between friendship and school life, particularly within the classroom, is further explored in the next section, where we consider the disconnection between home and school values in relation to educational success.

Mixed messages from school on learning and educational outcomes

Helen's set position in the classroom was in the front row, which appeared to have been a strategic seating arrangement as Mrs Duthie told me: 'Those who tend to be distracted I place at the front of the class, where I can keep my eye on them.' As such, Helen's physical placement in the classroom may well have made her feel uneasy given the vantage point of the teacher in monitoring her. Indeed, Helen's behaviour was erratic in switching between the two poles of engagement and disengagement. On the one hand she engaged in lively and sometimes playful behaviour, involving loud outbursts of excited on-task commentary during class, as her way of expressing enthusiasm for the topic. This was in contrast to the wilful disruption, evident through the outbursts of a couple of other boys in the class. On the other hand, when Helen was quieter, this was generally because she was disengaged and distracted from the activity. This manifested in an anxious, almost wistful, discomfort in which she could be seen to withdraw from the lesson. The shift in Helen's behaviour is illustrated in the following lesson excerpts:

> Mrs Duthie shows the class a video of a Muslim wedding, and children, including Helen, call out a couple of times remarking on the dress and music, which they find funny. After it has finished, the teacher explains the activity in which they are discussing, prayer. Helen starts squabbling with Ronan. Mrs Duthie tells her off and Helen responds angrily: 'tell him to get off'. The teacher replies sharply: 'Helen, Ronan, you have both already got one warning today, do you want another?' Helen responds 'No' and crosses her arms in an affronted manner. The teacher continues the discussion about prayer from a Muslim and Christian perspective. Helen just sits with her arms folded and looks cross. The noise level is a lot quieter and children listen to each other's comments. However, Helen zones out and gazes at the board

where the rewards and warnings are marked, she counts on her fingers; is she interested in her own points? Mrs Duthie has been interrupted several times by a pupil shouting out. He gets a warning and then a cross. Presently, the teacher asks Connor what he thinks and he isn't sure, she then asks Helen: 'What do you thinks about it all?' and she answers, 'I dunno'. She looks down.

(religious education (RE) lesson)

At other times Helen could be seen to engage thoughtfully in the lesson and make a valid contribution, even if she did lack some confidence in the value of her claims. This is illustrated in the personal and social education (PSE) lesson which picked up on the previous issue of prayer raised during the RE lesson from the day before:

The topic concerns morality, and the activity requires pupils to list the reasons for, 'why do people pray?' The teacher asks for volunteers to raise their hands. She then lists the reasons that children give on the board. Each answer given prompts responses and dialogue from the rest of the class. Helen and Connor call out and the teacher facilitates a debate between Helen and Connor about whether a person would pray if they had murdered someone. Helen thinks they would and Connor thinks they wouldn't. Mrs Duthie then intervenes, asking the class: 'Now just think about in your head, is it likely that a person would pray if they had murdered someone?' Although the question is posed so as to be open, her tone suggests that there is a correct and incorrect answer. A number of children murmur 'No', but Helen maintains she thinks they would and the teacher asks her 'Why?' in a surprised voice. (It is interesting that she didn't ask any of the children who answered 'No' to qualify their answers.) Helen replies: 'Maybe if they did it accidentally and didn't mean to do it'. Mrs Duthie responded: 'OK, so maybe if they didn't intend to do it, they may want to pray?' Helen then looks a bit unsure and replies 'I dunno' (possibly she picks up that this answer displeases the teacher?)[2] The topic is dropped as Mikey and Brynn call out that the window is leaking.

(PSE lesson)

Future aspirations

It was notable that for the duration of my time spent with Helen in Ivy school, she made no reference to the importance of doing well academically, and made no comment on her performance or attainment. She expressed no ambition to continue in education, and held work aspirations similar to Megan (chapter five):

CB: When do you wanna leave school? Have you got any plans?
HELEN: As soon as possible. Oh, um . . . I wanna look after children like in, well, I wanna look after children really. Like, um, like, there's like nurse . . .

Well . . . there's this like play-school or nursery kind of thing where you go and look after children.

Mixed messages from home on learning and educational outcomes

It may be that the sanctions system of warnings and crosses affected Helen's sense of being a valued member of the classroom community, as when threatened with a warning by the teacher, Helen's classroom behaviour changed from outspoken but engaged, to withdrawn and disengaged in the activity. It also caused some anxiety, for Helen, when sanctions led to a family intervention:

CB: Is there anything you don't like about school?
HELEN: Warnings and crosses.
CB: Yeah. Does it bother you getting them?
HELEN: Well, three crosses worries me.
CB: Really? So why is it that three bother you, but not one or two, or warnings?
HELEN: Well, I just don't like the letters sending home to my Mum. She gets annoyed if I behave bad.
CB: Why do you get them then?
HELEN: If you have, you get, um, a warning or a straight cross for not doing homework or if you're being naughty if you're breaking one of the school rules.
CB: So why would you get them then? What do you think you do to get them?
HELEN: Well last time it was mostly homework.
CB: Why weren't you doing your homework?
HELEN: Dunno.

This discussion highlights a tension between home and school. While Helen worried about her mother's response to her sanctions and this clearly caused her some concern, she did not consider homework to be important, nor did she object to missing out on taking her national assessments:

HELEN: I wasn't here for SATS.
CB: Where were you?
HELEN: Holiday.
CB: So you didn't do your SATS? Were you happy about that?
HELEN: Yeah.
CB: What did your Mum say?
HELEN: Well, they found out that I went on holiday so my Mum came in with me 'cause usually . . . Yeah, school found out and my Mum came with me because sometimes they like usually fine our parents and go to court and I was worrying.

CB: So are they taking your Mum to court?
HELEN: No it was OK in the end.

Despite evading court action, the potential financial penalty for her school absence had caused some concern for Helen. To withdraw her from school during examinations suggested that Helen's mother did not place a high value upon these standardized assessment tests, although she clearly objected to her misbehaviour in school. However, Helen's mother's own educational experiences may have explained her reticence towards Helen's schooling in Thornton: 'My Mum thought it was horrible [at Hollybush] as well so that's why she moved me here [to Ivy] 'cause she thought it was more nice, 'cause she's been there [Hollybush] before . . . when she was little' (Helen).

In explaining the low levels of parental involvement in school for children in poverty, Lareau (2001) found that parents 'did not believe that [the] child's academic progress depended upon his [or her] activities at home' (711). While the low-income parents of her study held the same educational values as those of middle-class parents, their views on the processes of educational success differed, in transferring the responsibility for educating their children wholly onto schools: 'Just as they depended on doctors to heal their children, they depended on teachers to educate them' (712). Accordingly, removing Helen from national tests, and not insisting on the completion of homework, is not to say that her mother didn't recognize the importance of Helen's education. It may say more about her disassociation between the spheres of school and family life. In illuminating the way that bind two may operate through a clash between home and school cultures and values, it is important to consider the way that schooling expectations may be passed down between generations.

Navigating the binds at primary school

In considering the binds against educational success that Helen faced during primary school, there is an interconnection between discordant home/school cultures and financial hardship, which impacted upon Helen's social relationships in school to the point of school transfer. Despite perceiving an improvement upon school life in Ivy, as her best friends were outside of the classroom, Helen felt variable with regard to her classroom membership, and lessons lacked relevance. We will consider how Helen continued to negotiate these binds upon transferring to secondary school.

Life in secondary school: Renegotiating the binds?

I followed up on Helen two years later when she was in year eight at the Maple secondary school (aged 12). Her parents had separated when she was in year seven, and her father had moved out of the family home. She continued to live with her mother in the same home that she had grown up in. Because she had been absent from school during her key stage two (KS2) standardized assessments tests (SATs), her results were teacher estimates:

Maths: Level 2
English: Level 3
Science: Level 3

These show that Helen's educational achievements were well below that deemed acceptable by national government,[3] indicating that at the end of her primary schooling she had experienced a significant educational penalty. In the Maple school Helen was currently placed in the bottom groups (6 of 6) for all set classes, which were English, maths and science. Helen's most recent assessments at the end of the third term in year eight are provided below.

At the end of year eight, Helen should be achieving at level 5A or 6C in at least five subjects, in order to be online for the national benchmark of 5 GCSE grades A* to C, including mathematics and English.[4] However, if Helen's achievements were to increase by two solid levels from KS2, this would constitute appropriate progress within secondary school (DfE 2011: 37). According to her prior attainment teacher estimations, she should therefore be achieving 4A or 5C in maths, and 5A or 6C in all other subjects. These results suggest that Helen had continued to make educational progress that was significantly below national attainment targets and below her expected progress rates (according to KS2 results) in 10 of 11 curriculum subjects. This indicates a cumulative educational penalty across Helen's primary and secondary schooling. Furthermore,

Table 7.1 Helen's educational achievements at the end of year 8, the Maple school

Subject	Attainment	Attitude
English	4C	2*
Maths	4C	3*
Science	3A	3*
Information Technology	4C	3*
Drama	6C	3*
Art	4B	2*
Design Technology	4A	3*
French	3C	4*
Geography	4B	3*
History	3B	3*
Music	4A	3*
European Studies	3C	2*

in four of her subjects (science, French, history and European studies), she was not even attaining at the level (4) considered a minimum national target at the end of KS2.

Helen's attitude results show a majority response of three out of five, which indicates that her attitude was considered by most teachers to be 'satisfactory'. However in English, art and European studies her attitude was 'unsatisfactory', and in only one subject (French) was Helen's attitude considered to be 'good'. Given her low attainment, these attitude scores do not indicate that Helen was an engaged and motivated learner. We will now reflect on these learning outcomes in light of Helen's experiences at secondary school.

Fear of bullying alleviated by friends

Mirroring her experiences at Ivy, Helen's sense of shame at her family's financial hardship caused her concern when starting secondary school. Again, this was in relation to her school uniform, a hand-me-down from her sister who was eight years older and who had also attended the Maple:

> I thought they would take the mick 'cause it's pleated [the skirt], and no-one wears it like that anymore, but at least it's 'New Look' [High street fashion shop] not nothing really crap or from the jumble sale or like that.
>
> (Helen)

Helen's anxiety about her uniform connected to a fear that she would be physically singled out and bullied:

> I was nervous when I first came and thinking I was gonna get picked on . . . I have been like hearing that year 11's put you in the 'Grundens' bins [school waste bins] and that, but it didn't happen.
>
> (Helen)

Upon joining the school, therefore, Helen was relieved to find that her fears were not realized. Her friendships with Lorna and Kirsten had survived through the summer holidays and made her first day 'a bit better': 'I was quite excited but quite nervous [because] I went with my friends, I walked with my friend, Kirsten' (Helen). Not only was the support and continuity in her friendships significant in generating a more positive experience of school transition than the turbulent move, but this stability in her social relationships had solidified over the last three years, and can be seen to have played a key role in her engagement and well-being in school. Helen was no longer regularly absent from school, indicating the strength of secure friendships as a buffer against exclusion within and from school. This connection between bind one and bind three will be further explained in the following discussion.

Social inclusion bridging between home, school and the community

Upon joining the Maple, Helen was reunited with Samantha and Kirsten, and despite being separated by a school year, she still considered them to be her best friends. Samantha had dropped a year, and was in the same class as Helen in maths and English. The strength of Helen's friendships with these two girls was unique from the other children in this book, in that she was the only pupil to consider friends among those people she could trust:

CB: Who have you gone to talk to about something personal over the last year or so?
HELEN: My friends Samantha and Kirsten maybe.
CB: Samantha? Kirsten? Anyone else?
HELEN: Well me and Samantha's Mum get on as well.
CB: Samantha's Mum?
HELEN: Yeah, 'cause my Mum and her Mum knew each other anyway and I went to Kirsten's sister's wedding reception, so I got on with Kirsten's Mum and Dad and called 'em Mum and Dad.

In discussing the foundation for this trust it was apparent that out of school contact with friends was important, as was the affirmation of social bonds between parents. Later it will be discussed as to what extent these bonds could be seen to offer a direct advantage in her school life, but the importance of Helen's relationship with Samantha's mother may well be contextualized against changes in her own family life.

Disruption in home life

Earlier disruption in Helen's home life may well have been a contributing factor to Helen's educational penalty. Following her parents break-up and subsequent paternal departure a year and a half previously, Helen had experienced quite a challenging time, which had instilled a sense of responsibility for her mother:

HELEN: Well it's a bit hectic at home 'cause like my Dad left, and my Mum lost her ring that she got from my Dad for her birthday, and I just want my Mum to find a man and that. I know it will take time and that. . .
CB: Must be hard.
HELEN: Yeah.
CB: Do you talk to your Mum about it?
HELEN: Not really.
CB: Do you talk to your friends about it?
HELEN: Sometimes, with Samantha and Kirsten, that helps.

While Helen's friendships with Samantha and Kirsten had become stronger in their role as confidantes, it was apparent that this was not without some cost within the friendship group. The closer bonds between Helen and Kirsten appeared to have resulted in the loss of Helen's friendship with Lorna:

CB: What happened there with Lorna?
HELEN: Oh we just had like a fall out and that, kept falling out, get together and then falling out.
CB: What was that about?
HELEN: I dunno she thinks that I was like taking Kirsten away from her.

Ridge and Millar (2000) discuss the value of friendships, and in particular the role of confidante, as an important emotional resource for children. Helen's account suggests, however, that there may also be a cost in terms of the politics of girls' friendships; the emotional closeness between certain members may consequentially threaten others within the group.

A place for social inclusion within school

While the ties between Helen and her two closest friends were very tight, they also socialized within a wider group of mixed boys and girls: 'People out of school . . . Kieran, Ross, Samantha and that come on my trampoline'. When asked why they were her friends, Helen's response was telling: 'cause sometimes they knock for me'. The consolidation of the home–school link was in contrast to Ivy school in which there was greater detachment between community and school friendships. Helen's social group extended to a group of seven pupils across year nine and ten, which met and socialized during break times and lunchtimes, in a small courtyard area outside the maths block:

CB: Where's your favourite place in school?
HELEN: Out there near maths, it's like just us, we just like mess around and hang around with each other.
CB: So it feels like your space?
HELEN: Yeah kind of like that.

It was notable that Helen's favourite place in school was next to the maths block. Maths was one subject that Helen enjoyed (as will be expanded upon later.) Her acknowledgement of a sense of ownership over school space was associated with positive feelings about school. When asked how she was doing at school, Helen responded:

HELEN: This one? Fine.
CB: In what way?

HELEN: Got lots of friends and like I aint really getting picked on . . . And so I've done well in my lessons, done better than I did in year seven.
CB: How does that you make me feel?
HELEN: Happy.

These comments reveal that Helen's primary gauge of 'doing well' in school was in terms of her social relationships. Given her broader and more stable group of friends and that she was no longer bullied, Helen's self-perception was of greater success in her school life. She also attributed her more secure social network to her better performance in class. Overall, Helen can be seen to have renegotiated bind three with a more successful outcome than in Ivy school, in gaining a more secure sense of security within her friendship group, and with stronger bridging between friendships at home, school and the community. In spite of Helen's acknowledgement that more settled friendships resulted in feeling happier at school, however, this had not brought her in line with national targets. In the next section we will consider the ways in which home life and friendships penetrated her experiences of and engagement within lessons.

The importance of teachers and friends in enjoying lessons

It was apparent that Helen hadn't altogether relinquished her friendship with Lorna: 'I sometimes have arguments and sometimes try to keep things smooth' (Helen). The weakening of their friendship, however, constituted a loss in terms of Helen's bridging into the classroom. This is because in being in the same registration class as Lorna, they shared all lessons except for English and science. Indeed, the only lessons Helen enjoyed in the Maple were maths and English:

CB: Do you enjoy lessons here?
HELEN: I like maths and English 'cause I get to be with Samantha, and I like the teachers.
CB: Is that the most important aspect of liking lessons then, friends and the teachers rather than the subject?
HELEN: Yeah, but maths is a good subject.
CB: What is it you like about maths particularly then?
HELEN: I dunno we do fun things together, and like work on different things in pairs and like work off sheets. Miss Best gives off sheets and we work off those.

Of all her teachers at the Maple, the only ones that Helen liked were Miss Best and Miss French, her maths and English teachers. This was significant as Helen believed that the most important thing that determined doing well at school at the Maple was 'getting on with teachers'. Yet for the vast majority of her subjects

Helen didn't feel she had a good relationship with them. In explain her good relationship with Miss Best, Helen made the following comment:

> I dunno it's like me, my friend Samantha, me and her get on with Miss Best well, like when Miss Best's dog was dying we was asking her how her dog was and that, and then like I dunno we got on really well with her, and she's a laugh and that.
>
> (Helen)

As in her relationships with friends, the home–school connection was important in consolidating positive relationships with teachers. Helen could relate to her maths teacher as a person, because Miss Best trusted Helen and Samantha to discuss intimate home-life matters. In reflecting upon Helen's attitude scores in maths and English (3*, 2*), it was apparent that as of yet her enjoyment of lessons had not been perceived by teachers as a positive attitude towards work, nor had it led to her attainment in these lessons being in line with progress targets.

The relevance of feeling liked by teachers is important to consider in reflecting upon Helen's previous experiences of feeling persecuted by teachers at Hollybush school, and her sense of classroom membership:

CB: What about the lessons other than maths and English?
HELEN: Lessons are a bit boring without Samantha, and the teachers aren't really that nice.
CB: What about IT, you used to like that at Ivy?
HELEN: It was good at Ivy but here we have Mr Porter, we don't really like him, he's horrible. Nasty, sends us out for no reason.
CB: Does that stop you enjoying the lesson then?
HELEN: Well it does a bit really because of some of them in there are my friends and I try to stick up for them, 'cause they don't really do anything just play on sims [online computer game].

It was interesting that Helen did not perceive off-task activity to warrant teacher disapproval. Perhaps she felt that unless pupils were being disruptive, this didn't constitute inappropriate classroom behaviour. Again, this suggests the limited value of schoolwork for Helen. Outside of maths and English, Helen's behaviour in lessons was disengaged from the teacher and pupils; she was quiet and withdrawn and appeared to take little pleasure from the learning exercise:

> The class are sat on their computers, some are conferring quietly with their partners, but Helen is staring out of the window. The task is to work in pairs to use the internet to scan Google Earth in answering some basic geographical questions. Helen is sat next to Lorna, but both are staring at the screen,

although they don't appear to be very active. The teacher is involved at his own screen and there is no interaction with the class. One boy pokes Helen to get her attention, a couple of children are looking at a game on screen and she turns and smiles but does not get involved. Mr Porter shouts at a boy who is messing around. This is the third time and he takes him out the room. Other children start chatting, but Helen is more interested in looking at her house on Google map. She turns to Lorna and shows her house on Google map, this is the first time they have conversed all lesson. They compare houses. The teacher comes back in and tells the class to get back to their own seats.

(information technology (IT) lesson)

Helen's performance in this lesson was very different from the way that she conducted herself in maths, where she was more extroverted, participative and louder:

The teacher comes in and Samantha and Helen call her over to the back of the class where they are sitting together. Miss Best chats to them for a couple of minutes and then moves to the front of the class. She addresses the class and asks them to take their jackets off. This takes three attempts before all the pupils respond. The teacher then tells them they are playing bingo. This involves giving the class a sum and the answer is a figure that needs to be crossed off. There is a chorus of, 'Oh Miss' when the teacher gives a more difficult sum. Helen bounces in her seat and makes some excitable sounds and then exclaims to the teacher that she's cold. The sum is 18 divided by six, Helen counts it out on her hand and then exclaims that she can't do it. The LSA then moves round from Samantha to Helen and talks her through it. Helen and Samantha are louder and more vocal than most of the other pupils, they good-naturedly spar off each other and make frequent vocal exclamations regarding the sums. They are engaged in the activity and there is a good atmosphere in the room as most pupils seem to be enjoying the task. Helen asks Mrs Niles [class LSA] if she has brought her sticker book and then uses the display of stickers to work out the answer. Mrs Niles tells Samantha to calm down as she has become very excited about working out a sum. There are cheers and exclamations of good natured frustration when anyone gets bingo. On one occasion Helen loses by one and shouts out and blows a raspberry, but the teacher doesn't seem to mind.

(maths lesson)

Despite the teacher and LSA occasionally checking Helen's and Samantha's exuberance, it was apparent that they enjoyed the learning activity and for the most part, were engaged in the work. Helen's easy rapport with these adults suggests she felt esteemed by the teacher and classroom assistant, and a valued member of the class. This was corroborated by Helen's maths teacher:

> She [Helen] has settled down a lot. I think she's growing up. She used to be very easily distracted, and now she does chat a lot, but she gets her work done. She can work and chat. She seems a lot happier and although she does chat she will now tell off Lorna for not getting her work done and distracting her. I like Helen. She's very close to Samantha, they get on really well and that's made a difference in lessons.
>
> (Miss Best)

It is notable that Mrs Niles (maths LSA) was the only other member of staff at the Maple that Helen acknowledged good relations with. She gave a similar account of Helen's progress: 'I sit with Helen in English as well and see the difference between when she started and now. She tries a lot harder now, she is a lot more settled. She does chat a lot, but she can do both' (Mrs Niles). It was unclear as to what extent Helen's friendship with Samantha affected or was affective upon her feelings towards adults. However, it was evident that in combination these positive relationships reinforced Helen's notion of being a deserving learner and participative member of the classroom community. This suggests the positive effect upon learning attitude of good relations between Helen and her friends and teachers.

In considering Helen's renegotiation of bind two, it would appear that social relationships with friends and teachers played a fundamental role in whether formal learning in lessons held any relevance. A recent shift in her attitude suggests that improved relationships could have a future positive effect upon Helen's attainment in formal learning outcomes, at least with regards to maths and English. However, in lacking core friendships in her other lessons, and in the absence of positive relationships with teachers, Helen's perception of the relevance of schoolwork was confined to these lower-set classes.

The long-term impact of school turbulence on trust in friendships and teachers

Lastly, it is necessary to consider the long-term effects of school mobility in orientating Helen towards her social relationships. For Helen, the turbulence bind was routed in her anxiety towards peers and teachers, and insecurity in her ability to initiate secure friendships following school relocation. In distinguishing Helen's pre-transition friendships from those of other pupils in this study, Helen did not feel sad about leaving her friends, but rather felt relieved to escape the partial friendship and bullying that they represented. Helen also had the advantage of prior connections with Samantha and Kirsten, friendships that proved to be very important over the course of Helen's primary and secondary schooling. However, in generating a positive and relevant experience of school, it was notable that over time, and in surviving transition to secondary school, Helen's core friendships strengthened in their emotional, educational and social value. In terms of the strength of these bonds, Helen was unique as the only pupil in this study who felt able to trust her friends with a matter of personal importance: ' 'cause me and Samantha got on very well and me and her Mum get on well and its also 'cause we've been friends for ages now' (Helen). Here Helen refers to the continuity and duration of her relationship with Samantha as a central component in cementing trust. These friendships that operated through the home sphere, as well as in school, could be seen to represent secure forms whereby the relationship was characterized by trust and emotional intimacy. Putnam (2000) argued that bridging social networks accrue social capital in resonating across different community contexts. In bridging between the home, community and school (in and outside of the maths class), Helen's social network enabled her to build a sense of belonging in school, community identity, and validation of her home life. Furthermore, these close attachments with her friends and their parents proved to be very supportive in discussing personal and sensitive issues about her home life, helping her to cope during challenging times.

Conclusion: Partially offsetting the binds of poverty

Helen's story is one of relative success, in having negotiated a secure sense of social inclusion within school. Navigating bind three also buffered bind one in view of Helen's abating shame and fear of stigma concerning the visual indicators of financial hardship. Furthermore, her secure and lasting friendships mediated bind two in tempering her disassociation of home from school life, with respect to homework and formal learning outcomes. This is because Helen's trusting relationships with Samantha and her teacher led Helen towards greater engagement in maths and English lessons, and brought home into the classroom with respect to Miss Best's stories about her dog.

Helen's escape from the binds of poverty, however, can be seen to be only partial. This is because her friendship group offered little endorsement of schooling values, and a peer culture of socializing and having fun, but where learning activities were frequently eschewed in favour of, for example, playing computer games. In having dropped a school year, we may speculate that educational attainment held little relevance for Helen's best friend, Samantha, either. Yet this represented a two-edged sword in that in moving into Helen's lower-set maths class, Samantha played an important role in reinforcing Helen's sense of inclusion within these lessons. As a result, Helen acquired a more confident role as a valued member of the classroom community. It is notable, however, that this was only possible in the lower 'ability' set lessons, maths and English, among other low-attaining pupils in the year. Helen's classroom behaviour did not change significantly between primary and secondary school, in that at times Helen was withdrawn and disengaged, and at others lively and enthused. In primary school,

Helen swung between these poles within the same lesson, while in secondary school, these two aspects of Helen's classroom orientations were mediated by lessons and teachers. The culture of Helen's low 'ability' maths group was more conducive to her manner of expressing herself (when happy) in class. It may be that shouting out to the teacher, lively dialogue and 'fun' activities tend to be features of lower-set lessons, whereby the culture in the mixed 'ability' lessons require more strict adherence to on-task activity. Here there may be lessons to be learned in that four of the six children in this study connected with the culture of maths classes, and the endorsement of their teachers Miss Best and Miss Bright. This raises the issue of school and classroom cultures and their inclusive value for different groups of children. The pedagogical implications will be further discussed in chapter nine.

Notes

1 This reflects findings by Lareau (2000) that children from low-income families were much less likely to take part in formal adult-structured activities outside of school than their middle-class peers, instead spending more time in unstructured activities and with the family.
2 Given the broad array of personal, moral and spiritual values held within culturally divisive society, it has been argued that moral and religious education could profitably focus upon 'enabling values' (i.e. values that are more personal, tentative and open to challenge and change) as opposed to 'prescriptive values' (Lenderyou 1995; Thomson 1997; Halstead and Taylor 2000), which are those clearly apparent in this lesson excerpt.
3 The national government target of level 4 in key stage two assessments is available on the Department for Education website at www.education.gov.uk/schools/performance/primary_12/p7.html [Accessed 14 April 2014].
4 Pupils' progress and achievement in key stage four (GCSE examinations age 16) is available in Ofsted guidance published February 2014, p. 12. Available at http://dashboard.ofsted.gov.uk/sdd_guidance.pdf [Accessed 20 June 2014].

References

Department for Education (2011) *How Do Pupils Progress during Key Stages 2 and 3?* Research Report DFE-RR096. Available at www.gov.uk/government/uploads/system/uploads/attachment_data/file/182413/DFE-RR096.pdf [Accessed 7 May 2014].

George, R. (2007) *Girls in a Goldfish Bowl: moral regulation, ritual and the use of power amongst inner city girls*, Rotterdam: Sense.

Halstead, M. J. and Taylor, M. J. (2000) 'Learning and teaching about values: a review of recent research', *Cambridge Journal of Education*, 30(2): 169–202.

Lareau, A. (2000) 'Social class and the daily lives of children: a study from the United States', *Childhood*, 7 (2): 155–71.

Lareau, A. (2001) 'Social-class differences in family school relationships: the importance of cultural capital', in A. H. Halsey, H. Lauder, P. Brown and A. S. Wells (eds) *Education: culture, economy, society*, Oxford: Oxford University Press, 703–17.

Lenderyou, G. (1995) 'School sex education, faith and values', in D. E. Massey (ed.) *Sex Education Source Book: current issues and debates*, London: Family Planning Association.

Lister, R. (2004) *Poverty*, Cambridge: Polity Press.

Nilan, P. (1991) 'Exclusion, inclusion and moral ordering in two girls' friendship groups', *Gender and Education*, 3: 163–82.

Putnam, R. D. (2000) *Bowling alone: the collapse and revival of American community*, New York: Simon and Schuster.

Ridge, T. (2009) *Living with poverty: a review of the literature on children's and families' experiences of poverty*, Department for Work and Pensions.

Ridge, T and Millar, J. (2000) 'Excluding children: autonomy, friendship and the experience of the care system', in *Social Policy and Administration*, 34 (2): 160–75.

Thomson, R. (1997) *Religion, Ethnicity and Sex Education: exploring the issues*, London: National Children's Bureau.

Chapter 8

Robin

School life with a hearing impediment and relocation due to paternal redundancy

Life in Ivy school

I first met Robin when he was in year six at Ivy school (aged 10). Robin lived at home with his mother, father and two older brothers in Thornton, having moved a year and a half previously from Hutton, a small town in central England, over 200 miles away.

The financial imperative to relocate in order to secure employment

Binds one and four are interconnected in Robin's case, given the financial imperative incumbent upon his family to relocate in order for his father to gain employment. Robin did not claim free school meals (FSM); he brought a packed lunch, but had claimed FSM in his previous school during the 18 months of his father's redundancy. Similarly to Codie, Robin's family had been reluctant to leave their previous community, but had been compelled to leave due to economic necessity. In being the single earner in Robin's family, his father had struggled to find any employment in their home town, before eventually securing a job in Little-town, a small town 15 miles from Ivy school. Having been unable to find affordable accommodation in Little-town, the family moved into a small terrace house in an estate on the outskirts of Thornton, after seven months of his father commuting from Hutton. The period of redundancy and consequential relocation was unsurprisingly, a stressful and traumatic time for Robin, and it was evident that the experience of moving school was significant for him. When asked what year he had joined Ivy school, Robin's response indicated that the date was poignant: 'In February, the 28th, I started here er February the 28th.' Like Clive, Liza, and Codie, Robin acknowledged with pragmatic acceptance the inevitability of moving: 'Well because my Dad lost his job and he got a new job in Little-town and it ended up being a long way to go up and down, at the beginning and end of the week'.

Robin's mother, Lorraine, provided a background to the pressure concerning what was clearly a difficult move for the entire family:

Very unwelcome move . . . we lived under a huge question mark for must be two years, so in the end when he was told his number was up, in a lot of a ways it was kind of a relief. But we never dreamt it would be 18 months before he got another job. For the kids as well it was hugely unsettling as they didn't know what would happen next, none of us wanted to move, we were close to my parents. I mean five miles from their front door was the furthest I've ever been . . . So 18 months later this job finally popped up, it was in Little-town which is extremely expensive . . . It was a long drawn out process . . . with nothing else coming up we didn't have a lot of choice but to move here, we didn't know anything about Thornton.

(Lorraine)

Robin's family had grown up in Hutton and left behind a strong social network of friends and family, resulting in significantly compromised social capital upon relocation (Coleman 1988; Pribesh and Downey 1999). To compound this, Robin's parents felt powerless over many of the factors associated with the move, including the job, the house and the area.

Synchronized educational values between school and home

Robin's mother and father had both left school without gaining formal educational qualifications. Later in life, Lorraine had gone back to college to continue her studies, in a course that had been interrupted by the family's relocation. It was evident that she placed a high value upon the education provided at Robin's previous school, and she spoke of the high SATs standards achieved: 'The fact that we were leaving a successful school, that was another big thing to me.'

Robin's previous school, St Paul's, was a larger than average sized primary. Ofsted reports indicated that the sociodemographic make-up of the school was fairly high and the proportion of pupils who were eligible for FSM was well below average. Almost all of the children were of White ethnic origins and special educational needs (SEN) were low. The overall evaluation for the school concluded: 'The ethos for learning is excellent, teaching is very good, pupils make consistently good progress and achieve highly. Pupils with special educational needs and those who are more able are supported and challenged very effectively.'[1] Robin's mother was aware of these achievements and approved of the 'performance orientated' culture that was geared towards high achievement:

It was academically a lot more demanding [than Ivy], we used to get reading every night, weekly spellings, maths homework at least once a week, projects kicked in year one. The older they got the spellings increased in difficulty and number of them, I must admit, I struggled a bit to help him at times.

(Lorraine)

In contrast to moral underclass disclosure (MUD) rhetoric that sees children in poverty as from families who fail to recognize the importance of formal learning outcomes (see chapter one), Lorraine's perspective illustrates the 'binds' against supporting their children's learning, that parents themselves experience, following their own lack of educational achievement.

Robin's memories or reflections about his previous school were similarly focused upon the learning environment:

ROBIN: Well, when I was leaving they were planning on putting projectors in year five and six classrooms, but not interactive whiteboards.
CB: Right, can you tell me anything else about it?
ROBIN: Well I can barely remember anything.
CB: Really?
ROBIN: Mmmm, barely remember anything.
CB: That's understandable . . . Did you have friends there?
ROBIN: Um, don't remember that one today.
CB: Can you remember how you felt when your Mum and Dad told you you had to leave that school?
ROBIN: Er, dunno.

Given Robin's precise memory of his starting date at Ivy, his forgetfulness about his friendships and moving, or perhaps his wish not to talk about them, could suggest that leaving St Paul's was painful. It may be that any emotional attachment to the school was subsumed beneath a pragmatic acceptance of the family situation, or as a coping strategy to adapt to his new school. In any case his interest in the formal aspects of school continued in Ivy school, and were clearly important for Robin, at least in relation to the subjects he liked and did well in. This was reflected in his response when asked his favourite thing about Ivy school: 'At my old one, there weren't interactive whiteboards in every single class room.' Nevertheless, Robin had a varied attitude towards lessons. He enjoyed those lessons that he performed well in: 'I like maths and ICT and I find science very easy' (Robin).

All the lessons that Robin did well in required a methodical and logical approach to the learning activity. However, he had a more negative experience of lessons involving a creative or philosophical approach, subjects such as art, religious education (RE) and history. When asked why he didn't enjoy these lessons, Robin replied: 'Because I can't barely enjoy it. I find it hard to think up what to do.' This didn't trouble Robin unduly, considering his nuanced understanding of the relative importance of subjects:

CB: Do you think that schoolwork's important?
ROBIN: No. I don't think all of it's important.
CB: No?
ROBIN: No because, because RE, history and geography, they aren't as important at the moment.

CB: Right, so what subjects are important?
ROBIN: Um, English, maths and science, they're the ones which we do SATs tests on.

With the exception of English, Robin felt confident in lessons that he perceived to have value for his educational career. These were also the lessons that he enjoyed in school. This may have been reinforced by the value that educational outcomes had within his family. Given the apparent harmony between Robin's home and school values, he did not experience bind two, and therefore may have had an educational advantage ahead of the other children in this study. However, a pro-schooling orientation was not enough to ensure Robin's inclusion within his new school, and as will be explored in the next section, the issue of social relationships played a key role in Robin's primary school experiences.

Failure to achieve social inclusion

While educational outcomes were important for Robin's mother, this was not to say that Robin's friendships and social inclusion were incidental:

> It took him years [to make friends], in fact it only really happened about a year before we moved, where his circle of friends seemed to get stronger and he'd go knock on their door. In that respect to uproot him was horrendous because he was only really finding his feet and consolidating a group of friends and getting the party invites, and then of course we had to pull him out of all that, and that was a horrible feeling as a parent just to whip him away from all that knowing that he doesn't find making friends easy.
>
> (Lorraine)

Additional penalty of a hearing impediment

Robin's difficulties in making new friends were in part connected to his hearing impediment, a total deafness in his right ear. This made communication challenging, in view of Robin's shyness in front of people that he didn't know. A key factor in Robin's parents' decision to send him to Ivy school was its good reputation for catering for pupils with SEN. For example, Lorraine believed that the school's 'buddying' strategy of pairing of new pupils with an existing pupil was a thoughtful and conscientious process, especially considering Robin's ambivalence in starting at Ivy:

ROBIN: I didn't want to come here. I didn't want to go to school. It was scary.
CB: What were the children like?
ROBIN: Errr . . . Errr nice they were . . . apart from two of them. They weren't nice. Well really only Danny was.

CB: No? How long did it take to make friends with Danny?
ROBIN: Well, Mrs Read actually told him to look after me for the day.

Danny was the only friend Robin seemed to have at Ivy school. It was notable that they shared a similar disposition, as both children were shy and quiet. In the playground they often stayed together and rarely socialized with peers. Within the lessons that the two sat together, they didn't engage much in conversation. When Robin was asked why Danny was his friend, he responded, 'Well, he likes me.' Research into the social integration of SEN children within mainstream settings has found that children with hearing impediments are more likely to feel rejected and have fewer friends than their hearing peers, leading to a sense of isolation and socially withdrawn behaviour (Wauters and Noors 2008; Kluwin, Stinson and Colarossi 2002; Musselman, Mootilal and MacKay 1996). In view of these findings, Robin's evaluation of his friendship with Danny may well have betrayed feelings of insecurity about his worth as a friend, and suggested that he did not make an autonomous choice in his friendships, because he believed that the peers who would accept him were limited.

Socially isolated out of school

Robin's self-value as a friend may have been connected to his relative isolation outside of school. He took part in very few social activities and seemed to spend all his time at home watching television or playing on the computer. Lorraine saw this as self-elective: 'Robin's very good with computers so usually he'd be able to sort out any problems . . . He does like his own company and he seems very content in his own company.' This may have compounded the limited bridge between home and school in his friendship with Danny:

CB: Do you ever stay at his house, or he stays at yours?
ROBIN: Well I've been round his once before and he's been round at mine one time.
CB: And do you have other friends outside of school?
ROBIN: Don't think so.

Peer group exclusion

Robin's feelings towards his only friendship in the school have to be couched in terms of his feelings towards other pupils in the year which were, 'Er, OK', apart from one child:

ROBIN: Well . . . he likes to . . . well basically he likes to annoy, quite annoy quite a lot of people.

CB: Really? He deliberately tries to annoy you?
ROBIN: Well, I'm not sure, but I think because he's been doing it to me before and at other people.
CB: Does he tease you then?
ROBIN: Well, before he kept on putting everyone's hoods up on them, I think, before on their coats. I think that happened before.

It is clear from this that Robin had experienced low-level bullying within Ivy school. Unlike Helen, Liza and Clive, he lacked a friendship group that offered a protective shield against bullying (Ridge and Millar 2000) and was arguably more vulnerable to this form of peer exclusion, with only limited social bonds at his disposal to act as a protective resource.

Reluctance to participate in lessons

For the lessons that he enjoyed, Robin preferred to work 'probably on my own' as opposed to with a partner or a group. Robin would often get on with his work without conversation with peers and was frequently distracted from the activity, as can be seen in this excerpt from a religious education lesson:

> Mrs Read asks children to get into groups. Robin does not respond and just stares into space. He is sat at the front due to his hearing difficulties and the seat next to him is vacant. However, he doesn't turn around to make eye contact with any potential partners. No one is volunteering to work with Robin so the teacher calls Mikey over to work with him who is currently messing about with his seat-mate. [Mikey is known for being disruptive in lessons and I wonder if this is a ploy to keep an eye on him and maybe she considers Robin to be unlikely to collude in any disruption].

There were other lessons, however, in which Robin didn't feel so confident in managing on his own. When asked whether he liked to work alone for all lessons he replied: 'Well it depends what work it is, because some work it needs help with it.' This applied to 'mainly literacy', as the only subject Robin identified as 'important' in which he felt anxious about his abilities:

CB: What sort of people, if you did get stuck would you ask?
ROBIN: Well for one thing I would ask the teacher.
CB: Would you ever ask any of the children?
ROBIN: Well I'm not sure.
CB: You might do, or not?
ROBIN: Probably not.

Reflecting his reluctance to work with peers in the class, Robin was uncomfortable in seeking help from them. This may in part have been on account of his hearing difficulties compounding his ability to engage in conversation. Furthermore, his seating position at the front of the class on the left, gave him less options concerning interaction with children around him. However, Robin's reluctance and lack of effort in building social relationships with peers could, perhaps, also be seen to reflect a more fundamental anxiety about his own worth as a friend. Perhaps he felt more confident in the response he would get from teachers, or perhaps in relation to the importance Robin attributed to literacy, help from teachers was considered more reliable?

One way in which Robin did get involved as an active and contributory member of the classroom was through the utilization of his information technology (IT) skills. On several occasions Robin volunteered without prompting to help sort out audiovisual equipment. Upon being asked about these technical difficulties, Robin was animated and enthusiastic:

ROBIN: Well basically it's very simple, you just follow the colours you do, because each port has a different colour.
CB: Oh right so were they put in the wrong places then?
ROBIN: No, well originally when she couldn't get the video to work it was plugged into the DVD port, so that had to be input from the back of the TV into the DVD. And also watching one video she had to actually hold the audio wire because the sound was dodgy, inside the box.
CB: So how do you know about that sort of stuff then? That technical stuff?
ROBIN: Because I actually saw, because she was actually holding it she was, because the sound kept on going . . . I think it might be a dodgy connection. It isn't the cable because it got changed.

Robin apparently valued this opportunity to be helpful in class. When asked whether he was often helpful with technical problems, Robin replied 'yes', and when asked whether the teachers liked this, he claimed, 'I think so'. Robin was then asked if he liked it when the teacher was happy, and he proceeded to describe an occasion where the IT teacher had been unhappy with the class and the positive impact of his helping:

ROBIN: Because Mr Henry when he's angry, he actually gets very angry.
CB: Right so you don't like that?
ROBIN: Well no, but when he's happy it's actually very good.
CB: Right, so you like it when you help him and he's happy?
ROBIN: Yes and he likes to play a game he does, on the board with a timer [laughs]
CB: Cool, so you like that game?
ROBIN: Well it's actually his idea of trying to not keep us in tomorrow break time.
CB: Really?
ROBIN: Yes, because loads of people aren't doing what they're told.

CB: Right. So do you think maybe you do things to make him happy to make him like the class?
ROBIN: Well probably.

Navigating the binds at primary school

In reflecting upon the impact of the varying binds that Robin had faced at primary school, it is evident that bind one, bind four, and bind three interconnected in creating a social penalty for Robin. Just as his mother had feared, the social disruption caused by moving home, school and community had not abated a year and a half following transition to Ivy school. We will see to what extent these binds prevented Robin from educational success at the end of primary school, but it is likely that his social exclusion may have been associated with his lack of participation within lessons, even those in subjects that he enjoyed. This discussion will also be evaluated with respect to the ways in which Robin engaged with and renegotiated these binds in secondary school, and the longitudinal impact upon school achievement, as well as social and emotional well-being.

Life in secondary school: Renegotiating the binds

I followed up with Robin two years later when he was in year eight (aged 12) at the Maple secondary school. He remained living with his mother, father and one of his older brothers, in the house they had first moved into in Thornton. Robin had performed well in his key stage two (KS2) national examinations and his educational achievements upon leaving Ivy school were:

English: Level 4
Science: Level 5
Maths: Level 5

These outcomes suggest that Robin had not experienced an educational penalty at the end of his primary education, as his achievements exceeded national expectations. However, in order to consider whether Robin had continued to make good educational progress it is necessary to turn to his achievements within secondary school. In year eight Robin had been placed in the middle set for English (3 of 6) and the top sets for maths and science (1 of 6). Robin's assessments at the end of his third term are provided below. Both in attainment and attitude, numbers ascend in value, and for attainment sub-levels, A is the highest and C the lowest.

To be online with national targets of two solid levels progress across key stage three (KS3) (DfE 2014: 37) Robin should be attaining around 7C or 6A in science and maths, and 6C or 5A in English and all other subjects, at the time when these assessments were taken. These results suggest that Robin was attaining just

Table 8.1 Robin's educational achievements at the end of year 8, the Maple school

Subject	Attainment	Attitude
English	5B	4*
Maths	8C	5*
Science	6A	4*
IT	6B	4*
Drama	5A	3*
Art	4A	4*
DT	6C	4*
French	5B	4*
Geography	6A	5*
History	6C	4*
Music	6C	4*

below target for English and French. But for eight curriculum subjects he was achieving according to national targets, and for three of these (IT, geography and maths) Robin's achievements were above target. In maths his performance even exceeded the good progress expected from his high KS2 results. Robin's attitude appraisals show a majority response of four out of five in eight subjects, which indicates that his attitude was 'good', while in maths and geography Robin's attitude was considered by his teachers to be 'excellent'. Robin's lowest attitude rating was in drama where he was considered to have a 'satisfactory' approach to work. Art was the only subject in which Robin's attainment was significantly below target.

Robin's test results and teacher assessments at secondary school can be seen to broadly concur with those of primary school, in having achieved above the national average in science and maths. While his achievement in English was shy of national expectations, the difference was only one sub-level. However, the degree of Robin's achievements in geography and particularly maths, indicate that in these key lessons Robin flourished in terms of his educational achievement. These results demonstrate that Robin was considerably higher attaining than the other pupils encountered in his book. It is also important to consider his attitude results, which suggest that Robin's orientation and participation in lessons had improved from primary school. However, the scale of these improvements are subject relative. While it might be expected that children may perform better in some subjects than others, it is interesting that his attitude was rated as 'excellent' in the two lessons where he excelled, suggesting that he was maximizing his abilities only in maths and geography. Nevertheless, unlike the other pupils in this book, Robin can be seen to have evaded an educational penalty, in being successful at school. However, these figures alone are but a small part of the whole story of Robin's experiences at secondary school. In considering the ways in which he renegotiated the binds at the Maple, we will consider how Robin managed to succeed where his peers failed, and to what extent educational success was consistent with success within the social as well as the emotional components of school life.

The social isolation incurred through living in low-cost housing

Four and a half years following Robin's relocation, his family were yet to fully settle into their home in Thornton. This was partly due to the isolated location of the only housing that they could afford. Robin's mother lamented the geographic positioning of their current house with respect to that of their previous house in Hutton:

> Both schools [in Hutton] were five minutes walk, I could walk to the town centre, I could walk to Asda if I needed to, and we had a small shopping parade on our estate so everything was really accessible. Coming here school was two miles away, Asda's eight miles away which is a big issue for me, I mean Sainsbury's got its uses but you can't go regularly, it's too expensive and I don't have a car.
>
> (Lorraine)

It was evident that religious faith was an important aspect of family life, and Lorraine had been hopeful that church could provide a link into the local community. However, this had proved impossible within Thornton:

> Finding a church which we wanted was not an easy issue, which was important to us as a family, what Jason [Robin's father] and I would settle for, the kids didn't like, they [the local church congregation] were standoffish, they weren't friendly.
>
> (Lorraine)

As a consequence, Lorraine and her husband were compelled to look outside of Thornton before they found an appropriate church 10 miles away and in another county. Religious institutions have been cited as a powerful producer of social capital, which can strengthen the individual's involvement in civic life (Putnam 2000: 408–10; Fukayama 2001: 19). Lorraine's account, however, suggests that faith-based social capital networks can extend local community from the immediate proximity of home location, beyond town and even county borders.

Although it did not generate a direct social benefit in his school life, since joining the church Robin had expressed some desire to participate in social activities and events. When asked whether he was involved with any social activities arranged by the church, Lorraine responded:

> No, the relevant age group he's for at the moment meet out of area, but in September he can join YP [young persons church group], which is years nine to second year six [age 14–18] so he can join then . . . and he seems quite keen, strangely enough, more so than his brothers. He had the chance to go to [residential trip away with the church] but it was just too expensive . . . He wanted to go but it was too difficult.
>
> (Lorraine)

Robin had also expressed a desire to integrate with other children outside of school, however, it was evident that this was not something that was supported by his mother:

> I think he did once want to go down to the skate park one evening to meet some friends, but he hasn't asked to do it again. So whether they weren't there or whether he wasn't keen on it I'm not sure. It's not something I particularly want to encourage with them. You do worry about who they're mixing with and what not at times.
>
> (Lorraine)

The outcome of these failed attempts to socialize was that Robin did not take part in many activities outside of school and spent a lot of time in his own company at home:

CB: Where do you like being best?
ROBIN: I dunno, I just spend a lot of time sitting down watching TV.
CB: Where?
ROBIN: In my bedroom.
CB: Why is that the best?
ROBIN: Because it means that I don't get disturbed by my brothers that much.
CB: Do you prefer doing that on your own or with friends?
ROBIN: Well I'm on my own most of the time.
CB: Why?
ROBIN: I don't know (. . .) because they're already doing things.

This final admission suggests that it was not out of choice that Robin spent so much time alone. Despite his best efforts Robin remained isolated out of school, and even within the home sphere felt separated from his brothers. His lack of social inclusion can be contextualized against the social isolation of Robin's mother from the community and school:

> I don't really know a lot about it [the Maple]. For me it would have been easier if we'd moved when the kids were younger to get to know people

at the school gates. I was told by the head-teacher I was never down with [accepted by] the gate gossips. I was never a gate gossip who are down there [accepted by the school]. So there's few parents I've got to know, and not a lot of their friends.

(Lorraine)

It may have been that Lorraine's negative experiences of the local Thornton church congregation challenged her trust in possible new social networks, with the result that she had become hesitant to get to know parents at the school gate. Failure to develop parental links had implications for Robin's mother, fostering her perception that rejection from parental networks presaged rejection by teachers and staff at the Maple.

In reflecting on whether Robin had been able to renegotiate the binds one and four from primary school, it is evident that they continued to persist while he was at secondary school. As a result of the limited options of financial hardship upon housing choices, access issues in Robin's home life clearly continued to prevent social inclusion in and out of school.

Transition to the Maple

Although there was little bridging between home, school and the local community in Thornton, nevertheless, Robin was clear that joining the Maple was a more positive experience than starting at Ivy:

CB: Did you know anyone from Ivy moving up at the same time?
ROBIN: Yeah Danny, Mike and Mark.
CB: Did that make a difference, knowing someone else?
ROBIN: Yeah because when you go where you don't know anyone it's different to where you know a few of them.
CB: How's it different?
ROBIN: Well it's more confidence in talking to people.
CB: Did you prefer it moving to the Maple?
ROBIN: Well it's easier because it was everyone else's first day at the Maple.
CB: So how does that make it easier for you?
ROBIN: Because we're all at the same stage being new in the school rather than I'm being new in the school and they've been there for a few years.

In view of the continued isolation of his family, the shared experience of transition was of added precedence for Robin, in buffering the strangeness of starting at a new school. In feeling himself to be on equal footing with his peers as a pupil at Maple school, we may reflect on his turbulent experience in challenging that view. With respect to the binds of a turbulent school move and the financial constraints upon housing location, Robin's educational achievements can be seen to be all the more remarkable. In exploring these achievements the following discussion will probe the development of

Robin's integration within secondary school, and it is to this bind that I will now turn.

Friendships that validate classroom membership

While out of school Robin saw little of other children from the school or community, nevertheless it was clear that he was more socially integrated at the Maple than at Ivy school, in spite of notable ambivalence towards the pupils:

CB: What do you think of the other pupils in the year?
ROBIN: Well some of them do disrupt lessons.
CB: Do you like them?
ROBIN: Not all the time but sometimes they just get on with their work generally fine.
CB: What do you think about the pupils at the school generally?
ROBIN: Well I don't think much about them.
CB: What about in comparison with Ivy?
ROBIN: Better (. . .) I've got more friends.

It is evident that Robin's social network at the Maple school was broader than it was at Ivy. Robin's friendship with Danny had stood the test of time and survived the transition to secondary school. In addition, Robin claimed another three friends: Dave, Mike and Mark. Robin's sociogram marked the four boys close to him, with Danny being the closest and all four clustered together in one corner, suggesting that the friendships were reciprocal. As in his time at Ivy school, Robin was not so vocal about the factors cementing his friendships:

CB: Why have you put Danny here closest to you?
ROBIN: I dunno, he doesn't annoy me that much, he doesn't annoy me as much as my other friends can do sometimes.
CB: How do they annoy you?
ROBIN: Well it depends, because sometimes they tend to be better than me at lessons I'm not that good in. Other times it's the other way round.

In speaking little of the emotional connection between Robin and his friends, this comment reveals that academic performance continued to have a high value for Robin. Unlike the other children in this study, who made no mention of schoolwork as a feature of their friendships, academic attainment was a key factor in Robin's sense of his position within his friendship group, as well as of his importance in school:

CB: What do you think it means to do well at the Maple?
ROBIN: Well it means that you get better grades at the end of your GCSEs and stuff.

CB: Do you think doing well at school means the same at the Maple as it does at Ivy?
ROBIN: There's higher expectations here of us.
CB: And is that good or bad?
ROBIN: Well it's good if you are very good at stuff or bad if you aren't that good, because then you have to do more work.
CB: So what about you, where are you then?
ROBIN: In the middle.

Having felt on the peripheries of classroom culture at the Ivy, it may have been that being 'in the middle' felt like quite a secure place to be, yet in terms of attainment, Robin was clearly above the middle in most subjects. While this suggests that Robin underestimated his abilities, the following discussion illustrates that Robin's confidence in his all-round abilities and enjoyment in subjects had grown since being at Ivy. This included in the subjects where previously in Ivy he felt incompetent:

CB: So what about the lessons here then, do you enjoy them at the Maple?
ROBIN: Yeah most of them.
CB: Which ones?
ROBIN: Pretty much all the ones I can actually do the work in (laughs).
CB: Which are those?
ROBIN: Maths, science, English (. . .) IT, geography, history and probably some others.
CB: What makes you enjoy those lessons?
ROBIN: They can be very easy and involve play games in them.

It is significant that this list of lessons he enjoyed had expanded from when Robin was at Ivy. There was also a direct correspondence between the lessons that Robin believed himself to do well in, and those that he enjoyed.[2] Robin's account of his abilities broadly supported his attitude and attainment data, indicating a consensus with school performance judgements. This raises questions as to what extent pro-learning values were shared within the culture of Robin's friendship group, and what effects they may have had upon his learning orientations.

Helping as a bridge into classroom participation

A significant development in Robin's learning orientation since primary school was in his demeanour towards group work activities:

ROBIN: Yeah I prefer work in groups, because it's much easier to think of something better than with just one person.
CB: What is it about group work that you like then?

ROBIN: You don't have to think of everything that happens, its all team effort rather than just individual.

One of the reasons that Robin might have felt more confident with his peers in the classroom related to his perceived ability to 'help' other pupils:

CB: Do you ever ask for help?
ROBIN: Well depends, I'm alright, sometimes people ask me [to help].
CB: But you never ask people for help?
ROBIN: Not really, most of the time I can just do the work.

In primary school 'helping' was a strategy that Robin employed with teachers in order to please, and it was evident that at secondary school Robin had extended this to his classmates. This was a significant development given that Robin had found the confidence to offer help even when it wasn't solicited: 'because sometimes they might ask you to help themselves and sometimes they might not' (Robin). Robin had mixed feelings about the benefit of helping, but from a personal point of view he felt it was an effective way to protect against victimization:

CB: How does it make you feel helping?
ROBIN: Well it depends, because sometimes they probably don't even know what it means, like when I've been copying and pasting they sometimes don't know what it means.
CB: So does that feel good?
ROBIN: Yeah sometimes.
CB: In what way?
ROBIN: Well it means that they aren't stuck and it means that they get their work done quicker.
CB: But does it make you feel good?
ROBIN: I think it probably does, it means that less people hate you.

It is clear that the classroom felt a safer place than it did in Ivy school where Robin had experience of bullying and little interaction with others. At the Maple Robin felt he had something to offer, which had increased his confidence and may have led him to participate more in lessons. His last comment is particularly significant because it suggests Robin's sensitivity as to how pupils felt about him. It is unclear whether Robin referred specifically to the people he helped, or rather a general sense of feeling more included in class. It may be, however, that the two were connected:

CB: Who do you help in lessons?
ROBIN: My friends, Mike, Dave, Mark and Danny.

CB: Do you think the people you sit next to can have an impact on how much you like the lesson?
ROBIN: It can do because if you sit next to someone who doesn't like it [the lesson] or asks stupid questions, it can get very annoying.

Here Robin could be seen to voice frustration towards seat-mates whom he felt didn't share his values with regards to the importance of learning outcomes, as well as an antipathy towards those much less able than himself. If however, the help sought was from his friends whom he observed to be of similar high attainment, the validation of his helping could understandably be seen to be of much greater consequence. The following classroom excerpt is from a geography lesson, one of Robin's most high attaining subjects:

> The pupils work in pairs to draw a map of the world and label correctly the given countries and capitals. Robin and his seat-mate Annie take it in turns to draw on the paper and discuss the task. Their conversation is limited but all on task. Dave and Mike are seated behind Robin and Annie and are discussing the activity in hushed voices, heads bent in a conspiratorial manner. A couple of times Dave calls to Robin and he turns round, answers a question and then returns to the task. After 10 minutes and three further questions, Dave calls and asks him something again but Robin shakes his head. When the teacher calls the class to order Robin turns and faces him immediately. The teacher goes through the questions and Annie puts her hand up for most of the answers while Robin puts his hand up occasionally. Robin and Annie get the highest mark in the class and when the teacher tells the class this Robin smiles and looks around the class. [I wonder why he didn't put up his hand as he obviously knew the answers].
>
> (geography lesson)

This excerpt reveals the inclusive effect of working with Annie and helping Dave. Here Robin can be seen to be far more participative in the classroom activity than he was at Ivy school. The four children shared a pro-learning orientation, and there is an element of competitiveness between the two pairs, such that while on some occasions Robin shared his answers, on other occasions he was reluctant to help. When questioned about the activity, Robin was clear to point out that he had contributed the most to the pair's success:

CB: I noticed that today in geography you did very well with Annie didn't you, top of the class?
ROBIN: Well yes (laughs) well actually the amount I did. She actually did the most of it, but ended up putting things in the wrong place, like New Zealand above Australia and Japan somewhere else.
CB: But you still did very well?
ROBIN: Well I know, only because I know so many countries.

At the same time as 'correcting' Annie's mistakes, Robin also had to negotiate the demands of Dave. He evidently felt that this process needed mediation. On a number of occasions Robin answered Dave's questions, yet there was clearly a tipping point whereby he felt that a request was unreasonable: 'Dave asked me to draw his map but I didn't' (Robin). This discussion reveals the positive effect of Robin's strategy of helping in building his confidence in his abilities, as well as in his sense of membership within a group of motivated learners who endorsed his 'ability' through help seeking. Nevertheless, Robin didn't lose sight of the attainment hierarchy within the class, and recognized that offered in excess or inappropriately, his help could also threaten his position within it.

The trade-off of helping

Alongside the positive effects of helping his classmates, there was evidence of some degree of trade-off for Robin. This was apparent in the occasions where Robin felt that his helping others negatively affected his own learning:

ROBIN: Well in some ways it's fine [helping] but in others I don't like it much, 'cause sometimes I just get fed up doing the same thing over and over again . . . Sometimes I don't really want to do it, because I've got my own work to do, gets a bit irritating because well, I've probably done more of other people's work than mine over the last few weeks.
CB: So why don't you say no to them?
ROBIN: Well I do occasionally, but it's much easier to say 'No' for people over the other side of the room.

Given that his friends were those who sat closest to Robin, his reluctance to refuse help may have been connected to their validation of his ability. In considering the impact of this trade off, the following conversation was illuminating:

CB: Does it make you feel good being good at maths, being good at geography?
ROBIN: It can do.
CB: When does it make you feel good?
ROBIN: Only when you're the first one to complete the work.

This suggests that helping others may have prevented Robin from being the first to finish in his class. As such his helping strategy was a two-edged sword, in that on the one hand he felt more confident and included in lessons, while on the other hand he perceived that his position in the classroom hierarchy was threatened when his momentum in lessons was compromised.

In view of Robin's test and teacher and evaluations, it may have been that the most significant payback was from helping his friends, Dave and Mike, who also shared his top-set maths, science and geography lessons. These were the lessons in which Robin scored so highly in attitude and attainment. Outside of these lessons Robin often sat next to Danny or Mark, as they shared his registration classes as well as middle-set English. Yet his helping strategy held less currency in these lessons for Robin: 'Sometimes it can be a bit annoying with [helping] Mark and Danny, 'cause they always asking things really obvious' (Robin). It may be that because he did not consider Mark and Danny to be equal in the attainment hierarchy, helping them did not validate his ability in the same way that helping his higher attaining friends, Mike and Dave, did. Therefore, Robin's lower attitude scores in these lessons may in part be explained through the frustrations he experienced in helping.

Limited nature of friendship bonds

Robin's helping strategy can be seen to have earned him a sense of inclusion within lessons that was not evident at Ivy school. This inclusion, however, did not extend outside of lessons. During lunchtimes and break times he tended to drift around the playground lacking a routine meeting place, nor indeed anyone to meet there:

ROBIN: I just walk around most of the time, I don't usually stay in the same place all throughout playground.
CB: Why?
ROBIN: Because it's easier to walk about, I walk quite a bit. I walk about without realizing it sometimes.
CB: So is there a place which feels more comfortable to be in than anywhere else?
ROBIN: No . . . Maybe outside the maths block, because the older people don't tend to go there that much.

Robin may have felt confined to the subject buildings where he felt comfortable in lessons, as it's notable that he perceived some spaces to be more accessible than others. Robin's account suggests a lack of autonomy within informal school spaces, his inclination towards the maths block was a default election not a positive choice, such as Helen's: 'Out there near maths block [because] it's just like us [there]' (Helen). His social exclusion outside of lessons may also explain why Robin could not recall an occasion in which he had discussed a personal matter with any of his friends, and speculated that the only people he could trust with a personal matter would be his parents.

Overcoming the binds against educational success

In evaluating Robin's negotiation of the binds of poverty, it is remarkable to see that in educational terms escape was in some way possible: judging by his formal attainments over four years, Robin was highly successful in view of national standards. In comparing Robin's schooling experiences with those of other children in this book, for whom the binds of poverty prevented such achievement, it is important to consider that Robin and his family shared the same values towards schooling and formal learning outcomes throughout Robin's educational career. Nevertheless, credit also must be attributed to Robin's strategy of helping within lessons, for the validation of his abilities, as well as the sense of inclusion this earned him as a valued member of the classroom community. There was also a trade-off to his helping strategy in that at times Robin felt his own learning to be compromised, holding him back from finishing activities quickly, and thus threatening his perceived position in attainment hierarchies. Notwithstanding this, Robin's gains from helping peers in lessons far outweighed his losses, in that Robin's confidence, enjoyment and learning in lessons increased significantly, particularly in the lessons where his achievements were highest.

While his ingenuity is laudable, Robin's success must be seen in the context of his whole schooling experiences, as the inclusion he earned was restricted to the formal aspects of school. Across his educational career Robin remained socially isolated, in that his friendship bonds did not extend outside of the classroom, let alone outside of school. It is with respect to the social and emotional aspects of schooling that the binds of poverty persisted. These concerned the interconnected binds of financial hardship and relocation, the social isolation of affordable housing, and the effect of this in curtailing Robin's opportunities (as well as those of his mother) to build social networks that could bridge between home, school and the community. The effects of these binds were further exacerbated through the additional bind of Robin's hearing impediment, which made communication difficult.

Of all the stories told here, Robin's can be seen to be the most successful in offsetting any educational penalty. However, his story represents an only partial success. Formal learning outcomes are not sufficient for a positive experience of school, where a child can still experience isolation and social exclusion outside of the classroom. It is clear that effort alone has not been enough for Robin. In the absence of external support structures, through resources from the school and family to aid community inclusion, he may continue to experience a social and emotional penalty.

Notes

1 This statement is from St Paul's Ofsted report 2007. The reference is omitted to maintain confidentiality.
2 Research into children's appraisals of their educational potential has highlighted the competitiveness of classroom culture and pupils' keen awareness of peer attainment hierarchies. This was associated with the performative culture of high-stakes testing and its influence upon children's sense of inadequacy concerning, and fear of, achieving educational performances that were less than their peers (Reay and Wiliam 1999; Booher-Jennings 2008).

References

Booher-Jennings, J. (2008) 'Learning to label: socialisation, gender and the hidden curriculum of high-stakes testing', *British Journal of Sociology of Education*, 29 (2): 149–160.

Coleman, J. (1988) 'Social capital and the creation of human capital', *American Journal of Sociology*, 94: 95–120.

Department for Education (2011) *How Do Pupils Progress during Key Stages 2 and 3?* Research Report DFE-RR096. Available at www.gov.uk/government/uploads/system/uploads/attachment_data/file/182413/DFE-RR096.pdf [Accessed 7 May 2014].

Fukuyama, F. (2001) 'Social capital, civil society and development', *Third World Quarterly*, 22 (1): 7–20.

Kluwin, T. N., Stinson, M. S. and Colarossi, G. M. (2002). 'Social processes and outcomes of in-school contact between deaf and hearing peers', *Journal of Deaf Studies and Deaf Education*, 7: 200–13.

Musselman, C., Mootilal, A. and MacKay, S. (1996) 'The social adjustment of deaf adolescents in segregated, partially integrated, and mainstreamed settings', *Journal of Deaf Studies and Deaf Education*, 1: 52–63.

Pribesh, S. and Downey, D. (1999) 'Why are residential and school moves associated with poor school performance?', *Demography*, 36 (4): 521–34.

Putnam, R. D. (2000) *Bowling alone: the collapse and revival of American community*, New York: Simon and Schuster.

Reay, D. and Wiliam, D. (1999) '"I'll be a nothing": Structure, agency and the construction of identity through assessment', *British Educational Research Journal*, 25 (3): 343–54.

Ridge, T. and Millar, J. (2000) 'Excluding children: autonomy, friendship and the experience of the care system', *Social Policy and Administration*, 34 (2): 160–75.

Wauters, L. N. and Noors, H. K. (2008) 'Social integration of deaf children in inclusive settings', *Journal of Deaf Studies and Deaf Education*, 13 (1): 21–36.

Chapter 9

Unpicking the binds
Learning (in) lessons from those that don't

> Infra-humanisation is a deliberate attempt to conceal what is common to us all and what therefore should provide the mortar of our lives. By these means, an inner life and range of sensibilities beyond those associated with the caricature of feckless idlers is denied to a swathe of our fellow citizens. If we are willing to be taught that they do not bleed, empathy is diminished. Fraternity is not only made difficult, it is presented as actively misguided, and whatever government then chooses to do in the name of 'fairness' becomes acceptable: we are made complicit in falsity and a failure of ethical obligation.[1]

This chapter reflects on two different accounts of the behaviour of children in poverty: the policy makers who believe children can be cajoled, regulated and monitored into behaving 'rationally', and the empirical evidence drawn from the stories of the six children presented in earlier chapters, in view of the varying ways in which they navigated the binds of poverty over time. The question will be raised as to why the moral underclass discourse (MUD) approach continues to be sutured into educational and social policy, and three explanations will be canvassed. Lastly, we return to the four binds in considering ways in which they might best be tackled.

Learning to label: MUD in the context of welfare reform

In the quote that opens this chapter, Jill Segger (2013) provides a definition of what she sees to be the strategy by which language is used by politicians in order to manipulate public attitudes towards welfare reform and perceptions of benefit recipients. Segger describes how the terms by which government officials refer to state-provided financial support have changed from 'social security', a label which recognized the cyclical nature by which recipients may pay in to a national system, and are therefore entitled to rely on that system for support in times of need. The concept of 'social security' was underpinned by a basis of mutuality and reciprocity. This meaning has been lost in the shift towards 'benefits', and 'welfare', labels embedded in a one-way understanding of state support as operating upon the passive recipients of government provision. More recently, political terminology has shifted again to employ the term 'hand-outs', in situating recipients as a net drain on society's resources. This positioning of welfare claimants as getting something for nothing is reinforced in the language used for welfare reform initiatives. An example is apparent in what protesters have called the 'bedroom tax' to refer to the reduction now applied to housing benefit for claimants living in a property with an 'unoccupied' room, while for politicians it is labelled the 'spare room subsidy'. Such language aims to invoke the public's sense of unfairness in emphasizing the superfluous nature of benefit payments but does little to acknowledge the needs and dignity of people whose children may return to the family home during times of financial hardship, who require another bedroom for health purposes, or for whom there is a scarcity of council property with fewer bedrooms.

As for the pervasiveness of the infra-humanization discourses used by politicians, it would appear that they are highly effective in changing public perceptions. Research into public attitudes to poverty and welfare over three decades shows that attitudes towards people claiming benefits have significantly hardened. For example, in conducting secondary analysis of British Social Attitudes survey data, the Joseph Rowntree Foundation (2013) found that 'Two-thirds (66%) of the public identify an explanation for child poverty that relates to the characteristics and behaviour of parents, compared to the 28% who say it is down to broader social issues';[2] and 'Fifteen per cent of the public in 1994 thought people lived in need because of laziness or lack of willpower, compared to 23% in 2010. Support for the view that people live in poverty because of injustice in society fell from 29% to 21% over the same time period.'[3]

Segger's account of the linguistic power of welfare discourse to affect public perceptions provides an additional impetus to the ways in which we might understand MUD to operate upon a social and cultural as well as a material level, with malign consequences not only for the living conditions of children in poverty, but also for the ways in which they are conceptualized and treated by others.

Learning from empirical research: Navigating the binds

In tackling infra-humanization discourses, the following discussion looks across the schooling lives of the six children in poverty encountered in this book, in considering the ways in which we might understand the four binds to operate as barriers against positive social and emotional experiences and educational success.

Bind one concerns the lack of material resources and the implications for excluding and disadvantaging children in school. The material consequences of poverty and their impact upon school inclusion manifested in a number of ways evident for five of the six children whose stories we've considered. For Liza, the consequences of financial hardship informed her choice between participation in social activities or purchasing a school lunch, underlining the impact of material hardship upon social participation for children. For Helen, the shame she felt in wearing a worn and outdated hand-me-down school uniform caused her to elect to exclude herself from social engagement to minimize the risk of being singled out and bullied. In Codie's case, material hardship shaped her family's decision to cancel her membership with the dance class that she loved. This had the multiple impacts of severing social relationships with her long-standing friendships and her community, but also strained her family relationships due to the frustration and powerlessness she experienced on account of this decision. For Clive, Robin, and Codie, bind one and bind four were interconnected in that financial hardship forced each of these children's families to relocate, which in Clive's case led to time out of school, and for each of these children placed limits on their opportunities for social engagement, friendship building and connection to the school and local community.

Bind two concerns the alien culture of schooling, and was most evident in the case of Megan on account of the gulf between her Irish Traveller background and the formal schooling culture, particularly at secondary school. Incompatibility between the systems that allocate school resourcing, in addition to Megan's nomadic lifestyle, resulted in a failure to deliver Megan the support she needed, leading to a cumulative educational gap. By the time Megan entered secondary education, one-to-one support was her only bridge into learning in school, but due to resourcing demands this was only possible in the core sessions (literacy and numeracy). As a result Megan was unable to access the curriculum and became a burden upon her classmates in lessons, creating greater social isolation and preventing her educational progress. To a lesser degree Liza, Clive, and Helen also experienced a disconnect between home and school cultures. While for Liza and Clive, talent in art and maths was interrupted by the classroom culture, for Helen schoolwork did not feature as a priority in her school life. In all children's cases the lack of resonance between home and school cultures could be seen in the context of their family's ambiguous or peripheral relationship to the school community. Even for Robin, whose home and school cultures were most closely aligned, the disconnect between home and school was expressed through his mother Lorraine, who felt her opinions were overlooked as she did not conform to the 'gate gossip' mothers, whom she believed to hold an influence over senior management decisions in the secondary school.

Bind three concerns the inclusive value of friendships as a vital means of social inclusion in school, but one that may not lead to inclusion in the formal contexts of the classroom or to educational success. As the only one unable to make any significant friendships, Megan's case reflects the importance of friendships in generating positive experiences of school, as evidenced in the isolation that she felt. On the other end of the spectrum, Helen's consolidation of a friendship group that socialized in school and in the community could be seen to play a key role in generating a positive experience of secondary school. While Clive, Liza and Codie were unable to develop friendships in which they felt secure, nevertheless all could be seen to invest in friendship building as a priority motivation in their schooling lives. Robin was the only child able to mobilize his friendship group into creating an educational advantage, through endorsing his abilities in key lessons. However, they were not sufficiently strong enough to generate social inclusion in the playground or out of school.

Bind four concerns the impact of irregular school moves as a common feature of life in poverty. For each of these children, school mobility was due to different factors but with the exception of Megan and Helen, it was never welcomed by children, nor their families. Both for Clive and Liza, school moves followed parental break-up, but while for Clive this was so that his mother could be closer to her family, for Liza it was in order for her father to care for her grandfather. For Codie and Robin, school moves were initiated by a lack of affordable housing in the communities that they had grown up in, so that moving schools also meant leaving behind family and friends. For Robin this was due to his father's redundancy, while for Codie, internal flooding had forced a move in rendering her family home unsafe for occupation. School relocation for Megan and Helen, however, did not involve a break from their community: in the case of Helen this was because school mobility was not associated with a move of home and community; for Megan, frequent movement was a feature of her Irish Traveller culture. We might understand these varying circumstances to uniquely contextualize the impacts of mobility in shaping children's experiences of school. Each child, however, shared the experience of being positioned as initially a stranger in school, so was at a disadvantage from their peers in terms of school inclusion, at least at point of entry.

In considering these children's stories it is evident that the 'four binds' were experienced to different degrees and in various ways. Yet, in understanding how they represent barriers against educational success, it is necessary to analyse their interrelation in preventing children from forming a meaningful sense of belonging within the school community. What is clear in considering the lives of children in poverty and their experiences of school is the profound frustration they felt at the near impossibility of navigating a way through the often clashing cultures of home, school and the community, which for many is alien and threatening. Much of the business of getting through the daily struggles that these children faced involved the inventive and ingenious strategies by which Clive, Liza, Codie, Megan, Helen and Robin set about tackling the competing expectations of teachers, friends and sometimes family. Taken from the perspective of children, it is possible to view the school (especially the new school) to be a site comprised of multiple territories concerned with the activity of learning, socializing with friends, practices of (not) eating, drinking, trading and exchanging of goods, engaging in sport, drama and art (Invinson and Duveen 2006). Access into such activities, however, can be seen to be much more complex than simply stepping through the threshold. While teachers may be the literal gatekeepers to schools as institutions, it is invariably the pupils who determine inclusion in the schooling activities, not just in the informal arenas of the playground, pond, maths block and lunchtime registration room, but also in the formal sites of the classroom. It was children's peers who validated Robin's abilities in maths and science, cajoled Liza's 'silliness', and blocked Clive's attempts not to be distracted in maths. Studying the experiences and orientations of Clive, Liza, Codie, Helen, Megan and Robin highlights the complexity involved in the making and sustaining of friendships and the ways in which this is mediated by material hardship, cultural background and inclusion in the local community. These children's stories broadly support the friendship literature, in that girls were more likely to orientate towards close dyadic friendships, while the boys socialized in groups, yet it was evident that all were engaged in friendships that required a continuous process of creating and sustaining trust. While all children's friendships were to some degree volatile, only Helen retained friendships that endured through primary and secondary schooling and were relevant within the home and community spheres. Possibly as a consequence, she was the only child to claim friendships that were wholly trusting. In the absence of trust, what has been termed the 'dark side' of social capital (Brown 2012) can be seen to be the result, where children enter into friendships that they perceive to be unstable and conditional upon often anti-learning behaviours. A history of ethnographic research shows how working-class peer groups are often in tension with the demands of schooling (Willis 1977; Brown 1987; Renold 2001). However, these insights are given greater prominence in light of the schooling lives of Clive, Liza, Codie, Helen, Megan and Robin. Therefore, in place of terms like 'resistance', what we see is a much more complex process in the construction of friendships, involving trade-offs or compromises of self.

Against the mantra regarding children in poverty getting 'ahead' in school, these stories show the difficulty in simply getting by. For these children, 'getting by' was a complex process fraught with the tensions and sacrifices necessary in order to balance inclusion in one area of school life against the requirements to be included in another. Sadly for some children, such as Megan, even navigating a place of belonging in one area of school life proved impossible, and the result was exclusion and even bullying. In face of such difficulty it was remarkable that these children found ways to 'get by' in school at all.

Three reasons for why MUD policies prevail

Such stories of social and educational exclusion sit in stark relief to the MUD perspective evident in Coalition policies. These are rooted in a neo-conservative rhetoric that young people in poverty are morally 'dangerous', in need of tighter regulation and control, and a neo-liberal/conservative logic of 'rational' human action: that people know what's good for them (i.e. education) and therefore, if they don't turn up to school, or once there don't work hard, they must be coerced and disciplined into doing what's in their own best interests. This prompts the question as to why the 'MUD' mantra – as Levitas (2005) coined it – can continue to persist in current policy making. There are three potential explanations that can be canvassed in answering this question. The first of these is that after 30 years of neo-liberalism, policy makers are ideologically locked into a 'rationalist' understanding of human motivation in which the best response is through neo-conservative moral outrage of those in poverty, and the neo-liberal policy tools through which to address this outrage, in relation to what is perceived to be in the best interests of those in poverty.

A second theory for why the MUD approach continues is that the relationship between research-based evidence and policy decision making has shifted from one in which evidence is used to *inform* policy to one in which it is used to *support* policy, where evidence is used in a selective and piecemeal manner in order to advance a preexisting political agenda. The empirical basis of government policy has been questioned in a range of cases, for example, with regards to Free schools, by the House of Lords Select Committee on Science and Technology report into the role and status of Chief Scientific Advisers (CSAs) in policymaking (HLSCST 2012). Here it was argued that the CSA represents a 'critically important voice' and, 'a source of independent challenge' (5) in policy decision making, which should be strengthened and underpinned by greater political independence and autonomy. In support of independent CSA representation, the report raised the example of the Free school initiative, in calling into question the Schools Minister (at the time) Nick Gibb, for his claim that policy should be based on evidence, because 'if they are not based on all the evidence available they will not go in the direction you expect them to go in'.[4] This comment was made with specific reference to the evidence that had been considered in the formulation of the Free school policy.[5] Undermining Gibb's claim, the report cited counter-research evidence submitted by policy analyst and educational leadership expert, Professor Pamela Sammons. Sammons pointed to the narrow and unrepresentative evidence base for the Free school initiative, which appeared to have ignored key findings on comparative schooling schemes such as the Swedish Free schools, as well as the Charter schools in the US:

> [I]t does not appear that the Government's Free Schools policy is based on robust evidence and it is not clear whether the DfE has provided an impartial review of the evidence base for the policy, and if so whether this was taken into account or ignored in developing the White Paper and in the subsequent implementation of the policy. A wider body of evidence provides a much less clear cut picture of the impact of Free Schools in Sweden and of Charter Schools in the US.[6]

It could be argued that such cursory treatment of evidence weakens the power of empirical work in explaining the lives of children in poverty. Indeed, the former Secretary of State for Education has been personally criticized for the evidence upon which he based his denigrating comments about the ignorance of teenagers: 'Survey after survey has revealed disturbing historical ignorance, with one teenager in five believing Winston Churchill was a fictional character while 58% think

Sherlock Holmes was real.'[7] Following a freedom of information request made by a retired teacher, the Department of Education admitted that the 'surveys' upon which these claims were made were based upon polls from Premier Inn and UKTV Gold press releases.[8]

In considering why politicians should misappropriate research evidence in order to drive social and educational agendas concerning children in poverty, it is germane to consider policy responses regarding the assumed needs of young people against a backdrop of national austerity measures. The treatment of the youth work sector is a prime lens for considering the Coalition's intentions regarding children in poverty, and how to respond to them. Previously under the auspices of local government, the youth work sector provided a dedicated set of services, universally available for children and young people in order to encourage them to take a more active role in their communities. Coalition policies have weakened the state's role in providing and funding these services, instead delegating provision to the voluntary or for-profit sector, and in being targeted towards crime reduction (Davies 2013). Here the argument of Mark Smith (2011) is compelling; that the government's treatment of the 2011 London riots and the young people involved, was a convenient form of scapegoating used to justify decisions on funding priorities and resource restructuring in the area of social and educational policy, that would ultimately dissolve the youth sector. Smith argues that: 'one of the key points to bear in mind . . . is the extent to which reaction to the "riots" will skew or be used as an excuse to keep policy away from some of the fundamentals.' The 'fundamentals' for young people include growing inequality and poverty (Wilkinson and Pickett 2010); the dearth of employment opportunities for young people; and the increasing cost of post-16 education. Smith is justified in his critique of policy responses for being targeted, punitive, and piecemeal, given the framing of youth work resources within a focus on 'dangerous behaviours around teenagers' (Higgs 2011).

A third reason for why the daily lives of children in poverty are routinely overlooked by policy makers may be due to the complexity of multiple factors which impinge upon children's life chances, thus engendering reluctance by politicians to commit the time to fully unpack the lessons we may learn from ethnographic studies, especially if these don't map onto easy solutions. There is something of an irony in the observation raised by Fiona Millar (2012) that while the Department for Education boasted spending £24.7 million on educational research between 2010 and 2012, much of this is 'cherry-picked' or 'ignored'[9] in relation to educational policy. Millar points to the Effective Pre-school, Primary & Secondary Education (EPPSE) study which followed 3,000 children longitudinally since the first year of the Blair administration. At the heart of this study were the factors in and out of school that can help reduce inequality. This was the focus of one such report to come out of the EPPSE study, which considered the influences on students' development between the ages of 11 and 14 (Sylva et al. 2012). Findings indicated that 'schools are not the only influence on students' development' (1), but family (background), communities, neighbourhood and preschool all affect educational achievement, social behaviour and dispositions for children aged 11 to 14.

Moving on from considering why the lives of children in poverty have been overlooked, the task is now to reflect upon what lessons can be drawn from studying the stories of these children, in casting out the policy tools which have so far only served to further alienate children and their families, and considering what are the policy implications from these stories as to how we may best support children in poverty. This involves drawing upon the lessons learned from the six stories encountered, and attending to these in relation to each of the binds detailed throughout the book.

Tackling bind one: Material deprivation and the consequences for social inclusion

First, in terms of the material bind, families need more financial support, rather than having financial penalties imposed upon them (such as school absence fines). Alan Milburn, social policy mobility advisor to the Coalition government, has warned that current social policies risk the creation of a class war between families of the squeezed middle and those on the lowest incomes.[10] In his report into social mobility and child poverty (SMCPC 2013) Milburn implored the government to stop debating whether to give benefits to families *or* help them find work, when both measures are required to offer a sustainable chance of escaping poverty. He advocated a multipronged approach including 'family incomes that are supported through decent levels of pay' through benefits and tax credits; job creation with 'good progression opportunities and fair recruitment processes'; the provision of 'high quality, affordable and universal childcare' (2); as well as working to reduce in-work poverty through 'looking again at the remit of the Low Pay Commission to enable the raising of the minimum wage' (7).

Further evidence in support of the complexity of the ways in which material deprivation impacts upon quality of life is offered in a Joseph Rowntree Foundation report (Ferragina, Tomlinson and Walker 2013), which links material manifestations of deprivation with social participation and trust. Drawing upon three large-scale UK quantitative data sets, Ferragina and colleagues identify two discrete social worlds separated by income, whereby 'the poorest 30 per cent of the population have to choose between basic necessities and participation in social activities' (1). The dividing line suggests a participation floor beyond which there is a break between falling income and social participation, meaning that at or beyond this line people find it difficult to afford all their basic necessities and so have to make hard decisions about which needs to neglect. This may have deleterious consequences for children's educational performance, through curtailing the amount of time that parents can spend with their children, for example, accompanying them in paid activities such as a museum, galleries or the zoo (33). The participation floor is significant in creating a two-tier society where for those above the dividing line, additional income gains have a tangible advantageous effect upon lifestyle. However, for those below the line, additional income makes little impact as it is absorbed in bolstering key basic needs, as opposed to meeting further essential needs required to increase social participation. Supporting Chase and Walker (2012), Ferragina et al. (2013) reflect upon the consequences of this analysis in relation to public discourses, through inverting the dominant 'something for nothing' critique of families on welfare, to reveal the material truth for families on benefit as more likely, 'nothing for something' because financial hardship is so great that additional income gains remain insufficient to meet all the basic survival needs (38). Furthermore, this situation is only set to worsen in current austerity Britain where rising living costs are coupled with welfare reform initiatives, with the result that for many receiving benefit payments, the only option is accumulative debt. This is the prognosis offered in the third report to emerge from the Real Life Reform (2014) study into the impact of welfare reform on households across the North, which found that the average household debt has increased by £670 to £2,943 since October 2013, which approximates £52 of additional debt per week.

In conclusion, we might reflect that the material penalty of poverty requires not simply an increase in benefit payments to ensure that life on a low income does not compromise human dignity, but also a revision of minimum pay wages at least in line with the rate of inflation, and a closer approximation of the Living Wage, an 'hourly rate [of pay] set independently and updated annually . . . according to the basic cost of living in the UK'. This has been set up by the Living Wage Foundation[11] so as to ensure all basic needs for families in poverty can be met.

Tackling bind two: The alien culture of schooling

In tackling the alien culture of schooling for children in poverty we might point towards the socially just pedagogy advocated by Lupton and Hempel-Jorgensen (2012). In highlighting the contextual pressures placed upon schools with high levels of poverty in their pupil composition, Lupton (2005) found that key elements of quality pedagogy were dampened, including 'creating a learning environment, focusing on teaching and learning, maintaining high expectations, teaching purposefully, and developing an effective home-school partnership' (601). In the face of such pressures two interventions were put forward by Lupton and Hempel-Jorgensen (2012). The first concerned changing the context, both of pupil composition and of the accountability regime under which schools are assessed. The authors acknowledge that while schools cannot move, admission pathways could be addressed so as to ensure schools received more balanced compositional intakes. It is arguable that this recommendation has never been more pressing, given a Sutton Trust report on the social selectivity of high achieving secondary schools:

> [Ninety-five per cent] of the top 500 comprehensives take fewer pupils on free school meals than the total proportion in their local areas, including

almost two thirds (64%) which are unrepresentative of their local authority area with gaps of five or more percentage points.

(The Sutton Trust 2013: 4)

Lupton and Hempel-Jorgensen (2012) also call for a broader basis for educational success than the current one based purely upon raw test scores, in order to support schools in their efforts to address the holistic development and well-being of children. They argued, however, that this would require the resourcing necessary to achieve pedagogical goals in high poverty settings. For example:

> smaller teaching groups, more teachers in the classroom, more non-contact time for front-line staff, a higher ratio of managers to staff, and substantially more investment in learning support, language teaching, pupil welfare or parental liaison roles.
>
> (602)

In reflecting upon the measures by which to tackle the alien culture of schooling, the work of Lupton and Hempel-Jorgensen (2012) points towards school-based interventions that aim to build understanding between teachers, learners and their families, through shifting the focus onto the whole child, as opposed to narrow attainment targets in the core subjects. This is only possible through adequate resources (particularly human ones) that build positive teacher–learner relationships, and within a policy context that distributes deprivation levels more fairly between schools, in order to release the time and resources to target family outreach strategies more effectively.

Bind three: Friendship as a social resource but a barrier to learning

In recognizing friendship as a refuge for children in poverty, but one that may be a barrier to educational achievement, this bind warrants consideration of the measures through which schools may become more inclusive and support friendships in ways that enable learning (as opposed to short-sighted measures such as the current policy idea of banning friends). Brett Laursen, an expert in peer relationships at Florida Atlantic University, has spoken out against school policies aiming to discourage children from forming close paired friendships, arguing that 'we [should] want children to get good at leading close relationships, not superficial ones.'[12] Laursen's work (1996) shows that close peer friendships through adolescence aid children's social development as well as support in the development of lasting romantic relationships.

In supporting the development of social relationships that may foster educational development, a more appropriate point of intervention may be found in the pedagogical approach advanced by Silvana Tiani Brunelli, a psychologist working for the Italian UNESCO member organization Club of Udine. The focus of Tiani's book *The Art of Education: Educating with Love and Firmness* (2007), and its associated training courses for students, parents and teachers (The Art of Education 2007–2013), is upon the means as opposed to the content of the pedagogical endeavor. Her work is underpinned by principles that inform the development of a trusting relationship between the learner and pedagogue: 'dignity, respect and human warmth based on love (11). This is because, for Tiani, relationships are the key medium through which learning is made possible. She gives the analogy of the relationship as a tube connecting two people:

> If the tube is intact and empty, we can roll a ball from one end until it reaches the person at the other end. However, if the tube is broken, or if it has a hole, the ball can fall out and doesn't reach the other person . . . Just like the ball in the example, this is how communication between two people takes place. Indeed, in a healthy and open relationship, messages leave one person and reach the other in an understandable manner. In a relationship which is compromised by interruptions, misunderstandings and resentment, messages cannot reach the other person, or reach them in a distorted and altered state.
>
> (Tiani 2010: 13)

The development of effective communication skills therefore provides the foundation of all school-based learning and the fulcrum for relationship building. In order to achieve a healthy learning relationship the learner must feel respected, recognized as an individual, cared for and supported. This is because when a child fears punishment, coercion and comparison, their internal motivations to learn are silenced and channels of communication are blocked (37). Given that such fears are often the attendant consequences of benchmarking strategies underpinning neo-liberal target setting, we might well apply this to children in poverty within the UK. However, within a trusting learning environment aimed to dispel fears, Tiani argues that the child's internal desire to learn and participate in class is activated as a precondition for effective learning. She believes that the development of positive learner–pedagogue relationships build a model for productive learning relationships that are transmitted upon the child's relationships with other learners, including classmates and peers. At the heart of all personal development, be it social, emotional or educational, lie the core skills of effective communication: 'the ability to relate, meaning obtaining educative results – that the child learns – using communication, respect, cooperation, [and] firmness [with others] . . . [that] opens up a new perception of ourselves, of others and of life' (74).

Key to the more positive friendship relations advocated in this pedagogical philosophy is the individual achievement of a balance in the quest for personal and collective gains, what Tiani calls an 'equilibrium between personal emancipation and socialisation, between private and public realms' (9). Through invoking her own internal motivations and identity within a learning community (44), the learner is included in class on her own terms and recognizes others accordingly. In such a learning environment classroom participation avoids the 'trade-offs' between the competing expectations from peers and teachers, in being directed towards classroom learning as both a personal and social enterprise.

In tackling bind three, the measures presented here are in line with those of Lupton and Hempel-Jorgensen (2012) in emphasizing the creation of a learning environment where positive and trusting learning relationships are promoted based on effective communication and shared goals. Such measures are a far cry from the former Secretary of State for Education's move towards a national grading system where individual pupil performance is made public. In his speech to the Ofqual standards summit (2011), Gove congratulated a London school for introducing an internal rank order grading system: 'if additional data and transparency can generate those beneficial results, is there a case for exam boards publishing more data about the performance of students, rather than less?'[13] Student accounts on performance ranking, however, are far less positive. Reflecting on the pupil ranking at John Cleveland College, Leicestershire, one teenager summed up a Radio 4 student report into exam pressure with the following statement:

> Last year the entire year 11 got asked whether the rankings were motivational. Most of my tutor [group], apart from only one person, actually said 'No'. It's so much pressure, you just want to crumble sometimes, just crumble onto the pillow, and just cry.[14]

We may well question how positive, pro-learning peer relationships can flourish in a policy environment where individual achievement is evaluated through an accountability system founded upon competition, and success and failure is relative to the performance of peers. It also points away from individual assessments towards a greater reliance on group work and collaborative learning in evaluating student performance.

Bind four: Turbulence as a disruptor of social, emotional and educational outcomes

In recent times the issue of irregular school moves, or 'turbulence', for children in poverty has taken on an increasing precedence with respect to the cap on housing benefit and other benefit changes, particularly for those living in social housing in high-cost areas of London. Margaret Hodge MP has described the current situation as presenting the 'potential for sudden and unmanageable movements of population',[15] while the National Audit Office (NAO 2012) has estimated that the reforms 'will result in around two million households receiving lower benefits, with a smaller number of households receiving substantially less' (8). The impact is not just felt on families but also on local authorities, in view of the pressure on the supply of affordable local housing, with current trends indicating that '36 per cent of local authority areas in England could face shortfalls by 2017' (NAO 2012: 9).

In tackling the turbulence bind, we might proffer insights from the literature into school leadership within mobile regions (DfEE 2000; DfES 2003a; Dobson and Pooley 2004; Brown, James and Lauder 2011; RSA 2013). High pupil mobility is an issue that is concentrated in key schools and education boroughs that serve highly mobile populations, which tend to be concentrated geographically. These include Travellers, children from homeless families, refugees and asylum seekers, economic migrants, those escaping domestic violence, and children in care. Research findings in schools with high pupil mobility have pointed towards interventions needed at the level of national government, local authority, and the school. The key points raised in these studies are discussed below and given greater prominence in light of the stories of the six children presented in this book.

Recommended intervention from national government (Department for Education)

The need for DfE support in tackling the turbulence bind has been founded primarily on financial grounds, with respect to the requirement for targeted additional funding for schools with high pupil mobility. This is in view of the resourcing and administrative support necessary for minimizing the disruption for students caused by transition (DfEE 2000; DfES 2003a; Demie et al. 2004). This includes record keeping and admissions; demands made on teaching and staffing in relation to assessment, planning and monitoring; as well as material resources such as books, equipment, uniform and information packs for parents. Resourcing demands are also reflected in the additional pastoral support required for the children's emotional and behavioural challenges, as well as a liaison with families and children's agencies.

Recommendations have also referred to mechanisms concerning the allocation and resourcing of schools that experience high mobility, to ensure that schools are neither financially penalized for admitting children at nonstandard admission points, nor incentivized to neglect the performance of these children (DfEE 2000; Demie et al. 2004; RSA 2013). This has included measures such as the revision of a funding formula to offer appropriate rewards to schools, and advisory support for local education authorities, such as strategies to spread new admissions more equitably. Recommendations have also concerned the national platforms to track and monitor pupils' movement more efficiently, and revising Ofsted's inspection framework to encourage schools to attend to the needs of mobile pupils. Lastly, national government can help tackle the turbulence bind in supporting further research into the needs of different groups of mobile children, and interventions testing in relation to key findings. Key lines of enquiry here are discussed later.

Recommended intervention from local government

Recommendations at the level of local government must be considered in light of recent central government revisions to school admission policies on the Code of Practice regarding Fair Access Protocols. These have moved towards a self-administering model whereby statutory local authority admissions forums have been abolished and the responsibility for managing mid-year transitions has transferred from the local education authority (LEA) to a growing number of schools that are their own admissions authorities (RSA 2013: 4). This means that local authorities will have less control in the allocation of pupils to schools, and weakened monitoring of the provision for children without a school place. This could result in an increasing unwillingness among successful schools to admit pupils outside of normal admission points, and reduces the obligation for schools to inform parents of their right of appeal. This could lead to a decrease in surplus places at a time of greater mobility and a less egalitarian division of new admissions among schools (RSA 2013: 10–11).

Recommendations at the local educational authority level, therefore, directly concern the platforms to support information sharing at a time of weakened control. In collecting and publishing data on length of time out of school, and in naming schools refusing new admissions, further schools might be discouraged from declining applications (Demie et al. 2004; RSA 2013). LEAs could offer schools training and expertise to manage their own pupil tracking and monitoring systems. This could also be aided in collecting regular information on school outwards mobility and in disseminating clear procedures for schools concerning when to remove children from school rolls (Demie et al. 2004). Information sharing could be achieved through tasking liaison managers to operate between departments (housing and social services) and other nongovernment agencies (Demie et al. 2004; RSA 2013). This could be supported through a forum on pupil mobility whereby the appropriate department and agency representatives can meet regularly to share information. Lastly, LEAs could provide better information to parents concerning the processes involved in school relocation, partly to discourage parents from unnecessary moves, and also to reinforce to parents the importance of advance warning to schools and the local authority of planned moves (Demie et al. 2004; RSA 2013).

Recommendations targeted at the school level

Tackling the turbulence bind at the level of school leadership also concerns the provision of tailored resources and information sharing in order to meet children's individual educational needs and well-being, and to enable the management of transitions as smoothly as possible. This includes embedding within school culture the policies and systems in place for the admission, induction and assessment of mobile pupils (Demetriou et al. 2000), as well as the appropriate tracking mechanisms to ensure progression both of the individual child, and concerning groups of children, such as those with English as an additional language (EAL) and those with special educational needs (SEN; DfES 2003a; Demetriou et al. 2000). Training and resourcing are also required for all staff in liaising between the different agencies required to support the needs of the child (DfES 2003a; Demetriou et al. 2000) as well as to gain understanding of family background and to build links with parents (DfEE 2000; Brown, James and Lauder 2011).

However, in the absence of requisite policy measures, the dedication needed from school leaders to achieve these ends has been found to require a continual and sustained level of professional generosity, in striving to meet the needs of pupils regardless of whether the cost of meeting these is returned to the school (Brown, James and Lauder 2011). This is particularly important in buffering transitions through extensive preparations before entry and after exiting the school. For example, one head of a military school visited the feeder primary school in order to take photos of all the mid-year transition pupils due to be deployed to the receiving school, and then displayed the photos of each child in their new classroom for them to feel a part of the school community immediately upon entry.

For many schools that serve communities with already complex needs, the capacity for head teachers to go to such extreme lengths to support mobile children is extremely challenging. One solution, therefore, may be to assign the responsibility for mobile pupils to a dedicated, school-based caseworker. This was the basis of a successful intervention trialled in 48 secondary schools, which involved funding the placement of an 'induction mentor', a nonteaching post with the specific objective 'to enable the pupil to integrate socially and begin to make good academic progress' (DfES 2003b: 3). The role of the 'induction mentor' was as a dedicated point of contact between the pupil and family, school, and other agencies, in taking responsibility for supporting the material, social and emotional effects caused by transition into, as well as out of, the school. This support was initiated from the point of notification about a new admission pupil, and involved five days of assessment, planning and preparation prior to the child's official first day at school, and careful monitoring of their needs and responsiveness to ensure this was achieved and the child was successfully included within the new school.

While in current economic times the likelihood of interventions such as the 'induction mentor' being funded through state provision is slim, inclusion measures may well benefit from building connections between the family, school and community. This is because the effects of mobility upon educational progress may be multiple and interact in different ways with the other binds discussed here.

Future directions in researching the educational binds of poverty

There are a number of questions to be raised as drivers for future research. Given the economic, social and policy changes that are likely to lead to an increasing context of mobility for children in poverty in the UK, further research in this area is arguably a priority line of enquiry in understanding the impact of poverty on children. This is all the more pressing in view of the relative dearth of research into the effects of turbulence on schooling outcomes for children, as well as the opportunities presented for considering the interaction of the turbulence bind on the other three binds discussed here.

In laying the foundations for a turbulence agenda, one line of enquiry is to explore the cultural factors that may mediate the impacts of mobility upon disparate mobile groups; for example, mobility may be experienced differently for Traveller children than for children from homeless families, or refugees. Second, we might consider whether there are experiences associated with the causes for mobility that may cut across mobile groups, for example family break-up, unemployment, seasonal or temporary labour patterns and caring for family members. Third, it has been suggested that the family unit can act as both a buffer or an additional stressor upon children's relationship building post-mobility (Brown and Carr 2014), given that adolescents' attachment relationships with caregivers are likely to reflect internal working models that function as a psychological template during the construction of new friendships (Carr and Fitzpatrick 2011; Weimer et al. 2004). It therefore follows that the strain of turbulence upon social and emotional well-being and educational achievement is likely to reflect broader pressures associated with the context within which families are mobile.

It is perhaps opportune to conclude in proposing that inclusion in school may be best considered as a whole family issue. While such a claim risks reproach for coming full circle from the starting block of tackling MUD moralizing against families in poverty, it should be emphasized that the role of parents and families in relation to children's educational achievement is best approached from the perspective of advocating support within, not ostracism from, their communities. This is in line with the British Academy endorsement through the Peter Townsend Policy Press Prize awarded to Professors Tracy Shildrick and Rob MacDonald, for their 2012 book which aims to debunk prejudiced portrayals of people in poverty by highlighting a lasting work commitment and hatred of welfare dependency by benefit claimants in the North East of England. In a similar vein we might usefully extend the bind analogy to consider the position of the family unit, and therefore, remedial strategies for the binds of poverty might best be couched within a consideration of their impact upon the family and community as part and parcel of children's schooling lives.

Conclusion

For mobile children from families living in poverty, the social, emotional and educational penalties associated with mobility can be understood through children's orientations to social relationships (Brown 2012), and as discussed in bind three may be explained through the severing effects of previous significant relationships and the consequences for building new trusting relationships with peers and teachers. Similar social and emotional penalties have been identified for children who are mobile between countries; for example Pollack and Van Reken (2009) speak of the unresolved grief caused by the severing of friendships left behind. This directs the measures by which schools can support transitions and protect against the most harmful effects of turbulence, towards supporting children in maintaining previous relationships. It is important to acknowledge that this may require more than simply the technical or financial means by which to support remote social connections, but also the psychological resources to build and sustain healthy, supportive relationships.

If one implication of the current wave in neo-conservative MUD concerning those in poverty is the incitement of a public denigration concerning those children from families claiming benefit, it is likely that the UK will experience a growing social divide between those either side of the poverty line. Such is the prognosis inferred from a report into the growing use of food banks in the UK (Cooper and Dumpleton 2013).

The implications of the likely effects of welfare reform for children in poverty are given additional impetus in light of the binds against educational success presented here. Given the tightening of state-provided support, coupled with a hardening in social attitudes, the likelihood is that schools and educational providers will become even less amenable to the structural factors that shape children's schooling lives. This requires a fundamental revision in the policy drivers by which educational opportunities are tackled, if we are to avoid children in poverty becoming even more alienated from their classroom peers – the 'squeezed' middle class, themselves in crisis over declining living standards (Parker 2013). Only by attending to the lived experiences of children can we begin to tackle the binds against educational success, in order to prevent the challenges of schooling becoming cumulative – because, in Megan's words, '[I]t gets harder to do anything every day.'

Notes

1 Jill Segger, 'Fraternity, propaganda and transformation: thinking about "welfare"', article adapted from a contribution given at the welfare and benefit reform Justice Forum in Oxford, 23 May 2013. Available at www.ekklesia.co.uk/node/18421 [Accessed 3 September 2014].
2 Joseph Rowntree Foundation, press release, 'Tough on people in poverty – new report shows public's hardening attitudes to welfare'. Available at www.jrf.org.uk/media-centre/tough-attitudes-poverty [Accessed 21 March 2014].
3 Ibid.
4 Nick Gibb MP, oral evidence provided to the committee cited in House of Lords report, HLSCST (2012), p. 25.
5 Nick Gibb MP, letter sent in evidence to the Committee from Nick Gibb MP cited in House of Lords report, HLSCST (2012), p. 25.
6 Pamela Sammons, individual submission to the House of Lords Science and Technology Committee inquiry (2012) made in response to a request from the Committee, December 2011, kindly supplied by personal correspondence.

7 Michael Gove, 'I refuse to surrender to the Marxist teachers hell-bent on destroying our schools: Education Secretary berates "the new enemies of promise" for opposing his plans', *Mail on Sunday*, 23 March 2013.
8 James Ball, 'Gove's claims of teenagers' ignorance harpooned by retired teacher', *Guardian*, 13 May 2013.
9 Fiona Millar, 'Education research exists, so why isn't it used in policymaking?', *Guardian*, 7 May 2012.
10 Alan Milburn quoted by Juliette Jowit, 'Social policies could spark class war, says social mobility advisor', *Guardian*, 10 July 2012.
11 Living Wage Foundation, www.livingwage.org.uk/what-living-wage [Accessed March 14 2014].
12 Brett Laursen quoted in Hilary Stout, 'A best friend? You must be kidding', *New York Times*, 16 June 2010.
13 Michael Gove Speech to Ofqual Standards Summit, 24 November 2011. Available at www.gov.uk/government/speeches/michael-gove-to-ofqual-standards-summit [Accessed 17 March 2014].
14 Student interviewee in 'Exam Pressure on Teens' student report, Women's Hour, *Radio 4*, 26 March 2014. Available at www.bbc.co.uk/programmes/b03ynf5c [Accessed 28 March 2014].
15 Margaret Hodge MP in 'Housing benefit changes: Warning over affordable housing shortfalls'. Available at www.bbc.co.uk/news/uk-politics-20162617, [Accessed 18 March 2014].

References

Brown, C. (2012) 'Exploring how social capital works for children who have experienced school turbulence: What is the role of friendship and trust for children in poverty?', *International Studies in Sociology of Education*, 22 (3): 213–36.

Brown, C. and Carr, S. (2014) *Understanding the educational penalties of irregular school transitions through the lens of social relationships*, Unpublished manuscript, University of Bath, Department of Education.

Brown, C., James, C. and Lauder, H. (2011) *Managing Mobility to Maximise Learning*, Nottingham: National College for Leaderships of Schools and Children's Services.

Brown, P. (1987) *Schooling Ordinary Kids: inequality, unemployment, and the new vocationalism*, London: Tavistock.

Carr, S. and Fitzpatrick, N. (2011) 'Experiences of dyadic sport friendships as a function of self and partner attachment characteristics', *Psychology of Sport and Exercise*, 12 (4): 383–91.

Chase, E. and Walker, R. (2012) 'The co-construction of shame in the context of poverty: beyond a threat to social bonds', *Sociology*, 47 (4): 739–754. doi:10.1177/0038038512453796

Cooper, N. and Dumpleton S. (2013) *Walking the Breadline: the scandal of food poverty in 21st century Britain*, commissioned by Church Action on Poverty and Oxfam. Available at http://policy-practice.oxfam.org.uk/publications/walking-the-breadline-the-scandal-of-food-poverty-in-21st-century-britain-292978 [Accessed 30 May 2014].

Davies, B. (2013) 'Youth work in a changing policy landscape', *Youth & Policy*, 110: 6–32.

Demetriou, H., Goalen, P. and Rudduck, J. (2000) 'Academic performance, transfer, transition and friendship: listening to the student voice', *International Journal of Educational Research*, 33 (4): 425–41.

Demie, F., Dobson, J., Lewis, K., McAndrew, E., Power, C., Strand, S., Taplin, A. and Thompson, A. (2004) *Pupil Mobility in Lambeth Schools: implications for raising achievement and school management*, Lambeth LEA.

Department for Education and Employment (2000) *Pupil Mobility in Schools*. Available at www2.geog.ucl.ac.uk/mru/docs/pupil_mobility.pdf [Accessed 19 March 2014].

Department for Education and Skills (2003a) *Managing Pupil Mobility: guidance*. Available at http://webarchive.nationalarchives.gov.uk/20130401151715/ and www.education.gov.uk/publications/eOrderingDownload/0780-2003.pdf [Accessed 19 March 2014].

Department of Education and Skills (2003b) *Managing Pupil Mobility: a handbook for induction mentors*. London: Author.

Dobson, J. and Pooley, E. (2004) *Mobility, Equality and Diversity: a study of pupil mobility in the secondary school system*, London: UCL, Migration Research Unit.

Ferragina, E., Tomlinson, M. and Walker, R. (2013) *Poverty, Participation and Choice*, Joseph Rowntree Foundation. Available at www.jrf.org.uk/publications/poverty-participation-and-choice [Accessed 29 June 2014].

Higgs, L. (2011). 'Conservative conference 2011: wellbeing boards to be "significant player" in youth service provision', *Children and Young People Now*, 3 October.

Ivinson, G., and Duveen, G. (2006) 'Children's recontextualisations of pedagogy', in R. Moore, M. Arnot, J. Beck and H. Daniels (eds) *Knowledge, Power and Educational Reform*, New York: Routledge, 109–25.

Laursen, B. (1996) 'Closeness and conflict in adolescent peer relationships: interdependence with friends and romantic partners', in W. M. Bukowski, A. F. Newcomb and W. W. Hartup (eds) *The Company They Keep: friendships in childhood and adolescence*, New York: Cambridge University Press, 186–210.

Levitas, R. (2005) *The Inclusive Society? Social exclusion and new labour*, Basingstoke: Palgrave Macmillan.

Lupton, R. (2005) 'Social justice and school improvement: improving the quality of schooling in the poorest neighbourhoods', *British Educational Research Journal*, 31 (5): 589–604.

Lupton, R. and Hempel-Jorgensen, A. (2012) 'The importance of teaching: pedagogical constraints and possibilities in working class schools', *Journal of Education Policy*, 27 (5): 601–20.

National Audit Office (2012) *Managing the Impact of Housing Benefit Reform*, Department for Work and Pensions. Available at www.nao.org.uk/report/managing-the-impact-of-housing-benefit-reform/ [Accessed 18 March 2014].

Parker, S. (2013) *The Squeezed Middle: the pressure on ordinary workers in America and Britain*, Bristol: Policy Press.

Pollack, D. and Van Reken, R. (2009) *Third Culture Kids: growing up among worlds*, Boston: Nicolas Brealey.

Real Life Reform (2014) *Report 3, March*, Northern Housing Consortium. Available at www.northern-consortium.org.uk/reallifereform. [Accessed 28 March 2014].

Renold, E. (2001) 'Learning the "hard" way: boys, hegemonic masculinity and the negotiation of learner identities in the primary school', *British Journal of Sociology of Education*, 22 (3): 369–85.

Royal Society of Arts (2013) *Between the Cracks: exploring in-year admissions in schools in England*. Available at www.thersa.org/__data/assets/pdf_file/0007/1527316/RSA_Education_Between_the_cracks_report.pdf [Accessed 19 March 2014].

Shildrick, T. and MacDonald, R. (2012) *Poverty and Insecurity: life in low pay, no-pay Britain*, Bristol: Policy Press.

Slyva, K., Melhuish, E., Sammons, P., Siraj-Blatchford, I. and Taggart, B. (2012) *Final Report from the Key Stage 3 Phase: Influences on students' development from age 11–14*, Effective Pre-School, Primary and Secondary Education Project (EPPSE 3–14), Department for Education. Available at www.gov.uk/government/uploads/system/uploads/attachment_data/file/181677/DFE-RB202.pdf

Smith, M.K. (2011) *Young People and the 2011 'Riots' in England – experiences, explanations and implications for youth work*, The Encyclopedia of Informal Education. Available at www.infed.org/archives/jeffs_and_smith/young_people_youth_work_and_the_2011_riots_in_england.html] [Accessed 27 June 2014].

Social Mobility and Child Poverty Commission (2013) *State of the Nation 2013: social mobility and child poverty in Great Britain*, London: Stationery Office. Available at www.gov.uk/smcpc [Accessed 14 March 2014].

The Sutton Trust (2013) *Selective Comprehensives: the social composition of top comprehensive schools*. Available at www.suttontrust.com/news/publications/selective-comprehensives-the-social-composition-of-top/ [Accessed 27 June 2014].

Tiani, S. (2010) *The Art of Education: educating with love and firmness*, Prepotto, Italy: Podresca Edizioni (English translation by personal communication).

Weimer, B. L., Kerns, K. A. and Oldenburg, C. M. (2004) 'Adolescents' interactions with a best friend: associations with attachment style', *Journal of Experimental Child Psychology*, 88: 102–20.

Wilkinson, R. and Pickett K. (2010) *The Spirit Level: why equality is better for everyone*, London: Penguin.

Willis, P. (1977) *Learning to Labor: how working class kids get working class jobs*, New York: Columbia University Press.

Index

Academies 2, 4
achievement assessments 51–2, 68–9, 90–1, 108–10, 128–30, 147–9
achievement gap 3, 92–3
addiction 7, 8
alcohol addiction 8
The Art of Education: Educating with Love and Firmness (Tiani) 170
Association of Teachers and Lecturers 11
asylum seekers 34, 172
attainment grades 52; see also achievement assessments
attitude grades 52; see also achievement assessments

Bateson, Gregory 36n1
Becker, Gary 9
behavior: assumptions about 15; attention seeking 105–6, 118; control of 11–12; disruptive 4, 45–6, 63–5, 72–4
Bernstein, Basil 27
best friends: ban on 11–12, 169; unreciprocated 75–7
'Binds': concept of 21, 36n1; Bind one 22–5, 49, 110–12, 130, 137, 140, 147, 151, 161–2, 167–8; Bind two 25–8, 67, 78, 89–90, 128, 126, 137, 143, 162, 168–9 ; Bind three 28–34, 67, 75, 78, 85, 90, 133, 137, 147, 162, 169–71, 175; Bind four 34–5, 67, 77, 78, 89–90, 110–12, 130, 136, 140, 147, 151, 162, 163, 171–4; in primary school settings 48–50, 67–8, 89–90, 92, 108, 128, 147; in secondary school settings 58–9, 78–9, 98, 118, 137–8, 157–8; unpicking 160–76

Blair, Tony 6, 166
Bourdieu, Pierre 26, 27, 28, 30, 45, 88; account of symbolic violence 15, 27, 28, 29, 30, 87, 88
Bousted, Mary 11
boys, friendships of 29–31, 42–3, 46–9, 55–8, 143–5, 149–53, 157
breakfast consumption 62, 79n1
British Household Panel Youth Survey (BHPYS) 24
British Social Attitudes survey 161
Brown, Ceri 29, 35, 115, 164, 172, 174, 175
Brunelli, Silvana Tiani 169–70
'buddying' schemes 44, 143; see also 'induction mentors'
bullying 23, 25; Codie's story 114–15; fear of 130; Helen's story 121–2, 130; Megan's story 86–7, 90, 99n8; of teachers 28

Cameron, David 7–8
care work 15, 24, 61, 62, 69, 163, 167, 170
Centre for Social Justice (CSJ) 7
Chicago School 9
Chief Scientific Advisers (CSAs) 165
Child Poverty Act 7
children: in care 172; middle-class 26–7, 176; working class 118n1; see also children in poverty
children in poverty 15, 36; educational binds of 36; influences on 166–7; and paid employment 24; perspectives of 23–4; public perceptions of 161; and social mobility 167; and turbulence 34–5; see also 'Binds'; individual stories of children by name
'circuits of schooling' 23

Index

classroom culture: student appraisals of educational potential 158n2; tensions in 47–8
Clive's story 15, 42; Clive as rule challenger 44–6, 47–8; continued school absence 50–1; cultural capital and knowledge of the powerful 51–5; disengagement with learning orientations 53–5; educational achievements 51–2; and the educational binds of poverty 52, 58–9, 162–4; enjoyment of maths 45, 48–9, 54–5; friendship dynamics and social capital penalties 46; primary school years, 42–9; relocation and changing schools 42–4; secondary school years 50–9; social capital and the role of friendship 55–7
Club of Udine 169
Coalition politics 1–2, 3, 4, 28, 164, 166
Codie's story 16; attempts to be an appropriate learner 103–4, 117–18; attention seeking 105–6, 118; bullying 114–15; dance lessons 102–3, 111–12; disillusionment with learning 115–16; educational achievements 108–10; effects of the binds of poverty 162–4; elaborate storytelling 107–8; family support for education 103; family tensions 101–2; material deprivation 101, 110–11; precarious friendships 106–7; primary school years 101–8; relationship with teachers 105, 116–18; secondary school experience 108–18; SEN placement 104–5; social exclusion 113–15, 118; valuing education 117
communication skills 170
conservatism 6
crime 8
Criminal Justice and Public Order Act 98n1
cultural assumptions 1
cultural capital 43–6, 51–5
cultural differentiation 26
cultural inequalities 34
culture of exclusion 89
culture wars 1

debt 7, 22, 23, 35, 168
Department for Education (DfE), recommended interventions 172
dietary deficiencies 23
disadvantage 6, 8, 23, 26, 27, 163
discipline 1, 2, 4, 7, 8, 9, 10, 11, 13–14, 56, 164
disempowerment 61
divorce 23; *see also* families, break-up of
domestic abuse and violence 35, 172
double-bind 36n1
drug abuse 8

economic rationality 9–10
economics: neo-classical 9; neo-liberal free market 6
Education Act (2011) 4
education: authoritarian policies in 10; family support for 103; and the labour market 2; neo-liberal policies in 10; raising standards in 9–14
educational binds of poverty 16–17, 21–2; and the alien culture of schooling 22, 25–8; effects of 161–4; future directions in research 174–5; the impact of 'turbulence' (irregular school moves) 22, 34–36; material deprivation and its role in exclusion 22–5; school friendships and their implication in learning 22, 28–34
educational differentiation 26
Educational Reform Act (1988) 23
educational reform: Coalition government's position on 4; goals of 2
educational triage 45, 105
Effective Provision of Pre-School, Primary and Secondary Education Project (EPPSE) 25–6
exclusion: and material deprivation 22–5; financial and social 23; material 24; social 1, 6, 93–5, 113–15, 118; in social groups 24, 30, 32–3; *see also* inclusion

Fair Access Protocols 173
families: break-up of 7, 35, 42, 61, 131; financial support for 167; homeless 172, 175; importance of connection with school 124; military 34; in poverty 15; single-parent households 42; support for education by 103, 141–3, 158; 'troubled' 8
free school meals (FSM) 43, 120, 140
Free Schools 2, 4, 11, 165

friendship and friendships: as barrier to learning 169–70; of boys 29–31, 42–3, 46–9, 55–8, 143–5, 149–53, 157; dynamics of 46–9; effect of turbulence on 56–7; fear of being ostracized 56–7; fluctuating 113–15; of girls 29, 31–3, 66–7, 75–7, 85–6, 93–5, 102–3, 113–15, 122–5, 130–3; and identity 47; impact of turbulence on 136–7; importance of in enjoying lessons 133–7; influence of 28–9, 152–3, 157, 169–71, 176; as means of including and excluding 15; of pleasure 77; precarious 106–7; rule-challenging culture 47; schools' interference in 12; secure 130–3; and social capital 55–7; as social resource 169–71; value of 162–4; *see also* best friends

Gibb, Nick 2, 3, 165
Gilbert, Francis 11
girls: friendships of 29, 31–3, 66–7, 75–7, 85–6, 93–5, 102–3, 113–15, 122–5, 130–3; oppression of 31
global economic crisis 7
Gove, Michael 2, 10–11, 12, 171, 177
Guy, Christian 7

Harvard Project 31
health problems 23, 35
Helen's story 16; bullying 121–2, 130; educational achievements 129–30; effects of the binds of poverty 162–4; financial hardship 120–1, 137; future aspirations 126–7; improved social relations 122–5; learning and educational outcomes 125–7; primary school years 120–8; relationship with teachers 136; secondary school experience 128–37; secure friendships 130–3; tension between home and school 127–8
Hinshaw, Stephen 36n1
Hobby, Russell, 12
Hodge, Margaret 171
homophobia 30
Hopkins, David 2–3
House of Lords Select Committee on Science and Technology 165
housing issues 16, 23, 101, 149, 151, 158, 161, 163, 171–2; temporary social housing 34–5

identity: community 137, 171; effect of friendships on formation of 30–1, 32, 56; individual 46, 49, 54, 73, 87, 88, 98; national 7; social group 15, 47, 49, 56, 58; Traveller/Gypsy 99n3
illness 23, 35
The Importance of Teaching (White Paper) 4
'Improving Attendance at School' (Taylor) 12
inclusion: social inclusion 46, 132–2, 162–3; strategies for new students 4; *see also* exclusion
'induction mentors' 174; *see also* 'buddying' schemes
inequality 1, 6, 8, 166; cultural 15; social 4
infra-humanisation 160–1
interventions: DfE 172; local government 173–4; school-based 169, 173–4

Joseph Rowntree Foundation 161, 167

knowledge, powerful or disciplinary 26
knowledge of the powerful 26, 43–6, 51–5

labour market: education and 2; exclusion from 6
Lareau, Annette 26
Lauder, Hugh 2, 3, 34, 172, 174
Laursen, Brett 169
learning disability 16, 62, 143–6, 158
learning support assistants (LSAs) 84–5, 97–8
leisure activities: 12, 26, 27, 46, 47, 63, 70, 87, 89, 103, 111, 123, 144, 150, 162, 167
Levitas, Ruth 1
lifestyle migrants 34
linguistic advantages 27–8
literacy issues 88, 99n4
Liza's story 15; changing schools 61–2, 67–8; distracted and disruptive classroom behavior 63–5, 72–4; educational achievements 68–9; effects of the binds of poverty 161–4; the importance of home 63–6; interest in art 64–5, 74–5; lack of positive affirmation 70–2; primary school years 61–8; secondary school

experience 68–79; tenuous social relationships 66, 76–7, 79
London riots (2011) 7–8, 166
Low pay Commission 167

MacDonald, Rob 175
marginalization 27
material deprivation, and exclusion 22–5, 34, 167–8
material resources, lack of 161–2
meanness 33
Megan's story 15; bullying 86–7; difficulty created by frequent absence 82, 90–2; educational achievements 90–1; effects of the binds of poverty 162–4; home vs. school culture 87–8, 95–7; love of horses 87–8, 98; numeracy ability 88–9, 97; one-on-one learning support 84–5, 97–8; primary school years 81–9; secondary school years 90–8; social isolation and exclusion 82–4, 85–6, 90, 93–5, 98; widening achievement gap 92–3
middle class: children 26–7; 'squeezed' 176
migrants, economic 172
Milburn, Alan 167
military families, and turbulence 34
mobility 61; as cultural norm 81–2; effects of 22; among low-income families 15; social 167; and the Traveller culture 91–2; *see also* turbulence
Moral Underclass Discourse (MUD) 1–2, 8, 9, 13, 21, 25, 58, 175; and the blame culture 4–9; and educational policy 160; reasons why policies prevail 164–7; and social policy 160; and welfare reform 160–1
Mossbourne Academy 10

National Association of Head Teachers 12
National Audit Office (NAO) 171
National Literacy Strategy 3
National Numeracy Strategy 3
neighborhoods, disadvantaged 23
neo-conservatism 6–7
neo-liberalism 6, 9–10, 14, 165
New Labour government 1–2, 3, 28; and the attitude of blame 5–6
New Right 6

New Zealand, issue of turbulence in 34
North of England Education Conference (NEEC) 2
Nursing Partnership Scheme 6

OECD (Organisation for Economic Co-operation and Development) 2, 3–4
Ofqual standards summit 171
Ofsted reports 2, 10, 42, 141
one-on-one learning support 84–5, 97–8
Ordo-liberalism 9

parents: blamed for truancy 12–14, 25; influence on curriculum and pedagogy 4; *see also* families
pedagogy and pedagogies 43–6; parents' influence on 4; performative 28: progressive 28
peer pressure 24–5, 29, 49
persistent absence (PA) 12–14; *see also* truancy
Phoenix Free School 11
PISA tests 2
policy makers and making: limits and possibilities of 1; perspective of 16; *see also* Coalition politics; New Labour government
politics, decline in public faith in 14
poverty: and bullying 121; cultural analysis of 1, 9;cycle of 22; family life affected by 22–3; in-work 7; issues associated with 23; linked to crime 7; linked to low social participation 121, 167–8; material penalties associated with 22–5; moral explanation for 5–6, 21; nonfinancial antecedents to 7; public attitude toward 5, 160–1, 175; relationship with inequality 1; virtuous vs. vicious poor 5, 14; *see also* children in poverty; educational binds of poverty
'poverty of the imagination' 18n31
primary school, effect of binds on 48–50, 67–, 89–90, 108, 128, 147

racism 29, 30
Real Life Reform 168
redistribution (RED) 1
redundancy 5, 16, 23, 35, 140–1, 163
refugees 34, 172, 175

religious institutions, influence of 149–50
Rethinking Child Poverty 7
Ridge, Tess 22, 23, 24, 42, 67, 70, 121, 132, 145
'riots, communities and victims panel' (RCVP) 8
Robin's story 16; difficulty of hearing impediment 143–4, 158; educational achievements 147–9, 157–8; effects of the binds of poverty 162–4; family valuing education 141–3, 158; importance of helping 153–8; primary school years 140–7; relocation for financial reasons 140–1; reluctance to participate 145–7; secondary school experience 147–58; social exclusion and isolation 143–5, 149–51, 158
rules, challenging 44–6

Sammons, Pamela 165
scapegoating 166
Schleicher, Andreas 2
school absences, and relocation 43; *see also* mobility; persistent absence (PA); turbulence
schooling and schools: alien culture of 25–8, 168–9; autonomy and control in 3, 4, 14
secondary school, effects of binds on 58–9, 78–9, 98, 118, 137–8, 157–8
Segger, Jill 160
sexism 29, 30
Shildrick, Tracy 175
SID (social integrationist discourse) 1–2, 6
'silly' behaviour 47, 48, 63, 66, 72, 73, 75, 77, 79, 105, 106
Smith, Mark 166
social capital: penalties 46–9; and the role of friendship 55–7; theory 35
social control 12
social exclusion *see* exclusion, social
Social Exclusion Plan 6
social housing, temporary 34–5
social inclusion *see* inclusion, social
sociogram 114, 119n3
special educational needs coordinator (SENCO) 82

standardized assessment tests (SATs): 2, 3, 51, 68, 90, 108, 127, 128, 129, 141, 143
'state theory of learning' 2–3, 28
students: high achieving and popular (HAP) 33; special educational needs (SEN) 43, 50, 104–5
Sure Start 1
Sweden, Free Schools in 165

Tackling the Causes of Disadvantage and Transforming Families' Lives 7
Taylor, Charles 12–13, 96
teachers: autonomy for 4; expectations of 15, 33–4, 67, 116, 176; as gatekeepers 163; ex-military as 10–11; government expectations of 28; importance of 133–7; student relationships with 24, 27, 63–4, 71–4, 78, 79n1, 105, 116–18, 136, 176; working together with learners and families 169
teasing 23, 30
testing, emphasis on 2–3
Travellers: culture 15–16, 34, 87–8, 98, 99n3; lifestyle 162, 172, 175, 81–2, 98n1, 98n2, 99n4
'troops to teachers' programme 10–11
'Troubled families' programme 8, 17n12, 17n14
truancy 24; parents blamed for 12–14, 25; reasons for 24–5
turbulence 34–5; effects of 163; longer term effects of 77–8, 136–7; longitudinal effects of 57–8; negative effects of 35, 171–2, 175; recommended DfE intervention 172; recommended local government intervention 173; recommended school level intervention 173–4

underclass, attitudes toward 5; *see also* poverty
underperformance, policy discourses on 2
unemployment 5, 16, 23, 35, 140–1, 163
UNESCO 169
United States: Charter Schools in 165; issue of turbulence in 34

values 36–7n1; of friendship groups 31; home vs. school 74–5, 103, 125, 128, 141–3, 158; moral and spiritual 138n2; of school success 27, 31, 35, 128, 137, 153, 155; of Travellers 88–9, 99n3; of working class 27
violence: domestic 35, 172; symbolic 27–8, 29–30, 88

Waiton, Stuart 14
welfare dependency 7
Wilshaw, Michael 10

Young, Michael: account of powerful knowledge/knowledge of the powerful 26, 36, 41, 43, 45